The University and Public Education

This book examines an important aspect of the relationship between higher education and the public (and especially secondary) system of schooling in Britain. Higher education has influenced secondary schools in a number of ways, and not least in the development of school examinations—once again a focus of public debate. Some university luminaries have become Ministers of Education; others have contributed powerfully to successive reform movements; some have used their status as members of that mysterious class called "the great and the good" to mould public policy and to chair prestigious commissions; others have chosen to centre their own research and scholarship on matters related to schooling.

No University has been more visible than Oxford in such fields: that is why it has been chosen as the focus for this case study. This book brings together leading experts in their field to assess and explain the contribution Oxford has made to public schooling over time.

This book was previously published as a special issue of the *Oxford Review of Education*.

Harry Judge has been the director of a university department of education and the head of a comprehensive school. He has written widely on the history of educational policies and held a number of visiting appointments at major universities in the United States.

The University and Public Education

The Contribution of Oxford

Edited by Harry Judge

LONDON AND NEW YORK

First published 2007 by Routledge
2 Park Square, Milton Park, Abingdon, Oxon, OX14 4RN

Simultaneously published in the USA and Canada
by Routledge
270 Madison Ave, New York NY 10016

Routledge is an imprint of the Taylor & Francis Group, an informa business

Transferred to Digital Printing 2008

© 2007 Taylor and Francis Ltd

Typeset in by Plantin by Genesis Typesetting Ltd, Rochester, Kent

All rights reserved. No part of this book may be reprinted or reproduced on utilised in any form or by any electronic, mechanical, or other means, now known or hereafter invented, including photocopying and recording, or in any information storage or retrieval system, without permission in writing from the publishers

British Library Cataloguing in Publication Data
A catalogue record for this book is available from the British Library

Library of Congress Cataloging in Publication Data
A catalog record for this book has been requested

ISBN10: 0-415-41364-8 (hbk)
ISBN10: 0-415-46413-7 (pbk)

ISBN13: 978-0-415-41364-0 (hbk)
ISBN13: 978-0-415-46413-0 (pbk)

CONTENTS

Notes on Contributors — vi

Introduction
Harry Judge — vii

1. H. A. L. Fisher: scholar and minister
   Harry Judge — 1

2. T. H. Green: citizenship, education and the law
   Raymond Plant — 19

3. Michael Sadler and comparative education
   David Phillips — 35

4. Cyril Norwood and the English tradition of education
   Gary McCulloch — 51

5. Anthony Crosland: intellectual and politician
   Maurice Kogan — 67

6. Alan Bullock: historian, social democrat and chairman
   Geoffrey Caston — 83

7. A. H. Halsey: Oxford as a base for social research and educational reform
   George Smith & Teresa Smith — 101

8. How élite?
   Sheldon Rothblatt — 123

9. Oxford and the mandarin culture: the past that is gone
   Vernon Bogdanor — 143

   INDEX — 163

Notes on Contributor

Maurice Kogan is Professor Emeritus of Government and director of the Centre for the Evaluation of Public Policy and Practice at Brunel University, where he has been Dean of the Faculty of Social Sciences and Acting Vice-Chancellor. He is the author of several books and articles on higher education and science, health and local government policy. His most recent major works are in a five-volume publication (2000), with Swedish and Norwegian colleagues, on changing policies and practices in higher education in the three countries, and the joint editorship, with Mary Hawkesworth, of the second edition of the Routledge Encyclopaedia of Politics and Government (2003).

Introduction
Harry Judge

The following pages present the portraits of seven distinguished and influential men. Those portraits are then interpreted, from two very different perspectives, and placed in both national and international contexts. The seven careers all represent, albeit in subtly varying degrees, a common pattern. That common pattern is of a career which blends and integrates a commitment to professional academic life with a powerful engagement in public affairs—in these seven cases specifically in the field of education. It is not a coincidence that the seven had few predecessors, and are unlikely to have many (or indeed any) successors. Nor is it an accident that they all had personal and professional roots in the University of Oxford rather than in other places of equally high learning and repute.

Much of the rationale for their beliefs and the motivation for their activity is embedded in the writings, and perhaps even more in the personal influence, of T. H. Green (1836–1882). Green, a Fellow of Balliol College in the years when under the formidable Benjamin Jowett it was at the height of its influence, substituted for the traditional Christian beliefs which he had inherited a 'religion' of civic commitment, and a vison of the State as a potentially benevolent agent of social and moral improvement. Michael Sadler (1861–1943) acknowledged the depth and range of his debt to Green and was instrumental in redefining the mission of the University to a wider world—notably in continuing education, in promoting the serious study of comparative education and securing its influence on the making of policy, and in guiding the evolution of national educational development after the passage of the great Education Act of 1902. He ended his career, back in Oxford, as the head of one of its colleges. His contemporary, H. A. L. Fisher (1865–1940), was a professional historian of the highest standing who (like Sadler and many others, openly acknowledging the influence of Green) wished to play his full part on a wider stage. He was abruptly translated from the sequestered life of a scholar and academic administrator to serve as Minister of Education between 1916 and 1922—a six year tenure which established a record unbroken to the present day. He too returned to Oxford as the head of his own college there. Cyril Norwood (1875–1956) began his academic life in Oxford (as did they all, except the most recent of the seven) before launching himself into the world of secondary education, presiding over national bodies, and writing one of the most influential of the last century's official reports on education. He, too, ended his career as the head of the college at which he had been an undergraduate.

Tony Crosland (1918–1977) taught economics as an Oxford don, and of all seven subjects was perhaps the least rooted in the place and the least affected by its habits of mind. He moved rapidly from Trinity College into the career of a professional politician, and as a leading intellectual did much to redirect the flow of thinking about Labour Party policy. As Secretary of State for Education and Science for two years in the 1960s he imposed reforms which changed the structures of both secondary and higher education. Alan Bullock (1914–2004), like Fisher before him, flourished in Oxford as a historian, founded an Oxford college, and was drawn into public life as one of nature's consensual chairmen. Chelly Halsey (b.1923) closes this apostolic circle, but in a way peculiar to him. He is, in this company, unique in not beginning his academic life in Oxford, but later choosing to join that particular tribe partly because he believed it would increase his own capacity to do good. Acknowledging the importance of the values promoted by T. H. Green and mediated to him through Tawney, he applied to the design of progressive policies the novel (to Oxford) skills and insights of the social scientist.

It could therefore be argued that Halsey represents a transition from one 'university and public affairs' culture to another. The more recent tendency is to emphasise the importance of specialised knowledge, of technical expertise in the resolution of policy choices. In these changing contexts the universities may have an important part to play. But the earlier and very different tradition was rooted in the complementary yet contrasting values of privilege and of duty: a privilege inherited though superior schooling and family networks and implying a right to leadership status, as well as a derived duty to serve the public good in a selfless spirit. Universities in general, and Oxford in particular, were well attuned to such cultural values, which had little to do with expertise or specialised knowledge. Six of the seven began their university studies with an immersion in the classics and the ancient languages, while five of them (including the two historians of international repute) took their first degrees in the dominant disciplines of 'Greats' (ancient history, philosophy, and classical literature). This was therefore their common basis, and several of them were relatively unsympathetic to the study of science.

All of them were men. Women in Oxford, across the decades relevant to this discussion, became progressively more central in their university and in public life, and many of them rose to positions of considerable importance and influenced educational development a great deal more than did the majority of their male contemporaries. The decision (in itself questionable but defensible) to focus on Oxford dons who had an impact on education and public life at the highest level inevitably excluded otherwise impressive Oxford-educated candidates (notably Margaret Thatcher and Shirley Williams as Secretaries of State for Education). But the unpalatable fact remains that these pages do reflect the achievements of a university and of a culture that was still, as a matter of harsh fact, masculine as well as traditional in its underlying assumptions. Nor were even the most liberal of its leaders as sensitive to such issues as we might now wish them to have been: even Fisher, and this in spite of the strongly expressed principles well-articulated by his remarkable wife, was insensitive to the plight of those women teachers who were dismissed when they married. As is powerfully argued later, the world that is here described is a lost world of the mandarins, and the career patterns here recorded are unlikely ever to be replicated. And most of those mandarins were men.

It is therefore important to make explicit the reason for the selection of these seven lives. They did not emerge from some kind of clandestine competition to find the most worthy candidates for inclusion in a gallery of dead worthies. They were identified specifically as examples of Oxford dons who became engaged in issues of national education and in order to provide the raw material for the analysis at which later pages are directed. To some extent, of course, the choice of subjects was dependent on the availability of scholars willing and able to write about them. Equally relevant was the editorial obligation to provide a broadly representative selection across the whole period of time under review. Other names might of course have served these purposes. Two other Oxford dons in the later 20th century, for example, became Ministers of Education with cabinet rank. Henry Hadow (1859–1937) would have chimed well with the underlying themes of this discussion: so obviously would James Bryce (1838–1922) and the two Aclands, father and son (1809–1898 and 1847–1926). John Maud (1906–1982) was an Oxford academic who became a senior civil servant, notably at the head of the then Ministry of Education in the years of reconstruction after the end of the second world war, before launching into a diplomatic career and returning to Oxford as a college head. The addition of such eminent figures would not, however, have modified the concluding analysis, in which the recurring themes relate to the shared ideologies and the institutional circumstances which, across a limited period of time, combined to propel academics from a single university into public life and responsibilities. These pages should not be misconstrued as a covert celebration of their virtues, or of the superiority (in either status or ethics) of their parent university. Nor do they pretend to provide a full account of all that that university contributed (for good or ill) to the educational life of the nation. If that had indeed been the intention, then a biographical approach would have frustrated it, and only a very different thematic analysis could have clarified what the university has attempted to contribute to that field of activity. Such a presentation would have focused on, for example, its critical role in the development of school examinations, its contribution since the 1880s to the training of teachers, its more recent efforts in developing and applying educational research, the expansion of extramural education, the evolution of policies related to the admission of undergraduates, perhaps even the foundation and continued support from across the whole University of *The Oxford Review of Education*, and certainly the unparalleled educational projects of the Oxford University Press.

But attention has instead here been focused on a distinctive, if short-lived, engagement of professional academics in the education of the nation. That phase in the history of the university is now ending—partly no doubt because a less deferential world is no longer willing to revere the wisdom of an idealistic mandarin class, partly because increasingly specialised academics themselves have neither the time nor the motivation voluntarily to devote themselves to public causes, and also because quite different sources of advice and policy formulation are now more readily available. Curiously, however, the importance of Oxford in securing access to and success in public life—as distinct from its recent but now disappearing importance in offering mixed careers to its dons—seems much less likely to diminish or disappear. This more general relationship between Oxford and public (but especially political) life did, of course, in the past (but not it seems any longer) gently ease the passage—of a Fisher, a Sadler, perhaps a Bullock or even a Halsey—from the quadrangles of a college into the corridors of Westminster and Whitehall. Yet many of the factors which assisted such transitions remain potent. Of the 20 Prime Ministers who have held office since 1900, ten have been graduates of Oxford University (compared with two from Cambridge, two from Glasgow, one from Birmingham—albeit in its pre-university stage) while no less than five attained the highest office without the benefit of higher education. Stanley Baldwin was the last Prime Minister who went to a university other than Oxford. Of the 51 Ministers of Education over the same period, 21 were educated at Oxford. Of the special relationship between Oxford and public life, and within the narrower focus of this discussion, no example is more central than that of Herbert Fisher—classicist and professionally educated historian, cabinet member and Minister of Education, and finally Warden of New College Oxford.

H. A. L. Fisher: scholar and minister

Harry Judge

The Oxford Don

On a cold night in December 1916 the Vice-Chancellor of Sheffield University was summoned by telephone to London to meet the new Prime Minister, David Lloyd George, who then invited him to become his country's minister of education. H. A. L. Fisher enjoyed that high office for six years (a 20th-century record) before returning reluctantly to an Oxford college. 'Oxford', he observed in his unfinished autobiography, 'had been my destiny from the first' (Fisher, 1940, p. 41).[1] His father and grandfather had both been Fellows of Oxford colleges. One sister married F. W. Maitland, perhaps the most distinguished historian of a remarkable generation of scholars, and another became the wife of Ralph Vaughan Williams. Virginia Woolf and Vanessa Bell were numbered among his cousins. But his background suited him equally well for distinction in public and political life. His mother's family was related to Gladstone, and his father had been private secretary to the Prince of Wales. The young Fisher went to school at Winchester, where Edward Grey (foreign secretary in December 1916) had been his senior, while his exact contemporary Amherst Selby-Bigge was in 1916 the most senior civil servant at the Board of

Education. While still an Oxford don, Fisher had married the daughter of Sir Courtenay Ilbert, a former Fellow of Balliol, and from 1902 Clerk to the House of Commons. If Fisher's destiny was indeed Oxford, it never became an exclusive one. No career recalled in these pages illustrates so well that ease of transition between Oxford academic life and metropolitan public service which was so characteristic of his age.

When Fisher arrived at New College as an undergraduate predestined to read Greats (Greek and Latin, followed by ancient history and philosophy), T. H. Green had just died. Fisher, like many of his contemporaries, identified Green as the most powerful intellectual influence on his development and attributed to him a deep-rooted commitment to public life and virtuous causes. But for the moment his preoccupations remained academic. Fisher, anxious to equip himself as a professional modern historian, went to study in Paris—the first English student, he believed, to recognise that the heart of historical scholarship had been transplanted there from Germany. In Paris he mingled with painters as well as several scholars, although the company seems to have been aesthetic rather than raffish. His lifelong friend, the painter Will Rothenstein, described him as having 'a somewhat grand manner' (Rothenstein, 1934, I, p. 47).

A short period of study at Göttingen—whose ways he found less congenial than had Haldane—led to a resumption of the placid life of an Oxford tutorial fellow (Ashby & Anderson, 1974). He regularly taught 18 hours a week—although never of course in the afternoon. Maitland wrote to him in March 1893: 'I hope to be in Oxford some time after three o'clock tomorrow. Please do not allow me to keep you from whatever your usual form of exercise may be' (FP/1).[2] In due course he married the spirited Lettice Ilbert, whom he had taught as a bright Somerville College student and who herself became a lecturer in history and economics. She later became active in promoting women's causes within Oxford and in society at large.[3] Although her father grumbled that Fisher 'ought not to remain for ever grinding away as a College Tutor', influential friends failed to secure for him either the Regius chair at Oxford or appointments in Cambridge or Scotland.[4] He was already something of a grand figure: these are the years when Virginia Woolf described him in a letter to Lytton Strachey as 'impossibly enlightened and humane' (Woolf, 1975, p. 378). Although his correspondence conveys a sense of impatience at the narrowness of his Oxford life, these were not unproductive years. Between 1898 and 1912 he published seven books, ranging more widely than would nowadays be wise (or even possible) from the medieval empire to Bonapartism.

In 1912 at the age of 47, Herbert Fisher left Oxford to assume his ill-defined responsibilities as Vice-Chancellor of Sheffield University. He was perceived as an effective supporter of local manufacturers and of their links with the university, to which he certainly gave a higher profile. He complained privately to his wife 'How unpleasant and gauche the people I have to work with here are'. One irritated Alderman complained that the University Council had not even been properly consulted about the appointment, and implied that Fisher had been given the impression that he was not expected to give excessive attention to his duties there (FP/2).

That view was shared by his own father-in-law, who wrote to Bryce that Sheffield: '... offers him much gold, vows that he shan't have to grind in her grimy mills, that all she wants him to do is to spread light, which is much needed, and declares that she wants him to go on writing history and that he shall have more leisure for this than where he is. So I expect he will pitch his tent in Gaza at least for a while.'[5] In the event, his interests turned away from scholarship.

His local duties were certainly neither onerous nor prestigious enough to satisfy the new Vice-Chancellor. In August 1914 he wrote to the wife of a former President of Trinity: 'I feel horribly useless here, seeing nothing and doing nothing.'[6] Yet in his first year in the North he was granted leave of absence from Sheffield to join the Commission on the Indian Public Services (for which his name had been suggested by the Marquess of Crewe). Two years later he found himself on another national commission, under Bryce, to enquire into the alleged German atrocities in Belgium. He was clearly by now more interested in the world of action and in taking part in the making of history rather than in writing it. In September 1915, Gilbert Murray told Fisher of his efforts to inform the Prime Minister, Asquith 'that you and I wanted public work'.[7] In 1916, as he enjoyed recording in his diary, he prepared a government report on French propaganda. In August he was invited to breakfast with Lloyd George, then Secretary of State for War. No questions affecting domestic policy were raised. Lloyd George enquired first, 'Who are the Slovaks?' and then, 'Where are they?', observing that he was 'attracted to the Serbs. They are like the Welsh'—apparently because their legends reminded him of the Mabinogion (FD/27.8.1916). In the same month, Fisher was appointed to the prime ministerial committee on the teaching of foreign languages, and paid a visit to the Board of Education over which, to his professed surprise, he was shortly to preside.

The Minister

On becoming Prime Minister, Lloyd George claimed that he needed an educationist rather than a politician to push ahead with long anticipated educational reforms. In any case, Crewe (who had as recently as August replaced an ineffective Arthur Henderson as President of the Board) was too close to Asquith, the ejected Prime Minister, to remain in office. Lloyd George had great difficulty in enlisting enough experienced Liberals in his new coalition ministry. In the new War Cabinet the PM himself was the only Liberal, with Bonar Law, Curzon and Milner powerfully representing the Conservatives, and Henderson as the voice of Labour (Butler & Butler, 2000, pp. 6–9). Although the Liberals had dominated the now defunct Asquith coalition, too few of this old guard were willing to serve a new and controversial master. Outsiders like Fisher were therefore needed to swell the Liberal ranks. The 'special advisers' of the Garden Suburb—led by W. G. S. Adams, the Gladstone Professor of Government in Oxford and later Warden of All Souls, and by Philip Kerr—accelerated the shift towards a presidential form of government, while outsiders like Fisher (with or without parliamentary credentials) were injected into the government itself (Grigg, 2002, pp. 231, 409).

The newspapers were now busily ventilating the names of possible Ministers of Education—that was already the term commonly used, 30 years before the title was formally created. Fisher and Michael Sadler (a fellow Vice-Chancellor and later Master of University College) were both mentioned. Responsibility for the final decision was claimed by Tom Jones, a Cabinet official who described himself as 'a rather fluid person moving among people who matter', and dismissed Sadler as 'too viewy and wordy'. Fisher later claimed that he was ignorant of what was afoot and expected a consultation on other areas of policy. Tom Jones, writing at the time to the quietly influential Sir Henry Jones, Professor of Moral Philosophy at Glasgow, observed: 'You can tell Fisher he owes his election to *you*, for it was I who first put his name forward on Tuesday midnight to Dr Addison who pronounced it "an inspiration"... Some are afraid that Fisher will be too timid'. Henry Jones is significant, for he was himself much influenced by Edward Caird, the contemporary and colleague of T. H. Green, and Jowett's successor as Master of Balliol. Lloyd George told Tom Jones that Fisher had seemed 'frightened' and the two Welshman had therefore considered Hadow, yet another Vice-Chancellor and another Oxford man (Jones, 1969, pp. 10–15). But Fisher accepted, encouraged by many supporters—including the sceptical Balfour, who nevertheless told him during an after dinner stroll that he 'thought it rather a waste of an able man's time to be at the Education Department' (FP/3).

The senior officials of that Department were well qualified to support the new minister's reforming efforts. At their head was Selby-Bigge, formerly Lecturer in Philosophy at University College Oxford, a cautious civil servant who often welcomed Fisher to his country house near Banbury. Not everyone thought well of this mandarin: Haldane, in a letter to Crewe, dismissed him as 'a black-browed man, very jealous, and full of red tape and sealing wax' (Sherington, 1982, p. 179). He was ably seconded by W. N. Bruce, the head of the secondary division. More colourful and original were John Dover Wilson and E. K. Chambers, both literary scholars of high repute. Chambers had a tongue as sharp as his mind: when Dover Wilson announced to him in 1924 that he was leaving the Board to become Professor of Education at KCL, Chambers snorted: 'Education? A disgusting subject!' (Wilson, 1969, p. 93). These men of letters were supported by the poet and scholar J. W. Mackail, sometime Fellow of Balliol and later President of the British Academy, and by Owen Morgan Edwards, for 14 years a Fellow of Lincoln and now Chief Inspector for Wales. Fisher was pleased to inherit the ubiquitous Haldane (who had recently presided over a Cabinet committee on educational reconstruction), and added to this impressive team Gilbert Murray and, a little later, Albert Mansbridge. Above all he enjoyed the support, and won the unconditional loyalty, of the astute and idealistic Herbert Lewis, whose role as parliamentary secretary to the Board was later to find a neat parallel in the relationship of Chuter Ede to Rab Butler.

Fisher was further strengthened by the promise of support and money from Lloyd George. He inherited not only collaborators of quality but also a well-developed reform agenda. Indeed, one former Minister who had introduced an unsuccessful Bill as early as 1913 complained in a mildly envious spirit of plagiarism.[8] Haldane had spoken too soon when in 1913 he announced that education was the next of 'the great social problems' which the Government was about to address. He later conceded that before the War there had been insufficient 'breeze' to carry educational reform forward (Haldane, 1929, pp. 218–219). All the efforts of the Liberal ministries between 1905 and 1914 had been frustrated by the religious difficulty: the powerful nonconformist wing of the Liberal party was wholly preoccupied with correcting what they saw as the grave injustices of the Balfour Act—injustices which Lloyd George himself had so brilliantly exposed and exploited. Moreover, after the 1910 general elections the Liberal government was inconveniently dependent on the support of the Irish Nationalists, while the Baptist leader Dr John Clifford insisted that without the ending of Rome rule in England there could be no home rule for Ireland.[9] Fisher optimistically believed that the War had changed all that, and that it would at last be possible to address educational problems in a non-sectarian spirit.

A new mood of national solidarity was only one of the reasons for hoping that the time for a major educational reform had at last arrived. The War had also revealed, and not least to Lloyd George as Minister of Munitions, just how weak the British industrial base had become, and more specifically how dependent upon foreign imports and technical expertise British prosperity now was. Recruitment to the armed forces, and especially conscription, highlighted the problems of 'physical deterioration' and directed public attention to literacy rates that were low in internationally comparative terms. In a speech given at Manchester in the last months of the War, Lloyd George proclaimed:

> The most formidable institutions we had to fight in Germany were not the arsenals of Krupp, or the yards in which they turned out submarines, but the schools of Germany. They were our most formidable competitors in business and our most terrible opponents in war. An educated man is a better worker, a more formidable warrior, and a better citizen. That was only half comprehended before the war. (*The Times*, 13 September 1918)

Several scholars have explored the complex relationship between war and the imperatives of social policy, and the demand for educational improvement was certainly sharpened by a determination to build a land fit for heroes to live in (Marwick, 1974). The pivotal role in the planning of reconstruction assigned to Christopher Addison, who had himself been parliamentary undersecretary at the Board of Education and one of the key sponsors of Fisher as Minister, ensured that education would now move to the centre of the stage (Morgan & Morgan, 1980). Newly formed pressure groups, like the Education Reform Council in 1916, helped to raise the breeze which, as Haldane had wryly noted, had not been gusty enough in 1913. The report of the departmental committee on local taxation under the chairmanship of Sir John Kempe had now been published, endorsing the importance of percentage grants for educational purposes from the Treasury to local authorities. The committee chaired by Herbert Lewis on 'juvenile education in relation to employment after the War', produced an interim report anticipating the final report in 1917 which asked: 'Can the age of adolescence be brought out of the purview of economic exploitation and into that of the social conscience?' (Waterfall, 1923, p. 45; Ford & Ford, 1951, p. 459; Andrews, 1976, p. 10).

The Legislator

Fisher therefore inherited a detailed agenda, growing public support, the promises of a new Prime Minister, and a team of able and expert collaborators, but still needed—if he was now to steer a new Bill onto the statute book—a seat in the House of Commons. Tom Jones had observed that it would therefore be necessary to 'shove some nincompoop into the House of Lords' (Jones, 1969, vol. I, p. 8). This manoeuvre was swiftly executed and Fisher installed as Member for Sheffield Hallam. In February he presented his proposals to the Cabinet, and met no opposition. His maiden speech on April 19, delivered from notes and lasting for two hours and twelve minutes, was very well received. John Burns, the veteran Labour activist and former Liberal Minister, nevertheless warned him not to be too interesting: 'Send them to sleep, Mr Fisher. Send them to sleep!' (Fisher, 1940, p. 109). The Bill that followed was very much as expected. It did, however, unlike its pre-war predecessors, ignore the religious difficulty in the unrealistic hope that it would now prove to be irrelevant. The school leaving age was to be raised to 14, and part-time schooling abolished. Moreover, all young people between the ages of 14 and 18 who were not in full time education were to be required to attend part time Continuation Schools for eight hours a week for 40 weeks of the year—an annual total of 320 hours.[10] The purposes of these projected Continuation Schools have often been misunderstood. They were not to be vocational in emphasis (since such training was to be mainly reserved to the workplace and provided by the employer), but designed with a broader 'education' as the major objective. The stress was to be upon responsible citizenship and general culture: a later report, much influenced by John Dover Wilson, had the revealing title of *Humanism in the continuation schools* (Wilson, 1969, pp. 88–90). After a visit to the Cadbury Continuation School, Fisher himself reported that he 'saw some excellent work—gymnastics, Tennyson etc.' (FP/4).

Alongside these measures, most of which survived the parliamentary process, sat the less fortunate, so-called 'administrative proposals'. These were intended to secure a stronger regional and national coordination of services by transferring some powers from the smallest local authorities to the Counties and—even more controversially—by encouraging the creation of provincial associations to undertake strategic planning. Had these proposals flourished, many of Morant's aspirations for a rationally ordered national system would have been realised, together with a more effective integration of the voluntary (religious) schools with those which were fully funded by the State (Judge, 1984). Fisher embarked on an ambitious and largely successful round of speech making throughout the country. He was at his most successful, surprisingly perhaps, in addressing large audiences and recalled with special pleasure and pride his success at a Sunday morning meeting at Bristol, arranged by Ernest Bevin of the Dockers' Union: the men several times rose to their feet and waved their handkerchiefs (Fisher, 1940, p. 106). Although Fisher tried to distance his own administrative proposals from the much more threatening and university-centred plans promoted by Haldane, the local education authorities remained suspicious. Their administrators and elected members alike were unwilling to see their newly won power whittled away by a regional tier of government, and still less by a centralising Board in Whitehall.

The employers, and in some areas working-class opinion, had their own objections—especially in the north-west where the textile industry depended heavily on half-time and juvenile labour. Fisher did not mince his words in attacking such illiberal recalcitrance: 'the men who support these opinions inherit them in a right spiritual entail from the men who upheld the slave trade against Wilberforce …' (*Times Educational Supplement*, 10 February 1921; Waterfall, 1923, p. 61). Here indeed was the voice of Gladstone. But he was perhaps too subtle in arguing that, since higher educational standards would lead to a wider readership of newspapers, newsagents had nothing to fear from the threat to the employment of delivery boys. Sir Frederick Banbury, Member for the City of London and the head of a firm of stockbrokers, was in some danger of parodying himself: 'How is education going to assist a man who has to spread manure on a field?' he demanded to know. But he had more to say, aimed particularly at the former Oxford history don: 'My experience has ever been that the man who took a First at Oxford, if he comes into the City, generally comes out last, while the man who can hardly write his name very often comes out on top.'[11]

Fisher was disappointed that the spokesmen of the Labour Party, who might have come to his aid, were—with notable exceptions like the National Union of Teachers MP, Frank Goldstone—relatively cool, 'being' as Fisher gently observed, 'good conservatives' (Fisher, 1940, p. 111; Barker, 1972, p. 30). But he cannot have been surprised. The powerful writings of L. T. Hobhouse, the apostle of New Liberalism whose development had been influenced by T. H. Green, had misled Labour supporters into expecting more than any minister in a coalition government dominated by Conservatives could possibly deliver, even in wartime (Hobhouse, 1911). The more long-sighted Labour supporters detected in Continuation Schools a plot to keep the working classes in their place, inducting them into industrial and civic docility and robbing them of access to an authentic secondary education. In the very year of the collapse of the Coalition, R. H. Tawney ('my friend', as Fisher had correctly described him) published *Secondary education for all*, rejecting the very concept of the part-time Continuation School and gesturing towards the 1944 Act. Tawney dismissed Continuation Schools as 'a makeshift' and A. J. P. Taylor later protested that they would 'have made the class cleavage in education worse than ever' (Fisher, 1940, p. 10; Taylor, 1965, p. 184).

Although the churches, albeit for very different reasons, were also uneasy about the Bill, Fisher hoped to avoid any confrontation (Judge, 2001, pp. 144–148). He was well aware that the nonconformists would have been angered by any further subventions to the Anglicans and Roman Catholics, whereas these two churches knew that without additional funding from the State they would be unable to play a significant part in the expansion of schooling. Roman Catholics, concerned about the character of religious instruction proposed for the new Continuation Schools, were not reassured by Fisher's insistence that, since they were offered only part-time classes, the issue of institutional atmosphere simply did not arise. His own optimistically sceptical attitude was shared by Gilbert Murray who told Fisher of an Oxford meeting with

Catholic priests in July 1916: 'I listened to all they had to say, and merely said that, as they knew, all pious officials at the Board looked forward to a better world in which there would be no such thing as Religion: which they took in a friendly way and said they knew that would be a great convenience for the Board'. Fisher's comment on this, in red ink, was 'most interesting'.[12] In July 1919 he did finally convene a series of private meetings with nonconformist and Anglican leaders, from which, however, Roman Catholics (as seemed usual) were excluded. Four proposals were tentatively promoted but Fisher remarked that 'nothing would be more troublesome for me than having to defend this in the House of Commons'. In any case, Dr Clifford (described by Fisher in a letter to his wife as 'a grand old boy') was hostile to any such settlement. So nothing was done (Sherington, 1982, p. 156; FP/5).

Fisher took advantage of a delay in moving the Bill through its various stages in order to draft what was formally a new measure. From this Bill the contentious administrative clauses were dropped, and one powerful segment of opposition thereby appeased. Stormy debates also led to a serious weakening of the proposals for Continuation Schools: for an unspecified interim period, the application of the law to the 16–18 year olds was deferred, while LEAs could, if they wished, reduce the attendance requirements for younger people from 320 to 280 hours.

The Reformer

Many of Fisher's achievements have been obscured by an unhelpful emphasis on the Act which still bears his name, and by the post-war abandonment of many of its key provisions. While continuing to insist that Continuation Schools are 'what we principally require', he did provide more secondary grammar school places for the academic minority (Fisher, 1918, p. xiv). He accepted the recommendations of the Hilton Young report (1920) that there should be for the secondary sector more free places, more schools, more LEA planning and (eventually) the abolition of fees. Between 1917 and 1923 the number of pupils on the Board's school grant list rose from 216,765 to 327,601, while the number of free places almost doubled reaching 113,405 in 1923.[13] Fisher also encouraged the work of four influential official committees on the school curriculum, three of which had been established just before he assumed office. He had himself been an early member of the committee on modern languages, chaired by Sir Stanley Leathes, joint editor of *The Cambridge Modern History*. The committee on science teaching under Sir J. J. Thomson was much concerned with the balance between instruction and discovery, and led to the provision of school laboratories on a scale which was (for once) impressive by international standards. Its report was critical of what became the English disease of overspecialisation (from which the sciences in particular have suffered), urging that not more than one half or two-thirds of a sixth former's time should be devoted to specialised studies. Sir Henry Newbolt chaired the committee on English which enshrined the mantra 'Every teacher in English is a teacher of English', that echoes still in the Bullock report on the same subject. Newbolt canonised a 19th-century notion of literature. But there is no doubt that for Fisher himself the most important of the four committees was the one addressing the classics which he had himself established under the chairmanship of Lord Crewe and that included such luminaries as Hadow, Gilbert Murray (of course), Norwood and Whitehead. Fisher was alarmed by the precipitous decline of the classics: of the 444 secondary schools recently founded, only 33 offered Greek; and in 1919 Oxford abandoned that language as a matriculation requirement (Ford & Ford, 1951, I, pp. 475–476, 484).

Fisher, determined to introduce a national examination system as a means of raising standards in secondary schools and of opening up pathways to the university, accepted the recommendations of a 1911 committee. This had been chaired by Arthur Acland, another former Oxford don and Liberal minister who had been a close friend of T. H. Green (Ockwell & Pollins, 2000, p. 663). In 1919 Fisher therefore established the Secondary Schools Examination Council which substituted the School Certificate and Higher School Certificate for a bewildering variety of some 55 separate examinations (Ford & Ford, I, p. 313). These national examinations, the outlines of which survived the century, furnished the basis for a system of State Scholarships enabling some students from poorer families to gain access to universities. Fisher was, at least privately, clear that the main purpose of these scholarships was to protect the classics by focusing the provision of state support on the sciences—the older universities could then concentrate their own scholarship resources on nurturing the classics. In a letter to Gilbert Murray in 1917 he regretted the imprudent haste of Magdalen College in transferring such resources from the classics (FP/6). The expansion of university provision had already been accelerated by the financial support secured for ex-servicemen: Fisher had secured £8 million for this purpose and 27,000 students benefited (Fisher, 1940, p. 114).

As a result of that expansion, of earlier decades of under-funding, the depredations of the War, and the growth of cash hungry sciences, the universities were now in urgent need of enhanced state support. This need was widely acknowledged, even if Austen Chamberlain prophetically warned that 'It would be an evil day if the universities looked only to the government and not to the communities in which they were placed' (*The Times*, 18 September 1919). Fisher, anxious to protect a proper degree of autonomy, insisted that Treasury support should be as a general grant and not—as had frequently been the case in the past—as specific subventions to particular departments or projects. He formalised the University Grants Committee, which remained until the 1980s one of the brightest jewels in the British educational crown (Carswell, 1985; Shinn, 1986). Fisher, Minister and former Vice-Chancellor, argued that the Committee should not, however, exercise detailed control over the allocation of resources. He therefore encouraged the foundation of the Committee of Vice-Chancellors and Principals to undertake a coordinating role and specifically to block conflicting demands from the universities themselves. Parliament had, since 1889, been making annual grants to universities on an *ad hoc* basis, and in 1904 a committee under the chairmanship of Haldane had assumed responsibility for the distribution of grants. In 1911, the administrative oversight of that work was quietly transferred to the Board of Education itself, whose responsibilities were, however, for England and Wales only. It is misleading to suggest that Fisher and his advisers, or even the

Treasury itself, now wished the Board to be distanced from these tasks. Fisher in fact wanted the Board to preserve a dominant voice in such matters, but the extension of the Committee's mandate to all parts of the British Isles now made necessary the formal transfer to the Treasury of the responsibility for administering the grant. Not a few hallowed myths have gathered around this relatively unimportant change (Ashby & Anderson, 1974, p. 153).

Fisher nurtured the growth of graduate studies and the introduction of the PhD. Many American universities, following Yale's 1861 initiative, already offered this degree, although most serious students in the United States long continued to look to Europe and especially to Germany and France (as, of course, had Fisher himself). There was a widely shared hope that after the War the international flow of students towards Britain would increase, and not least from Canada (as ever, more than a little wary of its neighbour). In 1918, Balfour and Fisher met representatives of the British universities and, with unprecedented despatch and uncharacteristic unanimity, the British PhD and Oxford DPhil were launched (Rudd, 1975, p. 13). The peculiarities of Oxford received some attention from Fisher: in 1919 he appointed a Royal Commission on the two ancient universities chaired by Asquith, whom he always admired (Prest, 1994, pp. 27–44). Fisher entertained high hopes of its capacity to propel genuine change—he had after all signed a 'Reformers' Letter' as long ago as 1907 (*The Times*, 14 July 1907). The Commission concluded that the University did indeed need more public money (although only as a temporary stopgap): dons were overworking, and impoverished professors compelled to adhere to their chairs until they were 70 or 80. But only modest efforts were made to reconcile the interests of the Colleges and the University, and even Asquith's most sympathetic biographer— who himself later became Chancellor of Oxford—found the report unadventurous (Jenkins, 1964, p. 483, n. 1). Fisher must have wanted more. For example, in a private letter in June 1919 he observed: 'There is nothing in the grant-aided universities so subversive of intellectual freedom as the association in Oxford of the Chairs in Divinity with Canonries' (FP/7).

But it was teachers in the elementary and secondary schools, rather than elderly Professors, who owed most to Fisher. Writing to Lloyd George as they were both about to leave office, Fisher placed his work for teachers first in the list of achievements: 'The whole Teaching Service has been lifted out of the pit and placed upon a securer level of comfort' (Sherington, 1982, p. 167). In words which should be hammered into the consciousness of all politicians and administrators, Fisher asserted: 'The young should not be entrusted to the care of sad, melancholy, careworn teachers. The classroom should be a cheerful place. The state which values harmony should begin by making its teachers happy.' This remained for Fisher a civil, as well as an educational imperative. In the speech introducing the estimates for 1918, which included a 60% Government grant towards teachers' salaries, he warned that 'An anxious and depressed teacher is a bad teacher; an embittered teacher is a social danger'. Nor should teachers be regarded as civil servants: teaching must be a liberal profession, and it was preferable that it should be disorganised rather than centralised (Fisher, 1918, p. 10; Fisher, 1940, pp. 97, 105). In 1919 and 1920 the salary negotiations were delegated to the Burnham committees, representing the unions and the employers. Equally dramatic was the improvement in superannuation arrangements: the Board at first proposed that teachers should make a 5% contribution to a fund to be administered by insurance companies, but—for once preferring clarity to economy—the Treasury insisted on a non-contributory scheme. As a result, whereas teachers' salaries had been doubled, their superannuation prospects had improved threefold (Gosden, 1972, p. 139). The crisis in teacher supply in 1913–14 had been caused largely by poor pay, and it would now be necessary to improve the provision for teacher training. Between 1900 and 1913 the number of teacher training colleges had increased from 61 to 80, including 11 University Departments of Education. The 1918 Act imposed upon the LEAs the duty to establish new colleges and to ensure a sufficient supply of well-trained teachers. Fisher had no doubts about where the emphasis should lie in the training of teachers. Pedagogical principles were all very well, but 'the main weight ... should be thrown on the handling of the principal subjects in the school curriculum' (FP/8). Early in 1922, Tom Jones—who had of course been instrumental in bringing him to the Board—observed that the improvement in the status of teachers had been 'the biggest thing that Fisher had been able to do' (Jones, 1969, vol. I, p. 192). It was certainly a sustained effort that was warmly appreciated by teachers. Unfortunately, as President of the Board, Fisher was less sympathetic to the cause of women teachers. Given his strong support for women's education, and the undoubted influence upon him of a strong-minded wife who was vigorously committed to raising the status of women in society, this seems surprising. Presumably he felt that there was a limit to the number of unpopular political battles that he could fight. At a time when all his carefully matured plans were under attack in the economically difficult post-war years he wrote a private note as Minister supporting the ban imposed by many local authorities on the employment of women teachers.[14]

Return to Oxford

After the end of the First World War, Fisher remained an MP for eight years, half of them as a Minister. The Cabinet to which he belonged was weakened by the fragility of the coalition alliance between the Liberal followers of Lloyd George and the powerful Conservative party: well characterised by wags as 'a flock of sheep led by a crook, and a flock of crooks led by a sheep' (Kinnear, 1973, p. 4). Fisher, 'that austere symbol of academic rectitude', dutifully polished some fine phrases for its 1918 election manifesto (Morgan, 1979, p. 36). Lloyd George won, but only on a small electoral turnout (the lowest until 2001), and Fisher soon began to doubt his wayward leader's capacity to deliver either the money or the Conservative support needed to protect the reforms for which he had fought so hard. But he had no wish to leave public life, finally resigning his Sheffield appointment, and hoping in vain for a new and more prestigious appointment: the India office, the foreign office, or the Washington embassy. But Lloyd George concluded that he was politically too valuable where he was. Education nevertheless absorbed less of his time and attention: he became chairman of the Cabinet home affairs committee as well as one of the British representatives at the League of Nations, and immersed himself in the tangled affairs of Ireland and India.

There was therefore plenty to keep Fisher occupied, even if his attention strayed far from the educational landscape. On the first day of 1920 the *Times Educational Supplement* complained that 'Mr Fisher seems to have lost the first fine frenzy of reconstruction. He sees a great educational epoch but sees it on a far horizon'. The collapse of the short-lived economic boom in that year rapidly refocused his attention, for the vulnerability of his reforms was suddenly exposed. Even the ever-friendly Tom Jones admitted that the Minister had miscalculated badly in suggesting that the 1918 Act and associated reforms would cost three rather than 30 million pounds a year (Jones, 1969, p. 192). The launching of The Anti-Waste Campaign encouraged the old enemies—especially of the Continuation Schools—to remobilise their forces (Cowling, 1971, p. 115). The opening of any more Continuation Schools was indefinitely postponed, and the few that existed faded away (although one at Rugby managed to survive in some form until 1969). Early in 1922, the government's Geddes committee of businessmen wielded its axe, proposing massive cuts of £46.5 million in defence and of £18 million in education. Such economies would require raising to six the age of starting school, closing small schools, worsening the teacher/pupil ratio to 1/50, abandoning the Continuation School project, cutting teachers' salaries, levying contributions to the superannuation scheme and—perhaps most threatening of all—ending the percentage grant system.

Fisher engaged in 'a week of wrestling with the Axe-Bearer', threatening that both he and Herbert Lewis would resign, and won valuable concessions—not least because it was clear that education cuts were damaging the government in by-elections (FP/9). The threatened cut was reduced to £6 million, 'to the infinite disgust of Banbury'. Lloyd George was not helpful to Fisher, declaring himself '... sure that the brightest children would learn as readily and as quickly in a class of seventy as they would in a much smaller class' (Morgan, 1979, p. 292). On May 16 1922 the Government was defeated on the issue of superannuation contributions, Fisher arguing in vain that relief from contributions had been part of a formal agreement within the Burnham Committees: yet again he threatened to resign. But the government itself did not have long to run, and within a year the superannuation levy was imposed and teachers accepted a voluntary percentage cut in their salaries. Lloyd George and the moderately progressive cause which Fisher represented had been seriously weakened by the departure of Addison, Montagu and Henderson. The alliance with the Conservatives had been undermined by the retirement of Bonar Law and his replacement by the less adroit Austen Chamberlain. Fisher, who had in 1919 disapproved of Lloyd George's proposals for a 'fusion' of the Coalition Liberals with their Conservative allies, was now persuaded that Lloyd George should resign, thereby pushing the Conservatives into an impossible position and then securing an electoral victory (FD/28.3.1922).

At the Carlton Club meeting on 19 October 1922 the crumbling alliance of the two parties finally collapsed and three hours later Lloyd George resigned. Fisher, of course, departed with him but in the subsequent general election kept his seat in Parliament: he had no wish to leave politics and deputised for Lloyd George alongside Asquith in November 1923 at a meeting in the Queen's Hall. In the following year the fractured Liberal party was formally reunited, but never recovered power. Fisher needed a career and an income, telling Bonar Law and Balfour of his interest in appropriate offices (Cowling, 1971, p. 323). He waited in vain. Five years later Tom Jones strolled with Abraham Flexner in St James' Park and yet again suggested Fisher for the Washington embassy: '... too colourless and negative', Flexner interjected (Jones, 1969, II, p. 159). By then Fisher had been elected as Warden of New College, after sighing that 'it may come to that' and in February 1928 reluctantly resigned his Commons seat (Harrison, 1994, p. 82). This exile from Parliament he described to Gilbert Murray as 'a great wrench', adding less plausibly that 'the moral atmosphere ... is there so much higher and more serious than it is in a university'(FP/10). Fisher, now 60 years old, returned to the College he had left 13 years earlier. He never recovered from his sense of loss and had little sympathy with most of his peers: 'I confess that I find it somewhat difficult to fill in my time at Oxford. The College business can be transacted in the twinkling of an eye. ... Really there is no excuse for Heads of Colleges not making important contributions to learning. Some of them of course do, but the majority find it easier to fill up their time with sawdust' (FP/11).

He successfully filled his own time with lecturing, public service, university and college affairs and scholarship—publishing a two-volume life of Bryce in 1927, and a lively and ironic attack on Christian Science in 1929. The work which brought him most fame was the successful three-volume *History of Europe*, published in 1935 and written for the general reader but with an eye on the youthful candidate seeking a scholarship at one of the two older universities (FP/12). He had always been concerned about his health, complaining as early as 1918 that '[t]he worst of my life is that I've never had enough physical vigour to feel at ease with my work' (FP/13). For the first three months of 1936 he was out of action with some kind of nervous collapse and the Warden's duties were undertaken by Richard Crossman—one of the young men, like Isaiah Berlin, upon whom he depended for stimulation (FP/14 and conversation with Mary Bennett 22 May 2002). Nevertheless on the outbreak of war and at the age of 75 he was ready to accept an extension of his tenure at New College for ten years or for the duration of the emergency 'whichever should be the shorter' (FP/15). But in March 1940, walking to a tribunal for conscientious objectors, he was knocked down in a road accident in London, and ten days later died in hospital in the city where he had lived and worked for the most memorable years of his life. It was in London, and not Oxford, that he found the greatest satisfaction, and in his last years he recalled a youthful holiday spent in Scotland with Gilbert Murray:

> The weather was lovely, the scenery was beautiful, the talk eager and wide-ranging. On the last evening of our visit, as Murray and I were taking our leave, Morley said, 'I will send you away with a text', and kneeling on the floor by the light of a single candle, read out from a well-worn little copy of Bain's life of J. S. Mill the master's prescription for a happy life; that we should never expect more from life than life can give, and that the happy life is three parts practical. (Fisher, 1940, p. 88)

Fisher never quite recovered from his deep but temporary immersion in practical affairs: the rest of his life was something of a disappointment. Virginia Woolf once laid a bet on how long it would take her cousin to let slip in conversation the phrase 'When I was in the Cabinet ...' (three minutes in fact), while Lionel Robbins recalled the embarrassment of Fisher's younger colleagues when the Warden launched into his political reminiscences: he was like 'a good man who had unwittingly entered a brothel—and rather enjoyed it' (Jones, 1969, II, p. 206; Robbins, 1971, pp. 112–117).

Although many of his reminiscences were of high politics and international affairs of state, his achievements in education were far from negligible. He was, of course, no revolutionary and sat sedately in a tradition of Gladstonian liberalism tempered with an admiration for Lloyd George's early reforming zeal and grounded in a rigorously classical education. Inevitably he disappointed his friend Tawney who hoped for much more. If he had been impolite enough to interrupt, he would also have disappointed King George V when the monarch lectured him on the need to 'Get the Latin and Greek out of the schools. Teach them engineering—something useful.'[15] He was deeply interested in the content and purposes of education: his Continuation Schools were intended to promote the humanities rather than vocational training, and of the four major reports on the school curriculum which he promoted, for him the most important dealt with the classics. State scholarships at the universities were to enable the ancient universities to use their own endowments to preserve the classics. Grammar Schools were to be allowed to grow, but their traditional academic character scrupulously preserved. The significance of the 1918 Act (one of a handful of British education acts destined to be known by the name of their principal sponsor) has been obscured by the vicious economies of the early 1920s: cuts which Fisher stoutly resisted and managed to limit. The school leaving age was raised to 14 and part-time schooling abolished whatever Sir Francis Banbury may have said. There were great improvements in the health of schoolchildren. The British universities were given a new lease of life, fortified by an injection of public funds and a minimum of political interference and control. A system of school examinations was established, sound enough to survive the hammerings of a long century. Above all, Fisher dramatically enhanced the status of teachers in elementary and secondary schools, securing for them improved training, a decent salary and a dignified retirement. The building of a well coordinated system of public education continued to be impeded by the religious difficulty, but Fisher can hardly be blamed for that. An agnostic who regularly attended his college chapel while believing that 'religion rots the mind', he understandably failed to understand the deep animosities which divided Christian denominations (Hart, 1998, p. 204). The sustained improvement of educational opportunity, while doubtless still inadequate, was made possible by a new system of educational financing based on a percentage grant arrangement which enabled local education authorities to realise at least some of their ambitions. Fisher, Oxford don and Liberal minister, deserves to be remembered more for his acts than for his Act. Four years after his own death the Butler Act of 1944 made its way to the statute book.

Notes

1. Much of the material for this study of Fisher was drawn from his unfinished autobiography (Fisher, 1940) supplemented by the short life written by his historian colleague at New College (Ogg, 1947). As with other sources, a precise citation is given in the text or a footnote only where there is a direct quotation, or clear identification is needed. Particularly valuable for the background to Fisher's work is Morgan (1979) and, on matters educational, Sherington (1982) and Andrews (1976). The Fisher Papers in the Bodleian Library in Oxford have been extensively consulted. References to this collection (as also to the Bryce, Gilbert Murray, and Margaret Louise Woods Papers, all referred to in later footnotes) are made with the consent of the Library, which is gratefully acknowledged. A particular debt is owed to Fisher's daughter, Mrs Mary Bennett (sometime Principal of St Hilda's College Oxford) who graciously gave permission for her father's papers to be cited, and whose conversations over the years were invaluable to the author. She died in November 2005. As these pages were written, Professor Russell Bryant was completing for publication his important edition of Fisher's diaries (see References). Since a paginated version of this edition had not been available to me, references to the diaries are given by date only, in the form FD/dd.mm.yyyy. Official papers are identified in the notes as National Archives.
2. Bodl MSS Fisher: Maitland to Fisher 4 March 1893. Letters and other documents in the Fisher Papers are here identified by date (and an excellent catalogue now exists in the Library itself). To avoid cluttering the text, this first reference is identified in the text above simply as (FP/1). Subsequent references are similarly coded and represent:
   FP/2 Herbert to Lettice Fisher 13 June 1916
   FP/3 Herbert to Lettice Fisher 3 February 1917
   FP/4 Herbert to Lettice Fisher 17 or 18 June 1917
   FP/5 Herbert to Lettice Fisher 7 January 1920
   FP/6 Fisher to Gilbert Murray 5 August 1917
   FP/7 Fisher to Gilbert Murray 11 June 1919
   FP/8 Handwritten note by Fisher on evidence to the Departmental Committee of the Training of Teachers 28 May 1923
   FP/9 Fisher to Gilbert Murray 12 January 1922
   FP/10 Fisher to Gilbert Murray 15 February 1926
   FP/11 Fisher to Lord Irwin 15 March 1928
   FP/12 Fisher to Douglas Jerrold 17 January 1934
   FP/13 Herbert to Lettice Fisher 1919 (n.d.)
   FP/14 New College Record 1936–37. Recollections of Mary Bennett
   FP/15 David Ogg to Fisher 10 February 1940.
3. Mary Bennett believed that her mother may have been Fisher's only Somerville pupil, and that she was accorded the privilege of being taught by him only because he held her father in great esteem. The Fishers later moved from no. 34 to no. 37. Their daughter was born in 1913.
4. Bryce Papers: Bodl MS Bryce 13, fol. 158, 6 June 1909.
5. Bryce Papers: Bodl MS Bryce 14, fol. 67, 8 November 1912.
6. Margaret Louise Woods Papers: Bodl MS Eng.lett. e.26, fols 175, 176.
7. Gilbert Murray Papers: Bodl MS Gilbert Murray 28, Murray to Fisher 25 September 1915.
8. Cleary's history of the Education Bill, National Archives Ed24/2077 cap XIX (see Note 10).
9. National Archives Ed24/624.
10. Many of the details relating to the passing of the 1918 Act are ably summarised in the unpublished paper (National Archives Ed24/2007) written by the young civil servant, William Cleary, who later played an important part in the planning of the 1944 Act.
11. National Archives Ed24/2007, cap. XII.
12. National Archives Ed24/799.
13. Report of the Board of Education for 1923–24, p. 67.

14. National Archives Ed24/1744.
15. Margaret Louise Woods Papers: Bodl. MS eng.lett. e.26, fols 189, 190.

Notes on contributor

Harry Judge is an Emeritus Fellow of Brasenose College Oxford and was, from 1973 to 1988, Director of the Oxford University Department of Educational Studies. Recent publications include: 'The Muslim headscarf and French schools', *American Journal of Education*, 111(1), 2004, and *Faith-based schools and the state: Catholics in America, France and England* (2002).

References

Andrews, A. (1976) *The Education Act of 1918* (Routledge & Kegan Paul).
Ashby, E. & Anderson, M. (1974) *Portrait of Haldane at work on education* (London, Macmillan).
Barker, R. (1972) *Education and politics, 1900–1951: a study of the Labour Party* (Oxford, Clarendon).
Bryant, R. (in press) *The coalition diaries and letters of H. A. L. Fisher, 1916–1922: the historian in Lloyd George's cabinet* (London, Mellen).
Butler, D. & Butler, G. (2000) *Twentieth century British political facts* (London, Macmillan).
Carswell, J. (1985) *Government and the universities in Britain: programme and performance 1960–1980* (Cambridge, Cambridge University Press).
Cowling, M. (1971) *The impact of Labour 1920–1924: the beginning of modern British politics* (Cambridge, Cambridge University Press).
Fisher, H. A. L. (1918) *Education reform* (London, Oxford University Press).
Fisher, H. A. L. (1940) *An unfinished autobiography* (London, Oxford University Press).
Ford, P. & Ford, G. (1951) *A breviate of Parliamentary papers, 3 vols* (Oxford, Basil Blackwell).
Gosden, P. (1972) *The evolution of a profession* (Oxford, Basil Blackwell).
Grigg, J. (2002) *Lloyd George: war leader 1916–1920* (London, Penguin).
Haldane, R. B. (1929) *An autobiography* (London, Hodder & Stoughton).
Harrison, B. (1994) College life, 1918–1939, in: B. Harrison (Ed.) *The history of the University of Oxford, vol. VIII* (Oxford, Clarendon Press), 81–108.
Hart, J. (1998) *As me no more: an autobiography* (London, Peter Halborn).
Hobhouse, L. T. (1911) *Liberalism* (London, Oxford University Press).
Jenkins, R. (1964, rev. 1986) *Asquith* (London, Collins).
Jones, T. (1969) (Ed. K. Middlemas) *Whitehall diaries, vols. 1, II* (London, Oxford University Press).
Judge, H. (1984) R. L. Morant, in: P. Barker (Ed.) *Founders of the welfare state* (London, Heinemann), 61–67.
Judge, H. (2001) *Faith-based schools and the state* (Wallingford, Symposium Books).
Kinnear, M. (1973) *The fall of Lloyd George: the political crisis of 1922* (London, Macmillan).
Marwick, A. (1974) *War and social change in the twentieth century* (London, Macmillan).
Morgan, K. (1979) *Concensus and disunity: the Lloyd George coalition government 1918–1922* (Oxford, Clarendon Press).
Morgan, K. & Morgan, J. (1980) *Portrait of a progressive: the political career of Christopher, Viscount Addison* (Oxford, Clarendon Press).
Ockwell, A. & Pollins, H. (2000) Extension in all its forms, in: M. G. Brock & M. C. Curthoys (Eds) *The history of the University of Oxford, vol. VII part 2* (Oxford, Clarendon Press).
Ogg, D. (1947) *Herbert Fisher: a short biography* (London, Edward Arnold).
Parkinson, M. (1970) The Labour Party and the organisation of secondary education 1918–1965 (London, Routledge & Kegan Paul).

Prest, J. (1994) The Asquith commission, 1919–1922, in: B. Harrison (Ed.) *The history of the University of Oxford, vol. VIII* (Oxford, Clarendon Press).
Robbins, L. (1971) *Autobiography of an economist* (London, Macmillan).
Rothenstein, W. (1934) *Men and memories* (London, Rose and Crown Library).
Rudd, E. (1975) *The highest education: a study of graduate education in Britain* (London, Routledge & Kegan Paul).
Sherington, G. E. (1982) *English education, social change and war 1911–1920* (Manchester, Manchester University Press).
Shinn, C. H. (1986) *Paying the piper: the development of the University Grants Committee 1919–1946* (Bascombe, Falmer Press).
Tawney, R. H. (1924) *Secondary education for all* (London, George Allen & Unwin).
Taylor, A. J. P. (1965) *English history 1914–1945* (Oxford, Oxford University Press).
Waterfall, E. A. (1923) *The day continuation school in England* (London, George Allen & Unwin).
Wilson, J. D. (1969) *Milestones on the Dover Road* (London, Faber).
Woolf, V. (1977–84) (Ed. A. Bell) *The diary of Virginia Woolf, vols I–V* (London, Hogarth Press).
Woolf, V. (1975) (Ed. N. Nicolson) *The letters of Virginia Woolf, vol. I* (London, Hogarth Press).

T. H. Green: citizenship, education and the law

Raymond Plant

Introduction

T. H. Green, who was a Fellow of Balliol College Oxford from 1860 (and Whyte's Professor of Moral Philosophy from 1877), had an immense impact on both philosophical life and public policy, and particularly in the sphere of education. He died in 1882 at the age of 45. Green was an influential tutor at Balliol in its heyday under the inspired Mastership of Jowett. Although Jowett came eventually to disapprove of what he saw as Green's excessive influence on young minds, the two were closely linked in developing what they saw as the mission of Balliol, both within Oxford and in the wider nation and Empire. Indeed Asquith, who had been at Balliol as Green's pupil and under Jowett's Mastership, confessed himself unable to separate them in his mind. Over 90% of Balliol undergraduates in the 75 years before 1914 entered public service at the local, national or colonial level (Perkin, 1989, p. 369): Green's philosophical and ethical views provided a strong and inspiring underpinning for such a commitment to public service.

The scope of Green's influence

Green exercised great influence in philosophy. Many of the succeeding generation of philosophers—including John and Edward Caird (the latter succeeding Jowett as Master), F. H Bradley, D. G. Ritchie, J. H. Muirhead, R. L. Nettleship, W. Wallace, and B. Bosanquet—were among his disciples. Many other scholars—such as Arnold Toynbee the political economist, Alfred Marshall the economist, Sir Henry Jones of Glasgow University and a prominent Liberal, J. A. Hobson the economist, and L. T. Hobhouse the social theorist—all acknowledged their debt to him. His influence was equally potent on men who entered public service in one form or another, especially in the field of education: Asquith, Arthur Acland, R. B. Haldane (twice Lord Chancellor), Alfred Milner, Sadler, Morant, Fisher, Charles Loch of the Charity Organisation Society (Vincent & Plant, 1984, ch. 6). He was a major influence on leading figures in religious life, notably Charles Gore (later Bishop of Oxford) and the authors of the controversial volume of essays *Lux Mundi*, as well as on Henry Scott Holland—one of the most influential religious figures of the day—and Canon Barnett in Oxford. Their role in the Christian Social Union and the Guild of St. Matthew owed a very great deal to Green. Even a second generation Tractarian such as the saintly Bishop King of Lincoln recognised that among philosophers, Green had befriended Christianity in a way that Mill and Spencer had not. He argued that Green had allowed men to believe once more in the soul.

Green's vision of civic idealism had a great impact on the Settlement movement, particularly through Canon Barnett and others in the East End of London (Vincent & Plant, 1984, ch. 7). Toynbee Hall, which Gertrude Himmelfarb called the 'existential realisation of Green's philosophy' (Himmelfarb, 1992, p. 243), mediated the influence of Green's ideas on civic idealism and the common good into the political and social thinking of R. H. Tawney, Clement Attlee and William Beveridge. Tawney, Scott Holland, Haldane and Sidney Ball were influential in the founding and sustaining of the WEA. In Oxford itself, Green became the first member of the university to be elected to the city council, and played a critical part in the foundation of a secondary school for boys. As though so much thought and action were not enough for one man, Green attained fictional immortality as the revered Professor Grey in Mrs Humphrey Ward's *Robert Elsmere*, one of the best selling novels of the 19th century. The succeeding years have produced a rich crop of scholarly works amply attesting to the significance of Green in intellectual and public life (Bowle, 1954; Richter, 1964; Greenleaf, 1983; Vincent & Plant, 1984; Nicholson, 1990; Collini, 1991; Harris, 1992; Boucher & Vincent, 2000; Cater, 2003; Leighton, 2004; Wempe, 2004). R. G. Collingwood, himself an Idealist in philosophy, although with significant differences from Green, had good reason to claim that:

> The school of Green sent out into public life a stream of ex-pupils who carried with them the conviction that philosophy, and in particular the philosophy they had learned at Oxford, was an important thing, and that their vocation was to put it into practice. ...Through this effect on the minds of its pupils, the philosophy of Green's school might be found from about 1880 to about 1910 penetrating and fertilizing every part of national life. (Collingwood, 1939, p. 17)

What, then, were the principal themes of that philosophy?

The intellectual context: religion, philosophy and the common life

Green's distinctive Idealist philosophy can be understood only against its contemporary background of religious belief and doubt: in a sense it filled the chasm left by the decline of belief in the historic truths of revealed religion while helping to satisfy the spiritual appetite of what was, after all, a highly religious century. The Oxford—or Tractarian—Movement had revitalised the Anglican Church (although not in ways approved of by Green), and there were equally powerful and deep revivals among Evangelicals of all persuasions. But it was also, and characteristically, an age of doubt—fed by the growing popularity of Darwinian explanations of human evolution, geological discoveries which cast immense doubt on the creation stories in Genesis, the growth of historical understanding which caused doubts about the evidential nature of the Biblical record and of the reliability of the image of Jesus as exhibited in the Gospels, and the growth of philosophical interest in materialism, evolution and utilitarianism. Darwin, Colenso, Strauss, Renan, Baur, Huxley, Spencer, Mill, W. K. Clifford, and Bradlaugh were figures who in their very different ways all undermined what were taken to be the basic truths of Christianity whether in metaphysics or ethics. This sense of doubt is perfectly reflected in the poetry of the period, whether in Tennyson's outpouring of grief in *In Memoriam* or Matthew Arnold's evocative reference to the long withdrawing roar of the sea of faith.

Green, the son of an evangelical clergyman, addressed himself directly to the sources of religious doubt—particularly in the ambiguous theological legacy of Hegel, as developed in different ways by Strauss and Baur—and he used their own work to fashion Christian belief into a metaphysical system, the truth of which could be argued for independently of contested evidence (Vincent & Plant 1984, ch. 2). At the same time, for Green, this philosophical position would illuminate the religious beliefs that the common people still had to a large extent, despite the long term withdrawal of the sea of faith. These beliefs were, however, in Green's view, represented conventionally in the scriptures and in religious teaching in what had, under intellectual pressure, come to be seen as contested and misleading idioms. Green's mission was to be the same as that of Hegel: to transform religious consciousness—shot through as that was with contested idioms, narratives, historical claims and symbols—into a conceptual and metaphysical theory which would give a firm foundation for the beliefs so transformed. But he did not think that Hegel could simply be translated, as it were, into English: the Hegelian position had rather to be taken as an inspirational guide to a more home grown type of language and metaphysic, thereby transforming the beliefs that most people held. These beliefs would then become more defensible and more appropriate as the foundation of a common life and common moral experience. As Green asserted: 'Philosophy does but interpret with full consciousness and in system the powers already working in the spiritual life of mankind'. There was for Green no gap at all between the philosophical life, the life of religious discipleship and the ethic that flowed from that and which so influenced public (including educational) policy. The social and political philosophy which flows from his metaphysical theory is not to be understood as something abstract which, as it were, sought an entry into the social and political conceptions of ordinary citizens. Instead, such a philosophy makes articulate and rationally defensible central elements of that moral and spiritual consciousness *as it already exists*. Ideas like the sanctified life, the Christed life (Leighton, 2004, ch. 3), the movement from abandonment and death to resurrection and the glorified life, could be given an interpretation within Green's philosophy which enabled them to be used as ethical ideas which did not require the person engaging with those ideas to accept the full theological and doctrinal understanding of Christianity.

It follows that his own philosophical position can be broader than Christianity and its doctrines. Philosophy incorporates, but is not confined to, this religious belief system and its own internal understanding of the spiritual and ethical life. But it can cast its net wider since it is based upon rational principles which can be understood by all rational persons, even although many will still want to understand the basic principles of life and ethics in a religious idiom. This goes some way to explain one element of Green's educational philosophy, namely his strong opposition to denominational schools and sectarianism in education. Although he was in favour of the communication of a religious sense in schools—both for its direct spiritual effect on the pupil and as part of the basis of a common life in the nation—his whole view of the nature of religion meant that he was opposed to sectarian and doctrinal divisions. These differences become much less important from the standpoint of a philosophical grasp of religious faith. Given his own philosophical and humanistic understanding of Christianity, there would be little room for such doctrinal differences and these differences should ideally not be reproduced in schools. Green could therefore argue that 'Philosophy on its part is seen to be the effort towards self recognition of that spiritual life which fulfils itself in many ways but most completely in the Christian religion and is related to that religion as flowers to a leaf' (Vincent & Plant, 1984).

It is this effort to provide a firm intellectual basis for a spirituality which would be undogmatic and issue in practical social action which inspired those who followed Green, whether in the philosophical life or in the life of government and public service. Arnold Toynbee recognised that:

> Earnest and thoughtful people are willing to encounter the difficulty of mastering some unfamiliar phrases of technical language when they find that they are in possession of a sharply defined intellectual position on which their religious faith can rest. (Toynbee, 1969, p. 246)

Philosophical themes

Which of the many themes running through Green's philosophy bear directly on the way that ethics could underpin public service and education? The aim of his metaphysic is to produce what might be regarded as a humanistic reading of Christianity. It follows that his understanding of the nature of God is important for his account of the human personality, freedom and the common good which are, in turn, central to his moral and political thought. Green rejected the idea typical of classical theism that God is utterly transcendent, impassable, unchangeable and totally 'other' in respect of human life. Rather, following Hegel, he wanted to stress the interrelationship between God and man and the progressive revelation of the nature of God in and through human history and human consciousness, and in ethical and political activity. Most of the central themes of Green's ethical and political philosophy are bound up in this conception of God—or what in his more philosophical writings he calls 'the spiritual principle'. In his review of John Caird's very Hegelian *Introduction to the philosophy of religion*, Green argued:

> That there is one spiritual self conscious being of which all that is real is the activity and expression; that we are related to this spiritual being not merely as parts of the world which is its expression but as partakers in some inchoate measure of the self consciousness through which it at once constitutes and distinguishes itself from the world: that this participation is the source of morality and religion; this we take to be the vital truth which Hegel had to teach. It still remains to be presented in a form which will command some general acceptance among serious and scientific men. (Green, 1888, p. 146)

It was Green's self-appointed task to articulate this vision in an English idiom, and then to draw out its ethical and political consequences. Green believed that humanity shares a common nature as sharers in the incarnation of God in the world (Green, 1883, p. 208). In consequence, human beings have common goals and values and there is a common good between people to be found. In living mindful of the needs of others as equally embodying the divine spirit, we realise our own nature and this way of living is connected with human freedom (Green, 1883, p. 218). Our understanding of the demands of morality, in both personal and public life is progressive since the spiritual principle embodied in our lives is not at any single time fully comprehended in its complexity. Our ethical understanding will be developed in a rational way so that one age will make an ethical advance on previous ages as our understanding of the ethical demands of human life becomes more complex and develops. Green links this principle back to F. C. Baur's religious views, which he summarises in these terms:

> The revelation is not made in a day, or a generation, or a century. The divine mind touches, modifies, becomes the mind of man through a process of which mere intellectual conception is only the beginning but of which the gradual complement is an unexhausted series of spiritual discipline through all the agencies of social life. (Green, 1888, p. 239)

Moral concern at one stage of human development may therefore be confined to the family, then to the tribe and then to the nation, and eventually to the whole of humanity 'for whom Christ died' (Green, 1883, p. 238). Green perceives morality as a progressive revelation of the deepest springs of a common human nature, within which ideas about common good and personal freedom have to make sense. While recognising that different societies have different conceptions of morality and duty he is nevertheless quite definitely not a relativist since there is a metaphysical and religious underpinning to the idea of moral progress which does not simply reflect diversity and difference.

Green, in elucidating these ideas and in a way that has seemed scandalous to many subsequent philosophers, talked in terms of two types of selfhood. Alongside my actual self—of empirical desires, preferences, interests and prejudices which have not been tested against the rational and legitimate concerns that I should have for others—there is also the possible self, the self that I could become by the constant rational redirection of my desires and preferences to ends which include a recognition of the needs of others. This is my possible self, or my ideal self which for Green is identical with the growing revelation of the nature of God/the spiritual principle in my life. The more I live in terms of the demands of this ideal, the more I shall live what Green called a Christed life (Leighton, 2004, ch. 3). Sin is the moral state in which an individual is unwilling or unable to respond to the demands of his ideal self. Redemption from sin is to be found in pursuing the ideal self. This is what Edward Caird meant when he urged his Balliol undergraduates to 'die in order to live': to die in terms of the pursuit of private desires and forms of fulfilment in favour of the realisation of the ideal self. This was for Green the necessary setting for his ideas of the common good and for freedom. The pursuit of the ideal and the actualisation of the ideal self was for Green the service of God.

The common good

This is a fundamentally important concept for Green and one which must certainly not be understood in utilitarian terms as maximal preference satisfaction (Green, 1883, ch. 4). The utilitarian had to take preferences as given and incorrigible data. There were no ethical principles or values independent of happiness or utility. However, for Green such a formulation was utterly inadequate, since human fulfilment could only come through the pursuit of the ideal (1883, chs 3–5). His common good had to be seen as one in which all could share and this is because the ideal is, at any one period of ethical understanding, the same for all people. For Green it must satisfy the following criteria as set out in the *Prolegomena to ethics*:

i) it must be a good for all men [sic]
ii) no one should gain by another's loss
iii) loss and gain have to be estimated on the same principle for each person in society.
 (Green, 1883, p. 282)

What, in particular circumstances, will be the common good and meet these criteria, cannot be determined in advance. In certain circumstances the common good is to be found by looking no further than the best interests of your own family. At other times it may well involve promoting measures of social and educational reform which would enable others to find within themselves the mental and physical resources needed for their own development. Such a distinction bears directly on his educational thought. Because of the nature of human life, the ideals as understood at a particular time of human development and the theism which underlies all of this, a common good must be identified. But, as the second of the criteria set out above indicates, this common good cannot be found in things for which there is competition, or in things the pursuit of which excludes others. While the utilitarian 'common good' of utility maximisation could encompass both competition and exclusion, for Green this cannot be so: the notion of a theistically grounded common ideal would be fractured by competition.

> Civil society may be and is founded on the idea of there being a common good but that idea in relation to the less favoured members of society is in effect being unrealised and is unrealised because the good is being sought in objects that admit of being competed for. They are of a kind that they cannot be equally attained by all. The success of some in attaining them is incompatible with the success of others. Until the object generally thought as good comes to be a state of mind or character of which the approach to attainment by each itself is itself a contribution to its attainment by everyone else, social life must continue to be a war. (Green, 1883, p. 289)

Such a conclusion has, of course, very substantial consequences for his political and public philosophy. It means that to be consistent, the common good cannot be defined in terms of social justice—that is to say the just allocation of resources between individuals—because the operation of social justice could infringe criterion (ii). Indeed, Green makes a strong case for a right to the accumulation and transfer of property (on which see below). There can be no development of the personality according to Green without a recognised power of appropriating material things. This capacity will in turn vary according to talent and opportunity. It follows from this that there will be social distinctions in a Greenian society, and he is not seeking to understand the nature of the common good in terms of social justice or in terms of equality of condition or outcome. The ideal for the individual and its contribution to the common good is to be found in qualities of mind and character.

> ... the only good which is really common to those who pursue it, is that which consists in the universal will to be good—in the settled disposition on each man's part to make the most and best of humanity in his own person and the persons of others. (Green, 1883, p. 288)

But this will mean different approaches for people with different talents and aptitudes. What matters is that each has the capacity to develop moral character and moral sense and that this will ultimately be part of a common endeavour, within which each will play his or her part.

This conclusion determines his approach to education. It is the task of education to develop character in pursuit of this moral ideal. Education can be part of the common good only if it has this as its fundamental aim. Insofar as it is concerned with what nowadays is called credentialism—in which education is seen instrumentally as a means to material ends—it cannot be part of the common good, since it produces winners and losers. So the content of education as the development of character and the pursuit of the Ideal is part of the common good because this is not competitive. This is certainly not to suggest that he neglected the importance of educational provision. As an assistant commissioner on the Taunton Commission and a member of the National Education League he had far-sighted plans for national education and a ladder of opportunity (see below). However, for Green, educational provision satisfied the conditions necessary for the development of character and the common good:

it was not part of the common good itself. Nevertheless, he did attribute to the state a central role in securing educational resources for individuals since without education one could not develop one's character and pursue morally good ends. The distribution of these goods, however, was not itself part of the common good of society.

An analogy could be drawn between the provision of education and the law. The law was necessary to provide a framework within which individuals could pursue the common good, but it was not itself part of the common good. It removed obstacles to the achievement of moral self development but it did not embody the ideal in itself. So there is a close relationship in Green's mind between the role of the law and the common good. The law is not, as it was for the legal positivists of Green's day, a command of a sovereign backed up by the threat of force. Rather the law had an intrinsic moral aspect which was related to the common good as Green understands good—as the fulfilment of a moral capacity. So in *The principles of political obligation* he observes that rights—which it is the role of the law to enforce—might, from a liberal perspective such as Green's, be thought of as somehow basic or natural. But Green rejects this view in favour of the idea that a right is a power that depends on mutual recognition and it is this recognition of legitimacy that turns mere possession into property. A property right is a socially recognised right and to be legitimate it must be conducive both to the development of the person exercising ownership and be judged by the common good of society (under Green's non competitive understanding of that term) (Green, 1884, section N).

So the law is an instrumental good which has then to be assessed in terms of the common good, and part of that common good for Green is the development of personal character and a sense of independence. Along with many other late Victorians, Green was therefore concerned with the potentially deleterious effect of state provision and state support on moral character and the sense of independence and initiative. His main concern was that the state should normally seek to remove obstacles to moral self development rather than directly providing these resources. Nevertheless, by attributing a considerable role to the state in the case of education he allowed a partial exception, justifying this in terms of securing the conditions for self development, character and the realisation of the best (in moral terms) that one could become. Although Green's ideas can therefore be cast into the language of 'fulfilling one's potential', that potential is, for Green, essentially moral. Its achievement presupposes some freedom from anxiety about the basic needs of life and education. But the whole purpose of realising one's potential or ideal self is moral—and not the acquisition of an advantage in a competitive market (Green, 1883, p. 288).

Freedom and the common good

Green's complex view of the nature of freedom challenges in a number of ways the standard liberal view that freedom is negative—freedom means being free from coercion. If a liberal state is to act as a defender of freedom it will seek to limit as far as possible the opportunities for coercion whether by one individual over another or by the state. This negative freedom might appear to meet Green's requirement for the common good: it can be enjoyed equally by all people, all in possession of a set of equal rights to be free from coercion. As a social and political ideal, this view of freedom has been one of the major moral ideas guiding the evolution of liberalism.

While Green does not reject this understanding of freedom, he finds it deeply inadequate, for reasons implicit in the argument so far. On the negative view of freedom nothing is implied about the ends to which freedom from coercion is to be directed. It is quite literally a demoralised view of freedom: what I do with my freedom is a matter of choice so long as in exercising it I respect the freedom of others. Such a view is defective for Green since it makes no reference to the idea that there are objectively good social ends and ideals, to which human beings—when they are seeking to make the best of themselves—aspire. Freedom and the realisation of the ideal for the self must go together. In the best self, as Green defined it, reason redirects the passions in favour of the end or ideal. This is an exercise of freedom and for Green there could therefore be no demoralised account of freedom. So the idea of freedom, given its relationship to the idea of the best self, is itself part of the common good. It is also closely linked to the idea of character. Given that character and the realisation of the best self is part of Green's educational ideal, so too is a conception of positive freedom.

Green also uses the linked ideas of the common good and freedom to elucidate the role of other social and political institutions such as property. Property cannot be seen as an entirely unrestricted right because it has to be judged in terms of whether it will advance the common good and the realisation of the ideal self. It is not, therefore, to be justified in terms of utility or natural rights but rather to the extent to which it does or does not promote the set of conditions necessary for the development of the common good and the realisation of the ideal self which cannot be construed, as I have made clear, as some private form of self realisation. Green draws out the critical consequences of this in the following passage:

> A man who possesses nothing but his powers of labour and has to sell them to the capitalist for bare daily maintenance might as well, in respect of the ethical purposes which the possession of property should serve, be denied the rights of property altogether. (Green, 1883 p. 170)

Property rights, like all rights, have to be considered in relation to their role in the exercise of moral capacity rather than as being some kind of independent moral absolute. The idea that property is to be judged in terms of its social function in relation to the common good became extremely important for those like Tawney who was indebted in many respects to Green's ideas but wished to push them in a more radical or egalitarian direction.

Obviously, as we have seen, Green did not and could not believe in material equality whether it is seen in terms of outcome, welfare or condition. But it does follow from his conception of the human personality and his understanding of morality that each person must have an equal opportunity to develop the personal moral ideal. Given that all are equal in this respect the important question, for Green, relates to the social and economic conditions which are necessary to the realisation of this kind of moral equality. Green clearly does not think that there is a general answer to this kind of question. It depends on circumstances. In the context of Victorian Britain this meant a move away from a perception of freedom in purely negative terms and of government as having a duty only to protect negative freedom:

> ... the negative equality before the law, which is already established in Christendom, comes to be supplanted by a more positive equality of conditions. (Green, 1883, p. 317)

So the nature of social and educational provision has to be judged in the context of this ideal, and there can be no universal answer as to what it entails. But Green remains cautious in enlarging the role of the state. Since a more positive role for the state might undermine character, it should for the most part remove hindrances. It should also be concerned with basic standards of life rather than with some overall transformation of society in the interests of social justice: such an extension of its sphere would be incompatible with the idea of the common good. The task was well defined by Green in an address to Oxford Liberals shortly before his death:

> Society was becoming every day more complicated, and they wished so to order, so to arrange that complicated society that everyone, whatever his station, whether peer or peasant, capitalist or labourer, townsman or countryman, should have a fair chance of making the best and most of himself. (Green, 1997, p. 385)

This imperative had a profound impact on Green's view of education.

Green, liberalism and education

Green's moral and metaphysical philosophy is clearly the foundation for his educational views. Green's generally cautious approach to the role of the state in public life did not extend to the field of educational policy and provision. His conviction that the voluntary system had failed and was divisive led him to argue for a national organisation of schools in different grades to create a potential ladder of learning. Green accepted that if adequate voluntary schools had in fact been provided, and if parents chose to send their children to them, then arrangements which operated independently of the state might in principle be preferable. But different circumstances require different measures. Green further argued that there could be no objection to laws which required a parent to send a child to school. For a parent who would in any case have done that voluntarily, such a law is experienced—not as a constraint but as a powerful friend. But matters which are as important as this cannot be left to private choice. Green's ideal is the common good and the individual pursuit of the ideal. Since education is a vital precondition for the achievement of these ends it cannot ultimately be left to personal choice. As in the parallel cases of property and rights, the test of legislation is the promotion of the conditions necessary for the common good to develop. Green is clear that while the state cannot secure the common good or any moral purpose directly by legislation, it can directly affect the conditions necessary for achieving that purpose and for that reason he was in favour of compulsory education.

The compulsory character of popular education must have a substantial effect on its provision. For Green, the system prevailing before 1870 was inadequate since voluntary schools were built with joint funding from the churches and the state. Although in principle nonconformists could (and to a limited extent did) participate in such joint funding arrangements, in reality the overwhelming number of such schools were Anglican with a steadily growing minority of Roman Catholic foundations. Forster's Education Act of 1870 was specifically designed to 'fill the gaps', and to provide Board schools (as they were called) only in areas where the supply of voluntary schools was demonstrably inadequate. Although such new schools were not required by law to provide religious education, the elected authorities controlling them could make provision if they chose. If such religious instruction was provided it could, under the terms of the famous and often misunderstood Cowper-Temple clause, not be governed by the formularies distinctive of any particular denomination. A general association in the public mind of religion with morality ensured that education of a Christian character would normally be provided in such schools, which were certainly not expected to be in any modern sense of the term 'secular' (Green, 1888, pp. 418–455).

Green gave somewhat qualified support to the Forster Act. His guiding principle was that national education should be seen as a matter of public duty, not as an object of sectarian zeal: he argued that such sectarian loyalties undermined that common set of spiritual ideas and values that could now be represented philosophically and in a way that bypassed most, if not all, of the points of sectarian dispute. Green did not want what he called a merely secular education, believing that common ideas were necessary to keep society together and that the common good could be found only in what could be called, in a broad sense, a religious ethos. Green therefore accepted the Cowper-Temple clause, urging that it was vitally important to separate the interests of morality and religion in education. Unsurprisingly he was a strong supporter of the Board schools rather than of their Voluntary cousins.

He nevertheless regretted that the Forster Act had to accommodate existing arrangements and could not dismantle an education system which put so much power in the hands of the Anglicans, and to a lesser degree of the Catholics. To make matters worse, the supplementary provisions of the 1870 Act meant that for the next two years the denominations were given strong financial incentives to build more new schools of their own (Green, 1888, p. 435). The Act gave the denominational position the opportunity of, in Green's words, needlessly extending itself. Green also regretted the fact that, because outside the towns (where School Boards were, as in Oxford, most often established), the parish remained the standard unit of educational organisation (Green, 1888, p. 437). In many parishes, therefore, as long as a school room could be provided by the parson or the squire, the state did not seek to interfere. In many parts of England the only provision was that offered by the Anglicans, and Green detected a further injustice in the uneven distribution of such schools. He had also hoped that more rapid progress would have been made towards making elementary education compulsory.

Green also drew attention to the important relationship between the gradual extension of compulsion and the character of the education provided in the schools. As education was becoming compulsory, and in many areas the only schools available were denominational, a firmer measure of state control was required if the common good was to be served. A clergyman in whose parish a school was situated would be very likely to regard the school and what went on inside it as part of what Green calls 'the outwork of the church' (1888, p. 448), subject only to a conscience clause allowing withdrawal from specifically denominational religious education. Such a conscience clause could not insulate children from the essentially sectarian ethos of such a school—increasingly influenced by what Green regarded as a more superstitious element associated with the sacerdotal and ritualistic practices promoted by the Tractarians. Over time, such circumstances would require a greater involvement of public authorities in the monitoring of the education provided by such schools (1888, p. 449). Green accepted that the wholesale transfer to the Boards of such schools would be a step too far at the time at which he was writing, but hoped that the supervision of voluntary schools would gradually be strengthened. His response to critics of the Board schools who argued that such schools were less successful than the church schools was unequivocal: the Board schools started with a great disadvantage as 'all the neglected children were swept into them' (Green, 1888, page 453), whereas church schools became more selective than they had been before. Moreover, where the system had worked for some time—as in London and Birmingham, which he knew particularly well from his association with the Taunton Royal Commission—the level of achievement was higher than in church schools.

Green regarded the effect of sectarian education as being morally divisive, and not conducive to the common good, whereas religious education in a broader sense was central to that common good. School boards should therefore be favoured and could—and in the event did—also play a significant role in extending what might today be called a meritocratic approach to equality of opportunity. This argument is set out in his 1879 lecture 'On the grading of secondary schools' (Green, 1888, pp. 387 ff.). Without a national and universal system of education it would be impossible to respect the principle of equality of moral capacity, and to allow those with the appropriate educational abilities to develop that capacity to the full, up to and including university education. Green was consistently in favour of extending the range of candidates for admission to Oxford, asserting that many currently coming to the university did so in pursuit of a social cachet rather than from any commitment to learning and intellectual development. He therefore developed the concept of a ladder of learning, to be constructed by placing all schools in three progressive grades. Careful grading would allow progress from one level to another, and for the suitably qualified, scholarships should be provided to ease the paths of working class children who were capable of ascending to the higher grades. Such objectives obviously required a national system rather than a patchwork of local arrangements. The curriculum would have to be organised to ensure that each grade of school would lead naturally to a higher grade while at the same time offering a coherent and rounded education for pupils who were to finish their education at that grade. Obviously, this ladder of learning could work in rural areas, only if the basis of educational organisation were to be shifted from the parish to a wider geographical area. He urged, with some success, that at Oxford (which he naturally regarded as the pinnacle for such a system) there should be experiments allowing poor students to matriculate and study for degrees without incurring the costs of college residence—the *Scholares non Ascripti*. He gave up his rooms in Balliol for a time to preside over a house in St. Giles for non-residential Balliol students. Such initiatives led eventually to the establishment of St. Catherine's Society (founded in 1868 for unattached students) and in the longer term of St. Anne's College (which developed from the establishment in 1878 of the Association for the Education of Women in Oxford). It is significant that Green's Balliol was the first college to allow St. Catherine's Society members to attend honours classes in the College (Bullock, 2000, p. 196). The plaque which still stands at the entrance to the old buildings of the Oxford High School for Boys (while unaccountably mistaking the year of his birth) acknowledges Green's achievement in founding that school and so 'completing in this city a ladder of learning from the elementary school to the university'.

Although, therefore, Green was in general terms cautious about enlarging the role of government in private and public life, he saw education as being in quite a different category from other sorts of good. The content of education is part of the common good, and the conditions necessary for the development of the individual's cognitive and moral capacities have to be taken very seriously by the state. Education increases our rational and thus our moral capacities. Green's understanding of the nature of reason and the development of the spiritual principle in human life, and of the unitary nature of the common good, led him to a distinctive view of a common culture which will unite all classes. A national system of education—outside the independent Public Schools, about which he could be quite scathing—would help to achieve this in practical terms. Here, there are anticipatory echoes of the 20th century debates on comprehensive education as a means of generating greater equality of opportunity and forming a common culture. In a speech to the Oxford School Board on the subject of the High School for Boys, Green observed:

> As a rule, of course, the boy whose school time continues till he is eighteen will be the son of well to do parents, but such a boy might well receive his elementary education along with the children of poorer families in a primary school, if he was transferred from it at about the age of eleven to a school of a higher grade. The only hindrance to such an arrangement, apart from social prejudice, is that at present, the primary school, having to receive all comers, may often contain children, unclean in their habits and language, with whom parents of refinement might reasonably object to their children being associated. But as education begins to tell on the poorer classes, we may confidently hope that this difficulty will be removed, and that most of our elementary schools will become, as many of them are already, places to which children might be sent without scruple from the most refined and carefully managed homes. And, just as a boy intended from the outset for university, might without disadvantage begin his education in an elementary school, so by a wise application of endowments, a promising boy, who would otherwise have been put to manual labour at the age of thirteen, might be lifted to a school which should prepare him for the university. (Green, 1888, p. 462)

Education was therefore essential for the development of the common good, partly because that common good would be arrived at by the development of educated citizens and partly because a universal education system would lead to a higher degree of social mixing and intercourse which, in Green's view, would extend the idea of the common good. Later in the same lecture and in lyrical or even prophetic terms, Green takes the now largely archaic concept of 'the gentleman' to fuse together the idea of reasoned judgement, a concern for others, and service for a common purpose in the service of common citizenship:

> Our high school then may fairly claim to be helping forward the time when every Oxford citizen will have open to him at least the precious companionship of the best books in his own language, and the knowledge necessary to make him really independent; when all who have a special taste for learning will have open to them what has hitherto been unpleasantly called the education of gentlemen. I confess to hoping for a time when that phrase will have lost its meaning because the sort of education which alone makes a gentleman in any true sense will be within the reach of all. As it was the inspiration of Moses that all the Lord's people should be prophets, so with all seriousness and reverence we may hope and pray for a condition of English society in which all honest citizens will recognise themselves and be recognised by each other as gentlemen. (Green, 1888, p. 475)

This language may now seem quaint, but an ideal of education which links it inextricably with mutual respect and mutual recognition of value as the basis of a common life, and which places the realisation of individual moral ideals at its centre, is still one worth preserving. T. H. Green did more, in a comparatively short life, both to provide a theory of this and undertake practical steps to bring it about than most of us, who may well hold to such ideals, would have the energy to contemplate. His funeral procession on a wet and windy March day in 1882 was followed by 'the largest combined gathering of citizens and members of the university in memory' (Day, 1997, p. 467).

Acknowledgements

The author would like to thank staff in the House of Lords' Library for their help in the preparation of this paper and Harry Judge for his most helpful comments.

Notes on contributor

Since 2001, Raymond Plant has been Professor of Jurisprudence and Political Philosophy at King's College London Law School. Prior to this he was Master of St Catherine's College Oxford from 1994. Between 1979 and 1994 he was professor of Political Philosophy at Southampton University. He became a member of the House of Lords as Lord Plant of Highfield in 1992 and subsequently became a Labour spokesperson on Home Affairs from 1992–96. He has written around a dozen books on political philosophy including *Hegel: philosophy, politics and citizenship* (with A. Vincent); *Modern political thought*; *Politics, theology and history*. In 2006 he will give the Boutwood Lectures in Cambridge and will be a Fellow of Corpus Christi College; in 2007 he will give the Bampton Lectures in Oxford. He is an honorary fellow of St Catherine's and Harris Manchester Colleges in Oxford.

References

Bowle, J. (1954) *Politics and opinion in the 19th century* (London, Jonathan Cape).
Boucher, D. & Vincent, A. (2000) *British idealists and political theory* (Edinburgh, Edinburgh University Press).
Bullock A. L. (2000) The non collegiate students, in: M. Brock & M. C. Curthoys (Eds) *The history of the University of Oxford, Vol. VI Part 2, The nineteenth century* (Oxford, Clarendon Press).
Carter, M. (2004) *T. H. Green and the development of ethical socialism* (Exeter, Imprint Academic).
Collingwood, R. G. (1939) *Autobiography* (Oxford, Oxford University Press), 17.
Collini, S. (1991) *Public moralists: political thought and intellectual life in Britain 1850–1930* (Oxford, Oxford University Press).
Day, C. J. (1997) The University and the city, in: M. Brock & M. C. Curthoys (Eds) *The history of the University of Oxford, Vol. VI Part 1, The nineteenth century* (Oxford, Clarendon Press).
Green, T. H. (1883) *Prolegomena to ethics* (Ed. A. C. Bradley) (Oxford, The Clarendon Press).
Green, T. H. (1886) *Collected works* Vol. 2 (Ed. R. L. Nettleship) (London, Longmans, Green & Co).
Green, T. H. (1888) *Collected works* Vol. 3 (Ed. R. L. Nettleship) (London, Longmans, Green & Co).
Green, T. H. (1997) *Collected works* Vol. 5 (Ed. P. Nicholson) (Bristol, Thoemmes Press).
Greenleaf, W. H. (1983) *The British political tradition, Vol. 2, The Ideological Heritage* (London, Methuen).
Harris, J. (1992) Political thought and the welfare state 1870–1940: an intellectual framework for British social policy, *Past and Present*, 135.
Himmelfarb, G. (1992) *Poverty and compassion: the moral imagination of the late Victorians* (New York, Vintage Books).
Leighton, D. (2004) *The Greenian moment* (Exeter, Imprint Academic).
Nicholson, P. (1990) *The political philosophy of the British idealists* (Cambridge, Cambridge University Press).
Perkin, H. (1989) *The rise of professional society* (London, Routledge).
Richter, M. (1964) *The politics of conscience: T. H. Green and his age* (London, Weidenfeld & Nicholson).
Toynbee, A. (1969) *The Industrial Revolution* (London, Longmans, Green & Co) (reprint).
Vincent, A. & Plant, R. (1984) *Philosophy, politics and citizenship: the life and thought of the British Idealists* (Oxford, Blackwell).
Wempe, B. (2004) *T. H. Green's Theory of positive freedom* (Exeter, Imprint Academic).

Michael Sadler and Comparative Education

David Phillips

Introduction

Michael Sadler was Master of University College, Oxford, from 1923 to 1934. Opinions about his Mastership are mixed. Stephen Spender, an undergraduate from 1927 to 1930, was particularly critical:

> The Master of the College, Sir Michael Sadler, was a famous educationist whose interest in education seemed to stop or to be arrested when it came to governing his own college. (Spender, 1951, p. 38)

It is said that Arthur Poynton, a Fellow of the College, lunching in Norham Gardens and seeing Sadler passing on the street, jumped up from the table and rushed to the window exclaiming 'There goes the Master of University College!'[1]—the irony here being oblique and unkind in a particularly Oxford way. There is mention of 'ghastly breakfasts at 8 am' with the Master and his first wife (Logan, 1974, p. 372), and one of Sadler's successors as Master expresses the view that he could have been 'in little doubt that the more senior Fellows found neither his appointment nor his views and temperament much to their taste' (Redcliffe-Maud, 1973, p. 251).

Sadler was apparently a compromise candidate for the Mastership, the other contenders being Poynton, the then Bursar who was a classicist, and Arthur Farquharson, the Senior Tutor and a philosopher. In the archives of University

College there is a note on former Masters which records that another Fellow of the day, Ainley Walker, who was 'determined to thwart their ambitions', suggested Sadler for the Mastership. There were only ten Fellows of University College in post when Sadler was elected, and the voting must have been close, the result being of the unhappiest *tertius gaudens* variety. Poynton was to succeed him as Master in 1934 'elected as a kind of consolation prize in the knowledge that he could not serve for more than three years'.

Sadler's first appearance before the assembled College was evidently inauspicious:

> [He] was anxious to show his great respect for Oxford traditions and learning, but his carefully prepared address to the undergraduates in Hall was a little above their heads. The theme was the long history of the College, with phrases like 'When Dante was composing The Divine Comedy, Univ was already flourishing, when Giotto's school were painting in Siena the College moved to its present site, the front quadrangle was building while the school of Caravaggio were developing their chiaroscuro effects ...'[2]

This—if true—is revealing of the combination of sustained earnest endeavour and sometimes embarrassing lack of judgement which characterised Sadler as an administrator, as a writer, and as a public figure. While his energy, enthusiasm, knowledge, and sheer range of involvement could not be faulted, he was too often impulsive and curiously unworldly, failing as a result to impress and to convince, and having then to endure whatever snub might follow. Here is an account of his administrative style from Redcliffe-Maud (Dean and Fellow of University College, later Permanent Secretary of the Department of Education and Science and Master of University College):

> He was [...] constantly driven by his impulsive temperament to instant action. [...] [A]t any time of the day when an idea affecting me entered his head he would sit down and write me a note in his own handsome hand. One's week would therefore be divided into one-note, two-note, and three-note days. [...] [T]he Warden of New College (H. A. L. Fisher) claimed that thanks to efficient College messengers he once had three notes from Sadler on one subject in a single day. (1973, p. 251)

In trying to reach consensus he would, it seems, often create difficulties for himself: he was 'too sensitive and shrewd to miss unspoken criticism, and his constant efforts to appreciate a dissenting voice were mistaken at times for appeasement—or even humbug' (Redcliffe-Maud, 1973).

But his more positive and sympathetic attributes were also recognised. The historian Sir Llewellyn Woodward appreciated the logic of Sadler's decision-making:

> In the days when Sadler had been immersed in controversies and committees, [his] detachment was often disconcerting. He would appear to change his mind suddenly and without regard to the immediate consequences or to his own reputation for consistency. Yet these changes were an inner, artistic response to the whole of his environment. So far from being capricious, they had their own final and convincing logic. Sadler might seem to be acting on an impulse of the moment, but you could work out stage by stage the arguments which led him from one conclusion to another. (Woodward, 1944, pp. 51–52)

As a Briggs recalls, from his time as a young Oxford don in 1945, that Sadler was being compared with Beveridge and that the Delegacy of Extra-Mural Studies 'owed an immense debt to him'. 'To understand him is to understand much about English history and the traditions which ... have sustained it' (Briggs, 1979).

Redcliffe-Maud remembers that Sadler was intimately involved in all aspects of College life; and he also played a full part in the life of the city (of which he became a freeman), and especially with the Oxford Preservation Trust. 'At once a man of action and a man of faith', he supported throughout his professional life a huge range of activities of a benevolent and mind-enriching kind. He was *the* person to approach for an opening lecture, or to chair a meeting, or to write a preface or an introduction. And he did so with reliability and a certain presence. He gave authority to whatever he was involved in—and since most of his work was in education ('the dullest of all subjects unless it be illuminated by imaginative understanding', in Woodward's view), he counts as a very significant figure in the national debate about education in all its aspects over a very long period in his long life.

The principal published sources on Sadler's life and work are the biographies by his son, the novelist Michael Sadleir (1949) and by the one-time principal of Lady Margaret Hall, Lynda Grier (1952), and the many articles and papers by a former Warden of Sadler Hall in the University of Leeds, J. H. Higginson. On the whole these sources celebrate Sadler's achievements. There is also a recent account by Sislian (2002) and a comprehensive bibliography of Sadler's works by Pickering (1982).

Oxford

Sadler's Oxford connection began in 1880. Born in Barnsley in 1861, he was a pupil at Rugby School before matriculating as a scholar of Trinity College in 1880. He served as President of the Oxford Union in 1882, took firsts in Mods and Greats, and in 1890 was elected a Student (in all other Colleges called a Fellow) of Christ Church, where he was Steward (bursar) from 1886 to 1895. During these early Oxford years he became involved in educational administration as Secretary both to the Delegates for Local Examinations and for University Extension—even at Rugby his propensity for leadership and organising things had been observed by the headmaster who reported that the school ran well provided he took advice from Sadler, who was then head boy of School House (Lowe, 2004). His was the Oxford of Jowett and Pattison, respectively Master of Balliol and Rector of Lincoln when Sadler arrived at Trinity. Liddell was Dean, and Charles Lutwidge Dodgson (Lewis Carroll) was a Student of Christ Church during Sadler's time as Steward, when he had to deal with a deluge of complaints about domestic arrangements from the difficult Dodgson, 'a prolific malcontent' from whom 48 letters of grievance addressed to the Steward survive (Sadleir, 1949, p. 90).

As an undergraduate Sadler was much impressed by lectures he attended by John Ruskin and the social reformer Arnold Toynbee (Sadler, in Higginson, 1979, pp. 12–13). And he soon began to show the beginnings of the liberal—if not radical— leanings which, as Lowe argues, characterised his life's work in education (Lowe, 2004). He used to make much of the fact that the (Tory) politician and factory reformer Michael Thomas Sadler (1780–1835), who did a great deal to improve the conditions of the poor, was his great uncle. During his first year at Oxford, in his first recorded display of interest in education, he had advocated at the Oxford Union the higher education of women 'by a speech ablaze with undergraduate fireworks' (Grier, 1952, pp. 1–2). With his strong academic record he might have become a college tutor and gone on to be an academic and scholar of a more conventional Oxford kind (there was the possibility at one stage of a tutorial fellowship at Merton College). Instead, having decided against being a schoolmaster, he looked for opportunities to exert influence on policy making and development in education generally—in the early years especially through the University Extension Movement. He came under the influence of Arthur Acland (1847–1926), whose group the 'Inner Ring' he joined and in whose footsteps he followed both as Steward of Christ Church and (in 1885) as Secretary of the university extension movement in Oxford.

A character sketch of Sadler as an undergraduate (in *The Oxford Rambler* of October 1882) provides a satirical but not unfriendly view of his youthful seriousness of purpose:

> A lay figure, youthful in appearance, the hair carefully curled, the countenance ruddy, the nose up tilted, the mouth clean cut and prominent, a general appearance as of a cherub out of condition, such is the material embodiment of the popular Trinity orator. Dressed usually in dark clothes, with chin thrust forward and one hand projecting like a bow sprit from a wriggling body, the other grasping a roll of voluminous notes, he pours forth his smiling platitudes ... He is a kind of oratorical Pecksniff, and yet his persuasive skill deserves the attention it generally receives. (Sadleir, 1949, p. 37)

There was a suggestion that he might go into politics, as Joseph Chamberlain had encouraged him to do, and he was later to consider this option again. He declined offers of an academic position in India and the Secretaryship of the Co-operative Wholesale Society, with which Acland also had close connections (Lowe, 2004). And so Oxford kept him for some 15 years, and he proceeded to launch 'a vigorous campaign to introduce Oxford extension lectures on a large scale' (Ockwell & Pollins, 2000, p. 666).

The university extension movement had its beginnings around 1850, though ideas for facilitating wider access to university study date back to 1845 (Mackinder & Sadler, 1891, p. 1). Cambridge inaugurated its scheme in 1873, with Oxford following more modestly in 1878 but revivifying its efforts in 1885, when Sadler became Secretary (Roberts, 1891, pp. 1–2). Acland had been appointed Secretary of the Oxford extension (which was an initiative of the Delegacy of Local Examinations) in 1878. The chairman of the Delegacy, T. H. Green, inspired Acland to give lectures, principally in the north of England, on education for citizenship—often delivered before very large audiences (Ockwell, 2004). Acland retired in 1885 and became a Liberal Member of Parliament. When Sadler took over he employed all his organising skills effectively enough to '[turn] the Oxford Extension movement into an educational empire which stretched from Cornwall to Lancashire' (Ockwell & Pollins, p. 667). Student numbers rose remarkably once he was in post, from 6,000 in 1885–86, to over 13,000 three years later and to more than 20,000 in 1890–91 (Goldman, 1995, p. 61).

Sadler was himself an enthusiastic lecturer—he wrote to his father about 'grand work with a great and useful future'; 'I confess that I incline to it' (Goldman, 1995, p. 64). Syllabuses survive for an early course of 12 lectures which he delivered in 1885 on the 'Past, Present, and Future of the Working Classes, and how to Better their Condition' (Sadler, 1885). Four years later—to take another example of his contribution at a practical level—he was lecturing on the beginnings of modern socialism at a summer meeting of university extension students in Oxford (Sadler, 1889) and was among the first to talk authoritatively on Marx. In 1891 he was lecturing in the United States on university extension and arguing that 'the next step we have to take in England is that of Secondary Education' (Higginson, 1997, p. 457).

There is no doubt that Sadler played a very significant part in giving new impetus to university extension at a critical time. Tawney's view of him as 'more of a thinker than an administrator, and more of a missionary than either' (quoted by Asa Briggs in Higginson, 1979) is perhaps unfair with regard to his capacity to run things, but quite right in its emphasis on the driven aspects of his personality. He was not infrequently inspired, and he had—and still has, as I shall argue—the capacity to inspire others.

In 1893 Sadler contacted people in influential positions in the University of Oxford and persuaded them that the University's Hebdomadal Council should convene a conference on secondary education. In doing so he set into motion the procedures to arrange a meeting which the Vice-Chancellor of the day referred to as 'the first time that there has been such a representative Conference of persons interested in education called together' (University of Oxford Convocation, 1893, p. 14). Sadler had become involved in efforts to recognise the importance of secondary education when the first flush of universal elementary education was still being felt. The Oxford conference[3] was attended by representatives from all constituencies in education and was instrumental in the establishment of the Royal Commission on Education (the Bryce Commission), of which Sadler was a member (while still in his early thirties) and which reported in 1895. The Bryce Report in turn paved the way to the 1902 Education Act.

The 17 Commissioners continued the tradition of previous Royal Commissions and reported at length: their Report and its appendices fill nine volumes. Sadler has been seen as the Report's principal author (Gosden, 1989, p. 9). Higginson regards the inclusion in the Report of a survey of foreign practice as a 'particular feature' of the Commission's work (1997, p. 458); the gathering of information on provision in other countries (by means of a circular) enabled Sadler to become involved in the use of the foreign example in policy debate, and it was to lead to that aspect of his life's work for which he is now principally remembered—an engagement with comparative studies in education and their use.

London (Office of Special Inquiries and Reports)

Acland had become Vice-President (in effect minister of education) of the Committee of Council on Education, the forerunner of the Board of Education, and Sadler approached his old mentor with a proposal to establish a 'new organ of inquiry and report', attached to the Education Department in Whitehall, which 'might prove useful in stimulating public opinion'. This approach resulted in the setting-up of the Office of Special Inquiries and Reports, of which Sadler became the first Director. Acland described the work of the new body as follows:

> There is a large number of matters affecting education as to which the Department lives merely from hand to mouth, failing to record the knowledge it obtains for future use, and unable to obtain information as to what is being done elsewhere, whether at home or abroad, in an efficient manner. There is now much waste of power through this deficiency, and the appointment of an officer with a limited amount of help, whose duty it shall be to collect and supply information, and to make occasional reports on special matters under the direction of his chiefs, has become essential if the Education Department, including the Science and Art Department, whose field of work is now so large, is to do its work efficiently. (Selby-Bigge, 1927, pp. 213–214)

Sadler's appointment was not without controversy. There was a Commons question on the matter, and Lowe believes that 'protests of political jobbery ... must have weakened [Sadler's] position, and future relations with Conservatives, from the outset' (Lowe, 1996, p. 101).

When Sadler became Director of the Office of Special Inquiries and Reports in 1895, comparative studies in education were still very much in their infancy. It is true, of course, that comparative inquiry in education has a long history, stretching at least back to the early years of the 19th century, but it was Sadler, it can be argued, who instituted procedures of systematic research—within an official context—into well-defined aspects of education in a wide range of countries with the distinct aim of improving the situation 'at home', and who started a tradition of inquiry that survives today:

> Michael Sadler stands out as the forerunner of the methodological approach that characterized comparative studies in the twentieth century. Although his actual studies of the European national systems were essentially governed by the same principles as those of Arnold, Mann, and the others, his statements about what the investigator should look for in studying systems of education have become classic expressions in the field. [...] The Sadlerian principles have become the cornerstones of the theoretical orientation of twentieth century comparative education. (Kazamias & Massialas, 1965, pp. 2–3)

During the eight years that Sadler spent as Director of the Office of Special Inquiries and Reports he produced eleven volumes of 'Special Reports on Educational Subjects' which, in the view of a one-time Permanent Secretary of the Board of Education, 'made available for English readers a large amount of useful information otherwise difficult to get at, but served an even more valuable purpose in the way of suggestion and inspiration' (Selby-Bigge, 1927, p. 214). The first volume (1896–1897) contained a vast array of papers, six of them written by Sadler as sole or co-author.

Robert Morant, whom Sadler had appointed as his deputy in 1895, was the author or co-author of five of the papers in this first volume. Aspects of education in Germany are covered in seven of the papers, with Sadler writing two substantial accounts which have a focus on intermediate and commercial/technical education, subjects on which he would in future place particular emphasis. In September 1897 he spent time in Hamburg and Altona visiting schools and recording his impressions.[4] Volume 9 in the series was to be devoted exclusively to education in Germany; and Volume 10 covered the United States.

As early as 1847 the Committee of Council on Education had appointed a special officer whose task was 'to collect and arrange Statistical information respecting public education', and at that time a request was also made to the Foreign Secretary, Lord Palmerston, for statistical and other documents to be made available to it through the embassies and legations of a number of countries. And so around mid-century British officialdom was showing interest in collecting a range of factual data about educational provision in other countries, and it is clear that various states of Germany were figuring prominently among the countries where such provision was attracting attention. Both the Bryce Commission and Sadler's Office were thus continuing a tradition which had been long established, and Sadler was taking the work forward with great energy and with a determination for thoroughness in the analysis of educational provision elsewhere and in the possible application 'at home' of foreign practice observed to be successful.

But Sadler, like Matthew Arnold and Mark Pattison before him, saw no panaceas in foreign approaches to educational provision. 'I hope with time to convince people,' Arnold had written in a letter of April 1868, 'that I do not care the least for importing this or that foreign machinery, whether it be French or German, but only for getting certain English deficiencies supplied' (Murray, 1997, p. 240). And Mark Pattison, in his report for the Newcastle Commission on aspects of education in Germany, had argued for circumspection in trying to learn lessons and find solutions to problems from experience in Germany:

> The utility of ... study of a foreign system does not depend on the question: Are the German primary schools or training colleges better than our own? [...] But the same difficulties in the way of national education with which we have to contend have to be met in the several countries of Germany, only under conditions so altered and infinitely varied as to afford a most instructive lesson. [...] In this country we are little likely to err on the side of a hasty imitation of foreign modes, or to adopt a usage from a neighbouring country, forgetful that its being successful there is no guarantee that it will adapt itself to our climate. [...] Much rather is everyone, who has any information on foreign systems to give, called upon to come forward with it, not as precedent to be followed, but as material for deliberation. (Pattison, 1861, p. 168)

Sadler was to take a similar line in a famous lecture delivered in Guildford in 1900 on the subject 'How far can we learn anything of practical value from the study of foreign systems of education?' This has remained one of Sadler's most quoted texts, not because it was particularly profound or—at the time—significant, but because, in stating with absolute clarity and authority something which ought to be regarded as obvious, he laid down what should be the guiding principles of comparative inquiry in education:

> In studying foreign systems of Education we should not forget that the things outside the schools matter even more than the things inside the schools, and govern and interpret

the things inside. We cannot wander at pleasure among the educational systems of the world, like a child strolling through a garden, and pick off a flower from one bush and some leaves from another, and then expect that if we stick what we have gathered into the soil at home, we shall have a living plant. A national system of Education is a living thing, the outcome of forgotten struggles and difficulties, and "of battles long ago". It has in it some of the secret workings of national life. It reflects, while it seeks to remedy, the failings of the national character. By instinct, it often lays special emphasis on those parts of training which the national character particularly needs. Not less by instinct it often shrinks from laying stress on points concerning which bitter dissensions have arisen in former periods of national history. But is it not likely that if we have endeavoured, in a sympathetic spirit, to understand the real working of a foreign system of education, we shall in turn find ourselves better able to enter into the spirit and tradition of our own national education, more sensitive to its unwritten ideals, quicker to catch the signs which mark its growing or fading influence, readier to mark the dangers which threaten it and the subtle workings of hurtful change. *The practical value of studying, in a right spirit and with scholarly accuracy, the working of foreign systems of education is that it will result in our being better fitted to understand our own.* (Sadler, in Higginson, 1979, pp. 49–50 (original emphasis); see also Bereday, 1964, pp. 307–314).

Despite the success of the Office of Special Inquiries and Reports in publishing material which was to inform policy discussions in the run-up to the 1902 Education Act and subsequent legislation, Sadler's time there ended in spectacular disharmony and controversy. Morant left the Office in 1899 to become first the Personal Private Secretary to Sir John Gorst (Vice-President of the Committee of Council on Education, 1895–1902) and later to be appointed Permanent Secretary of the Board of Education, and in this latter position he fell into dispute with Sadler over the role of the Office, which he also kept short of funding. Sadler insisted that his task was to investigate educational issues dispassionately and not to shape policy on behalf of the government. After a series of lengthy scraps with Morant, Sadler resigned as Director in 1903, the circumstances of his resignation being the subject of a blue book (*Papers Relating to the Resignation of the Director of Special Inquiries and Reports*, 1903), and questions on the matter being raised in Parliament.

The Sadler–Morant dispute has been the subject of much analysis and speculation. From the hagiographic perspective of Sadler's son Michael Sadleir (1949), Morant was the villain of the piece—a view shared by Lynda Grier in her account of Sadler's work (1952). Norman Chester, on the other hand, saw Sadler's stubbornness as a problem:

> Miss Grier says 'Indelible marks were left on Sadler by his experience at the Board' [...] The same can be said of Morant's experience of this period. Had Sadler shown some of the Christian understanding and patience which he is said to have possessed in abundance instead of being so bitter and no doubt spreading his bitterness to others, the two men might have continued to work closely together for the good of public education. It was unfortunate for both that Sadler failed to rise to the occasion. (Chester, 1953, p. 54)

Sadler had earlier nursed the hope that he might head the newly constituted secondary department of the Board of Education, and had been snubbed by Sir George Kekewich (Secretary of the Education Department and later of the Board of Education, 1890–1903) when he raised the matter, since it was felt to be inappropriate for a civil servant to give the impression of applying for promotion (Grier, 1952, pp. 76–77); and in unwisely publishing an anonymous letter in *The Times* he had incurred displeasure from the President of the Board, Lord Londonderry. The problem here is one of judgement and decision, areas in which Sadler—largely through vacillation and a form of inner anguish—was often lacking. 'I see in [Morant] an early arrival of the Fascist mentality', Sadler wrote in 1941 (Sadleir, 1949, p. 195), a remark interpreted by Fry (2004) as 'born of the self-pitying bitterness of bureaucratic politics'.

Sir George Kekewich—with whom Sadler also fell into dispute and of whom he was quite critical (and who also, incidentally, eventually fell victim to Morant)—judged Sadler's time as Director in generous terms:

> Mr Sadler brought to bear on the questions and inquiries submitted to him, a knowledge of education, both generally and in detail, which was then, and is still, second to that of no man in this, or perhaps any other, country. When ... he found it necessary to resign his position, I could not help feeling that his resignation was a real loss to the State, and that it would be exceedingly difficult, if not impossible, to find a man who could adequately fill his place. Such cases are exceedingly rare. [...] Mr Sadler had to depend exclusively on his own knowledge and his own ability, and the excellence of the work that he accomplished stands as a testimony to the greatness of both. (Kekewich, 1920, pp. 90–91)

What is significant for comparative studies in education is that Sadler's work at the Office of Special Inquiries and Reports established the value of the systematic collection of data on a wide range of aspects of education in other countries and of the use that might be made of such data in policy development. Successive departments and ministries have continued to commission reports and studies of education in other countries; most notably there has been a succession of published reports from 1985 onwards, largely from HMI and Ofsted, on aspects of education elsewhere of relevance to current policy issues in England and Wales.

Manchester and Leeds

Following his resignation from the Office of Special Inquiries and Reports, Sadler accepted the post of Professor of the History and Administration of Education at the University of Manchester. This appointment, which required only one term's residence each year, allowed him time to write, and his output increased considerably during his years there. He lectured, in particular, on the history of education in England from 1800 and prepared detailed syllabuses for those attending his courses (*Outlines of Education Courses at Manchester University*, 1911). Plans to write a comprehensive history of education in England did not materialise (though he was later to write a short monograph on *Our Public Elementary Schools* (1926)).

While at Manchester he undertook a number of commissions to report on education in various local education authorities as a result of their being obliged by the 1902 Act to make provisions for secondary education. In 1904 he reported on Huddersfield, Birkenhead, and Liverpool; in 1905 on Derbyshire, Exeter, Hampshire, and Newcastle upon Tyne; in 1906 on Essex. The main focus of all of these reports was secondary education. They are remarkably full surveys of provision, with detailed recommendations, of the kind that large committees of inquiry might normally undertake. As the work of one man they are an impressive achievement over the three-year period in which they were written. It is said that Sadler's advice was adopted in all of the authorities for which he reported (Grier, 1952, p. 134).

Sadler moved to Leeds as Vice-Chancellor in 1911, when the University had been in existence for only seven years. He steered the University through the war years and the Depression, and is remembered as having 'imbued the institution with the confidence it needed so badly':

> The confident outlook, the enormous energy, the wide knowledge and contacts and deep understanding of education and of government which Sadler brought made a vital and essential contribution to its development as a university with international standing by the time of his departure. (Gosden, 1989, p. 16)

There had been talk of Sadler returning to the Board of Education in 1911 when Morant left the Permanent Secretaryship, but again this came to nothing. Selby-Bigge was appointed as Morant's successor, and there was much grieving in the Sadler household (Sadleir, 1949, pp. 215–219). In 1916, Sadler nursed high hopes of becoming President of the Board, the post eventually going to H. A. L. Fisher, Vice-Chancellor of Sheffield and later to join Sadler in Oxford as Warden of New College. The civil servant who proposed Fisher as President had regarded Sadler as 'too viewy and wordy' (Jones, 1969) for the post, as Harry Judge reports elsewhere in this collection. Fisher himself had protested to Lloyd George when offered the position that he had no parliamentary experience and that 'in any case Michael Sadler knew more about education than [he] did' (Fisher, 1940, p. 91). When there was speculation about his being offered the job, Sadler wrote to his father 'I know that there is no one else quite qualified for it, and that it may be necessary for me to go', though he anticipated that his tenure would be brief 'because both sides would in the end stone me' (Sadleir, 1949, p. 274). He speculated about the House of Lords. When the news of Fisher's appointment broke, in December 1916, Sadler's disappointment at being passed over again was palpable. He wrote to his son:

> We have to think of the country, not of ourselves. And in some strange way humiliation is part of the preparation for action.
>
> I cannot pretend not to feel it all very much ... From a personal point of view, it could hardly be worse. People being what they are, it lessens one's influence quite decidedly and suddenly. But I feel that in some way which we cannot understand, it is a preparation for something else. And what this is to be will be clearer if we have patience. (Sadleir, 1949, pp. 275–276)

His wife confided to her diary: 'A public and galling slight to my dear. He is very cut up' (Sadleir, 1949, p. 275).

And so Sadler had to endure seeing Fisher fulfilling the function for which he had felt himself destined. Some two and a half years later there was speculation that Fisher would go to Washington as Ambassador, and this caused further anguish for Sadler, whose name was again being mentioned as President of the Board. 'Fisher did the Bill better than I (with more knowledge) should have been free to do', he wrote to his son in June 1919 (Sadleir, 1949, p. 276), and he composed a lengthy soul-searching memorandum on whether or not he would now accept an appointment in Lloyd George's Coalition. He concluded: 'I may be able to do more to mediate if I stay outside than if I go in now' (p. 279).

Fisher became the architect of the 1918 Education Act, which contained at least one element dear to Sadler—the proposal to introduce 'continuation schools' (along the lines of provision in Germany) which would keep young people in part-time education until the age of 18. (This ambition on the part of successive governments to emulate the duration of vocational and general education provided in Germany continues to the present day.) Sadler had edited in 1907 a collection of papers on continuation schools in England and other countries, arguing for their importance in modern industrial and commercial states and citing the German example: 'It is in Germany that the most systematic and (so far as can at present be judged) the most successful efforts have been made to grapple with the question of the further training of boys and girls who have completed the course at the elementary day school' (Sadler, 1907, p. xvii). Sadler was acquainted personally with Georg Kerschensteiner, the leading figure in vocational education in Germany, in whose company he had visited the continuation schools in Germany (Sadler, in Higginson, 1979, p. 81).

The example of Germany remained a constant theme in Sadler's writing (see, for example, Sadler, 1912b, 1914, 1916). One particular article encapsulates his views on what might be learnt from educational provision in a country with which political relations were hostile throughout most of Sadler's life. It appeared in *The Times* in 1916, in the middle of the First World War and so not at the most auspicious time, and was entitled 'Need We Imitate German Education?' Here he cites the achievements of education in Germany:

> German education has made the nation alert to science. It has made systematic cooperation a habit. It has taught patriotic duty. It has kept a whole people industrious. Combined with military training, it has given them the strength of discipline. It has made profitable use of second-rate intelligence. It has not neglected the mind. (Sadler, 1916)

Mention of 'second-rate intelligence' highlights the strengths of a system which to this day preserves in the *Realschulen* a form of schooling below that of the academic *Gymnasium* but above that of the basic general education of the *Hauptschule*, the kind of education, in fact, that was later envisaged for the technical schools which might have been created in large numbers following the 1944 Education Act but which never constituted more than ten per cent of secondary schools in England. In an earlier piece, 'The Strength and Weakness of German Education', Sadler had written of the 'extraordinary precision of aim', the 'high standards of intellectual attainment', the 'liberal encouragement of organised scientific research' and the 'wide diffusion and convenience of access' of education in Germany (1915, p. 304), and had argued that 'in certain respects, the educational achievement of Germany has been unequalled in the world' (p. 306).

In 1917 Sadler chaired a commission on the University of Calcutta. He spent some 15 months in India and the Commission's report appeared in 1919. It was an exhaustive survey (in 13 volumes) of post-primary education in Bengal, Sadler being responsible for about a third of the text of the main five volumes (Grier, 1952, p. 217). For this work he was knighted in 1919. The 'Sadler Report', as it has become known, proposed in particular the establishment of universities of the 'unitary' type, many of which were established following its publication (Ghosh, 1939, p. 224).

Mention should also be made of Sadler's growing interest in art and the building-up of his extraordinary and very large collection of paintings, especially by the Impressionists and Post-Impressionists. His son dates the main impetus for the collection to the period following Sadler's resignation from the Office of Special Inquiries and Reports, when 'the early and reckless phase of his collecting life' began, and 'picture buying became partly a pleasure, partly a drug to keep depression at bay' (Sadleir, 1949, p. 226). Much distress was caused by his over-spending, which had to be underwritten by his wife. But especially in the 1910s and 1920s, and in the decades to follow, he became a discerning and adventurous collector, with a good eye for what was innovative and accomplished. And he shared his paintings, drawings and sculptures with others in an extraordinarily generous fashion, and gained the lasting admiration of the likes of Henry Moore, Herbert Read, and John Piper (Oliver, 1989). He appreciated the quality of Kandinsky's work at a time when the general taste found it unpalatable; he commissioned and paid for a controversial sculptural relief by Eric Gill at Leeds; at University College he displayed works by Henry Moore. The University of Leeds benefited from Sadler's gift of a substantial number of works of art in 1923. University College was later neglected: '[Sadler] was too shrewd not to detect the undercurrent of our indifference to great modern art', Redcliffe-Maud reports (1973, p. 253), and so on his death the remainder of the collection was sold by the family.

Oxford again

As we have seen, Sadler returned to Oxford and to the Mastership of University College in 1923. His immensely busy and productive professional life was thus enfolded by Oxford, where he also spent his years of retirement. He died in Old Headington in 1943.

During his Mastership of University College he continued to write on a broad spectrum of educational subjects, also publishing more essays on art, while showing the elder statesman's compulsion to write to *The Times* on various subjects. In 1928 he delivered the Rede Lecture in Cambridge on the 18th-century English disciple of Rousseau, Thomas Day. He threw his energies into a characteristically wide range of causes, including advocating the establishment of a chair of education at Oxford (achieved only in 1989).

'I don't think I shall ever get ambition eradicated from my mind', Sadler wrote to his wife in 1899 (Sadleir, 1949, p. 170). For someone who saw himself as ideally qualified to be minister of education, there was always a strong sense of what might have been. But a chair in Manchester, the vice-chancellorship of a major civic university, and the headship of an Oxford college would surpass the ambitions of most educationists, and Sadler's success in achieving those positions is not uncreditable. Much more than what he contributed to the institutions with which he was involved, however, it was his role in public life that enabled him to exert the influence in education he had envisaged from his early Oxford days.

Sadler's significance as an educationist is considerable. It can be argued that he identified the main policy themes in education and so determined the agenda for much of the debate in education in the first decades of the 20th century. He is important in particular because:

- he recognised the importance of adult education and what has become known as 'lifelong learning';
- he did not lose sight of the needs of teachers and children while engaged in lofty considerations of policy;
- he saw the need to make better provision for secondary education at a critical moment in the 1880s;
- he became a passionate advocate of the role of technical and vocational education, especially in catering for the educational needs of the middle range of ability;
- he unfailingly sought to learn from the examples of educational provision in other countries;
- he established the parameters of systematic comparative inquiry in education and thus can be counted as one of the earliest professional comparativists.

He also encouraged art education, had a sustained interest in examinations and in scholarships and their use, and supported the teaching profession generally. He became the first fellow of the Royal Society of Teachers in 1935.

Comparativists still turn to his writing to endorse a position they might be taking on ways in which comparison in education could or should be undertaken. He still inspires, since so much of his work—whether on education in Germany or the United States, or by way of an *aperçu* on the French system, or through understanding of the roles of the university or the function of secondary schooling or of examinations—even today provides us with a degree of wisdom that often forms the starting point for a fresh discussion. Sprigade (2005, p. 11) shows that in 15 German, French and English introductions to comparative education published between 1918 and 1996 which she consulted, there were one or more references to Sadler, and the same would be true of a huge number of individual papers in the field. He covered virtually every topic of importance in educational studies, from eurhythmics (1912) to moral education (1908) and examinations (1936), from elementary schools (1926) and secondary education (1930) to continuation schools (1907), from education in Ireland and Belgium (1896-7) to education in India (1919). And he wrote for the most part with elegance and authority, without a hint of the superficiality of the dilettante.[5] He did his homework.

Sadler can count as one of the most influential figures in education outside politics in the first half of the 20th century. That he did not attain the high offices to which he aspired was the result of the perspicacity of those who saw that he would not be a success in a political or quasi-political role. His destiny was to understand, to inform, to comment, and to inspire—and all of this he did with an enviable measure of success, but without the power to effect change at a national level that had been denied to him so often.[6]

Notes

1. University College Archives, UC:R2/MS1/5. (Handwritten reminiscences of University College by the Rev. Richard Ratcliff, who matriculated in 1920.)
2. For the Oxford conference and its context see Porter, 1994, pp. 479–486, and Grier, 1952, pp. 29–32.
3. National Archives: Ed 24/1880.
4. Sadler's notes on the visits are preserved in the Bodleian Library, MS.Eng.misc.c.906/1–4.
5. Sadler's written output was considerable, though there is no single major publication by which he is known. Pickering (1982) lists 631 items. The main archival material is at the University of Leeds, with further holdings in the Bodleian Library. Selections from his work are to be found in Higginson (1979) and Sislian (2004).
6. I am grateful to Christine Ritchie, Librarian of University College, Oxford, for her help in making available to me various texts in the possession of the College, and to Dr Robert Darwall-Smith, the College's Archivist, for much valuable information.

Notes on contributor

David Phillips is Professor of Comparative Education and a Fellow of St Edmund Hall, University of Oxford. He has written widely on issues in comparative education, with a focus on education in Germany and on educational policy borrowing. He served as Chair of the British Association for International and Comparative Education (BAICE) from 1998 to 2000, and is an Academician of the British Social Sciences Academy and a Fellow of the Royal Historical Society. He was for 20 years editor of the *Oxford Review of Education* and serves on the editorial boards of various journals, including *Comparative Education*. He now edits the on-line journal, *Research in Comparative and International Education*, and is series editor of *Oxford Studies in Comparative Education*.

References

Aldrich, R. (1996) *In history and in education. Essays presented to Peter Gordon* (London, The Woburn Press).
Bradby, E. (1939) *The university outside Europe* (London, Oxford University Press).
Brock, M. G. & Curthoys M. C. (Eds) (2000) *The history of the University of Oxford,* Vol. VII, *Nineteenth-century Oxford,* Part 2 (Oxford, Clarendon Press).
Bereday, G. Z. F. (1964) Sir Michael Sadler's 'study of foreign systems of education', *Comparative Education Review,* 7, February, 307–314.
Briggs, A. (1979) Foreword, in: J. H. Higginson (Ed.) *Selections from Michael Sadler, studies in world citizenship* (Liverpool, Dejall & Meyorre).
Chester, D. N. (1953) Morant and Sadler—further evidence, *Public Administration,* Spring, 49–54.

Diaper, H. (Ed.) (1989) *Michael Sadler* (Leeds, University Gallery).
Fisher, H. A. L. (1940) *An unfinished autobiography* (London, Oxford University Press).
Fry, G. K. (2004) Morant, Sir Robert Leslie, *Oxford Dictionary of National Biography* (Oxford, Oxford University Press). Available online at http://www.oxforddnb.com/view/article/35096 (accessed 28 Feb 2005).
Germany in the nineteenth century. Five lectures (1912) (Manchester, Manchester University Press).
Ghosh, J. C. (1939) The universities of India, in: E. Bradby (Ed.) *The university outside Europe* (London, Oxford University Press), 209–239.
Goldman, L. (1995) *Dons and workers. Oxford and adult education since 1850* (Oxford, Clarendon Press).
Gosden, P. (1989) Sir Michael Sadler, educationist and Vice-Chancellor, in: H. Diaper (Ed.) (1989) *Michael Sadler* (Leeds, University Gallery), 9–16.
Grier, L. (1952) *Achievement in education. The work of Michael Ernest Sadler, 1885–1935* (London, Constable).
Higginson, J. H. (Ed.) (1979) *Selections from Michael Sadler. Studies in world citizenship* (Liverpool, Dejall & Meyorre).
Higginson, J. H. (1997) Michael Ernest Sadler (1861–1943), in: Juan Carlos Tedesco (Ed.) *Thinkers on education* 4 (Oxford, UNESCO Publishing & IBH Publishing), 455–469.
Jones, T. (1969) *Whitehall diary*, Vols. I, II (London, Oxford University Press).
Kazamias, A. M. & Byron G. M. (1965) *Tradition and change in education. A comparative study* (Englewood Cliffs, Prentice-Hall).
Kekewich, Sir G. W. (1920) *The Education Department and after* (London, Constable).
Logan, D. W. (1974) Lubens Subscribo sub Tutamine Leys Farquharson et Walker, *University College Record*, 6(4), 367–376.
Lowe, R. (1996) Personalities and policy: Sadler, Morant and the structure of education in England, in: R. Aldrich (Ed.) *In history and in education. Essays presented to Peter Gordon*, 98–115.
Lowe, R. (2004) Sadler, Sir Michael Ernest (1861–1943), *Oxford Dictionary of National Biography* (Oxford, Oxford University Press). Available online at http://www.oxforddnb.com/view/article/35905 (accessed 21 Jan 2005).
Mackinder, H. J. & Sadler, M. E. (1891) *University extension, past, present, and future* (London, Cassell).
Murray, N. (1996) [1997] *A life of Matthew Arnold* (London, Sceptre).
Ockwell, A. & Pollins, H. (2000) 'Extension' in all its forms, in: M. G. Brock & M. C. Curthoys (Eds) *The history of the University of Oxford, Vol. VII, Nineteenth-Century Oxford, Part 2* (Oxford, Clarendon Press), 661–688.
Ockwell, A. (2004) Acland, Sir Arthur Herbert Dyke, *Oxford Dictionary of National Biography* (Oxford, Oxford University Press). Available online at http://www.oxforddnb.com/view/article/30327 (accessed 28 Feb 2005).
Oliver, W. T. (1989) Sadler as art collector, in: H. Diaper (Ed.) (1989) *Michael Sadler* (Leeds, University Gallery), 17–20.
Outlines of Education Courses in Manchester University (1911) (Manchester, Manchester University Press).
Paterson, W. P. (Ed.) (1915) *German culture. The contribution of the Germans to knowledge, literature, art, and life* (London, T. C. & E. C. Jack).
Pattison, M. (1861) Report of the Rev. Mark Pattison, B. D., in: *Reports of the Assistant Commissioners appointed to inquire into the state of popular education in continental Europe and of educational charities in England and Wales* (London, HMSO).
Pickering, O. S. (1982) *Sir Michael Sadler. A bibliography of his published works* (Leeds, Leeds Studies in Adult and Continuing Education).
Porter, D. (1994) A minor educational centenary: a note on the Oxford conference on secondary education of 1893, *Oxford Review of Education*, 20(4), 479–486.
Redcliffe-Maud, J. (1973) Master Sadler after 50 years, *University College Record*, 6(3), 250–253.

Roberts, R. D. (1891) *Eighteen years of university extension* (Cambridge, Cambridge University Press).
Sadleir, M. (1949) *Michael Ernest Sadler* (London, Constable).
Sadler, Sir M. E. (1885) Syllabus of a course of lectures on 'Past, present, and future of the working classes, and how to better their condition' (Manchester, Co-operative Printing Society Limited).
Sadler, Sir M. E. (1889) *Three Lectures on the Beginnings of Modern Socialism Delivered at the Summer Meeting of University Extension Students in Oxford, August, 1889* (Oxford, Alden and Co.).
Sadler, Sir M. E. (n.d. [1904]) *Report on secondary education in Liverpool* (London, Eyre & Spottiswoode).
Sadler, Sir M. E. (1906) *Report on secondary and higher education in Essex* (Chelmsford, Essex Education Committee).
Sadler, Sir M. E. (Ed.) (1907) *Continuation schools in England & elsewhere. Their place in an industrial and commercial state* (Manchester, Manchester University Press).
Sadler Sir M. E. (Ed.) (1908) *Moral instruction and training in schools* (London, Longmans, Green and Co.).
Sadler, Sir M. E. (1912a) Introduction to *The Eurythmics of Jaques-Dalcroze* (London, Constable).
Sadler, Sir M. E. (1912b) The history of education, in: *Germany in the nineteenth century. Five lectures* (Manchester, Manchester University Press), 103–127.
Sadler, Sir M. E. (1914) *Modern Germany and the modern world* (London, Macmillan).
Sadler, Sir M. E. (1915) The strength and weakness of German education, in: W. P. Paterson (Ed.) *German culture. The contribution of the Germans to knowledge, literature, art, and life* (London, T. C. & E. C. Jack), 301–314.
Sadler Sir M. E. (1916) Need we imitate German education? *The Times*, 14 January.
Sadler, Sir M. E. (1926) *Our public elementary schools* (London, Thornton Butterworth).
Sadler, Sir M. E. (1928) *Thomas Day. An English disciple of Rousseau* (Cambridge, Cambridge University Press).
Sadler, Sir M. E. (1930) *The outlook in secondary education* (New York, Bureau of Publications, Teachers College, Columbia University).
Sadler, Sir M. E. (Ed.) (1936) *Essays on examinations* (London, Macmillan).
Selby-Bigge, Sir L. A. (1927) *The Board of Education* (London, G. P. Putnam's Sons).
Sislian, J. (2002) *Sir Michael Sadler 1861–1943: England's interpreter and America's admirer* (Huntington, Nova Science Publishers).
Sislian, J. (2004) *Representative Sadleriana. Sir Michael Sadler, 1861–1943, on English, French, German, and American school and society: a perennial reader for academics and the general public* (Huntington, Nova Science Publishers).
Spender, S. (1951) *World within world* (London, Hamish Hamilton).
Sprigade, A. (2005) Where there is reform there is comparison. English interest in education abroad 1800–1839. Unpublished D.Phil thesis, University of Oxford.
University of Oxford Convocation (1893) *Report of a Conference on Secondary Education in England.* Convened by the Vice-Chancellor of the University of Oxford. The Examination Schools, Oxford, 10–11 October (Oxford, Clarendon Press).
Woodward, E. L. (1944) Sir Michael Sadler. An impression, *Oxford*, 8, Summer, 51–53.

Cyril Norwood and the English tradition of education

Gary McCulloch

Introduction

It was 23 June 1943, as the Second World War approached its decisive phase, when the Board of Education committee met for the final time in the familiar surroundings of Oxford. It had been deliberating on the future of English secondary education for nearly two years and, with its final report safely signed, the committee presented its chairman with a copy of the *Cambridge Ancient History*, 'duly acknowledging the contribution of an Oxford man to future history through his leadership and tact'. The chairman of the committee, Sir Cyril Norwood, completed this complacent scene with the award of 'prizes' to members of the committee (Norwood committee, 1943). If Norwood was indeed an 'Oxford man', it was not by virtue of a lengthy direct association with the University of Oxford. He had been an undergraduate at St John's Oxford for four years in the 1890s, returning at almost 60 years of age to take up the presidency of his old college. Even when ruminating on the prospect of this appointment, the last in a distinguished educational career, Norwood was undecided about not only his own contribution to Oxford, but also the university's significance for him. As he noted, 'I did not like Oxford as a young man, and it is at least doubtful whether I shall like it now. I know that I do not like the climate.' Moreover, he added, 'I do not believe that as President of a College it is possible for me to make any direct impact on undergraduate life. It is more likely to lead to official business e.g. statutes, investments, general policy. This does not attract me much.' On the other hand, although Oxford was in his view a 'smaller sphere' than the world of secondary education to which he was accustomed, it did offer other potential advantages, not least 'a position of comfort and dignity with abundant leisure' (Norwood, 1933).

Cyril Norwood, the 'Oxford man', was to all appearances the quintessential insider of English education in the first half of the 20th century, a pillar of the establishment in the University of Oxford and for education in general. He was an outstanding classical scholar, a successful headmaster, Master of Marlborough College, Head of Harrow, and was knighted for his services to education in 1938. He was also prominent in national education policy circles well before his career culminated in 1943 in the Norwood Report on secondary school curriculum and examinations (Board of Education 1943; on the report itself see for example McCulloch, 1994). Yet he was also an outsider, insecure because of the circumstances of his childhood and upbringing, never fully accepted in the public schools over which he presided, not fully trusted by the officials at the Board of Education or by many of his colleagues despite his decades of public service. Norwood became widely known through the Board of Education report that came to bear his name for his support for a differentiated curriculum based on a notion that there were three types of mind, best suited to different types of secondary school, and he was deeply conservative in many respects. This study will investigate the paradoxical nature of his contribution to and significance in English education, a victim of social class anxieties, insecurities and snobbery even as he became the most famous celebrant of the so-called 'English tradition' of education.

1. Biography and society

The most familiar image of Sir Cyril Norwood is as a rather aloof and detached figure who progressed in an unruffled fashion towards a position of power and authority in English education, and was thoroughly at home in the élite world of the educational Establishment. He was educated from 1888 to 1894 at Merchant Taylors' School in London, recognised as one of the leading Victorian public schools for the social élite, although unusually for a school of this status it was principally a day school rather than a boarding school. He went on to St John's College Oxford, where he gained an outstanding first class honours degree in classics in 1898. In short order, he was the leading candidate for Civil Service entry in the Civil Service examinations of that year, and was appointed to the Admiralty. He soon decided on a career in education, becoming a classics master at Leeds Grammar School, under the new regime of the

Education Act of 1902. In 1906, aged 30, he was appointed headmaster of Bristol Grammar School, long established but struggling to survive in changing circumstances. Norwood re-established the fortunes of the school over the next decade, to such an extent indeed that he is often regarded as the second founder of the school. He went on in 1917 to become Master of Marlborough College, an élite boarding school, and then in 1926 the Head of an even more famous and prestigious school, Harrow. In 1934, he returned to his old Oxford college to become its president, staying there until he retired in 1946. For a quarter of a century he was the chairman of the Secondary Schools Examinations Council, and in this capacity exerted a great deal of influence over educational policy in the interwar years (for further details of Norwood's life and educational career, see Turner, 1971; McCulloch, 2004).

In 1929, Norwood produced his best known authored work, *The English tradition of education* (Norwood, 1929a), while he was Headmaster of Harrow School. This book celebrated the long tradition of service provided by the élite public schools, tracing it back to the Middle Ages and the ideals of knighthood, chivalry and the English gentleman, and called for this to be developed also in the national state system of education (see also McCulloch, 1991; McCulloch & McCaig, 2002). It insisted that 'the ideal which the public schools are seeking, however imperfectly, is the true ideal, that it answers to our national needs, and has its roots far back in our national history' (Norwood, 1929a, p. 20). Its dominant theme of continuity and renewal of established traditions and ideals was echoed in the Norwood Report of 1943, which declared that:

> ... the tradition of secondary education is a fine tradition, that men and women of fine and unselfish character have built up ideals and institutions of untold value to individuals and to the nation, and that the present generation has been tried in the furnace and not found wanting: that education is necessarily slow in growth if it is to grow aright, that it would be an unforgivable wrong to those who come after us not to conserve what is good from the labours of the past. (Board of Education, 1943, p. ix)

This was in many ways a conservative and complacent viewpoint, comfortable with the established order and keen to see it survive into a new age. His contemporary, Fred Clarke, also educated at Oxford and conscious of established traditions, struck a much more critical note when he observed that England's success over the past few centuries in avoiding invasion or revolution had engendered a sense of 'security' which was only now coming under challenge with the onset of a second world war (Clarke, 1940). Norwood appeared the very embodiment of this tradition of security.

And yet a number of tensions underlay this formidable exterior, based in Norwood's own personal and family background as well as in the nature of English society. In order to investigate the significance of these tensions, it is necessary to identify connections between the biographical and the social. This relationship between individual life and the wider society was emphasised by C. Wright Mills in his classic work *The sociological imagination* (1959). The study of individual lives has often been developed in isolation from broader considerations of historical and social dimensions. At the same time, historical and social inquiries have been prone to ignore the personal and the individual in their depiction of major institutions. Mills pointed out the need to try to understand the relationship between the individual and wider structures as a key component of his ideal of the sociological imagination, which makes it possible to understand 'the larger historical scene' in terms of 'its meaning for the inner life and the external career of a variety of individuals' (Mills, 1959, p. 5). Indeed, according to Mills, 'The sociological imagination enables us to grasp history and biography and the relations between the two within society' (Mills, 1959, p. 6). Thus, he urged, a key issue was to develop the capacity 'to range from the most impersonal and remote transformations to the most intimate features of the human self—and to see the relations between the two' (Mills, 1959, p. 7). Mills also traced out a fundamental relationship, albeit often neglected, between 'personal troubles', in which an individual finds his or her values being threatened, and 'public issues', involving crises in institutional arrangements. The connections between biography and society thus provide a route of entry into private lives and their relationship to public careers.

These connections are exemplified also in Richard Selleck's biography of James Kay-Shuttleworth, one of the main architects of the system of elementary education developed in England in the 19th century. Selleck argues that Kay-Shuttleworth was an 'outsider' who 'sought acceptance from the urban, professional middle class among whom he worked and the landed gentry into whom he married' (Selleck, 1994, p. xiv). According to Selleck, he succeeded only partially, and 'became a victim of the social structure he had so sternly defended' (p. xiv). Overall, Selleck concludes, he was 'altogether more interesting than he himself, his supporters and his detractors have suggested', living 'a life crowded with achievement, contradiction and distress, a fascinating mirror of the cruel age of which it was a product' (p. xiv). Similarly, Goodman and Martin, in their historical study of women educational reformers, also stress the interweaving of public and private lives, and suggest that biographical research offers a particularly appropriate vehicle for exploring the lived connections between personal and political worlds (Martin & Goodman, 2004).

Norwood's life and career provide a further fascinating example of these issues. It is by no means a straightforward exercise to reconstruct the personal and family dimensions of Norwood's life. He was active and often prolific in communicating his ideas in public articles, books and reports, so his contributions to education can be traced in some detail. Nevertheless, in other ways Norwood's personal life is tantalisingly elusive, and it is often difficult to peer beneath his public persona which was so aloof and reserved. Despite this, it is possible to point to at least three aspects of his life and career that are at odds with the received image. The first is his family background, and particularly his relationship with his father, Samuel Norwood. The second is his period as Head of Harrow School, outwardly the pinnacle of his career but an unhappy experience. Third and last, his interactions with the educational policy community will also be assessed to discern the extent to which he fitted in comfortably with this élite circle. In general, it is proposed, these provide examples of an underlying insecurity, and of Norwood's position not as an insider but in some ways as an outsider to, or an intruder within, the English educational tradition that he celebrated.

2. Tom Brown or David Copperfield?

The character of secondary education in England in the late 19th century was highly diverse, but it is possible to identify a basic division between two distinct and separate spheres of activity. On the one hand, there were the élite public schools such as Eton and Harrow which became established during this period as the defining institutions of education. There, growth in social prestige and cultural authority is often attributed to the example and precepts of Dr Thomas Arnold, headmaster of Rugby School from 1828 until 1842. On the other hand, there were many local endowed grammar schools and private schools that often struggled to survive, and which were hardly distinguishable from the elementary schools of the poor. Norwood's career in education took him into the public schools, and he associated himself with the tradition that they represented. However, his own personal and family background was in the domain of the local grammar schools and private provision, aspiring to social respectability but always anxious and insecure.

The major commissions that were appointed to produce reports on different areas of educational provision in the 1860s had terms of reference that reflected an acute awareness of social differences. The Newcastle commission reported in 1861 on the state of popular education in England (Newcastle report, 1861), while at the other end of the social scale the Clarendon report delivered its verdict on the public schools (Clarendon report, 1864). The Taunton commission reported in 1868 on the schools that fell between these extremes. According to the Taunton report, distinctions between different forms of education corresponded roughly, but not exactly, to 'the gradations of society'. Those who sent their sons to the public schools were 'men with considerable incomes independent of their own exertions, or professional men, and men in business, whose profits put them on the same level' (Taunton report, 1869, vol. I, p. 16). It also noted a widespread social anxiety that expressed itself in education, whether among professional men who, 'having received a cultivated education themselves, are very anxious that their sons should not fall below them' (p. 17), or among the smaller tenant farmers who, it observed, feared being 'outdone by the class below them' (p. 20).

Perhaps the leading commentator in this period was Matthew Arnold, the son of Thomas Arnold, who was a prominent poet and critic as well as a schools inspector. He was acutely conscious of the gulf between the two major domains of English secondary education. The English middle class, he argued, was 'cut in two in a way unexampled anywhere else' (Arnold, 1865/1964, p. 309). On the one hand, the 'professional class' was brought up with its own education that produced 'fine and governing qualities', but lacking the idea of science. On the other, the 'business class', increasingly important for the future, had a different form of education, of the second rank, 'cut off from the aristocracy and the professions, and without governing qualities' (Arnold, 1865/1964, p. 309). He proposed that the education of this latter group, or schools for the middle class should be greatly improved and organised by the State. A new system of secondary education would liberalise this class with an 'ampler culture', admit it to a 'wider sphere of thought', and help it live by larger ideas (Arnold 1864/1969, p. 152).

Perhaps the most eloquent characterisation of these social differences in secondary education emerges from Victorian fiction. The world of the public schools was romanticised in Thomas Hughes' *Tom Brown's schooldays* (1857). This famous novel traced the school career of Tom Brown as a pupil at Rugby School during the headmastership of Thomas Arnold. It emphasised the role of the school as a community in forging the character of pupils. The tone is set early on as the narrator insists that the purpose of schools 'is not to ram Latin and Greek into boys, but to make them good English boys, good future citizens, and by far the most important part of that work must be done, or not done, out of school hours' (Hughes, 1857/1949, p. 55). Brown's first sight of the school evokes its traditions and authority in striking fashion:

> Tom's heart beat quick as he passed the great school field or close, with its noble elms, in which several games at foot-ball were going on, and tried to take in at once the long line of grey buildings, beginning with the chapel, and ending with the school-house, the residence of the headmaster, where the great flag was lazily waving from the highest round tower. And he began already to be proud of being a Rugby boy, as he passed the school-gates, with the oriel window above, and saw the boys standing there, looking as if the town belonged to them; and nodding in a familiar manner to the coachman, as if any of them would be quite equal to getting on the box, and working the team down street as well as he. (Hughes 1857/1949, p. 78)

The key figure in promoting this image of the school is of course Dr Arnold himself, whether in the pulpit giving a sermon, or punishing pupils for breaching school rules. Norwood's English tradition drew heavily on the stereotype of 'Tom Brown's universe', and gave Norwood the opportunity to style himself after Dr Arnold (see Honey, 1977, on the Victorian public school community; and e.g. Bamford, 1960 and McCrum, 1989 on Arnold's role and career).

Tom Brown's fictionalised experiences at Rugby School have little in common with those of David Copperfield in Charles Dickens' equally celebrated novel, published several years earlier (Dickens, 1850/1948). Here, Salem House is 'a square brick building with wings, of a bare and unfurnished appearance', with a schoolroom that is 'the most forlorn and desolate place I had ever seen', and in which there is a 'strange unwholesome smell ..., like mildewed corduroys, sweet apples wanting air, and rotten books' (Dickens, 1850/1948, pp. 77–78). The master at the school, Mr Creakle, is depicted as ignorant and cruel. Equally significant is the brittle character of the school's respectability, evoked when another master, Mr Mell, is denounced by a pupil because his mother lives on charity in an alms-house, and is instantly dismissed from his post (pp. 98–100). According to Fred G. Walcott, Matthew Arnold, when he read *David Copperfield* for the first time in 1880 recognised Mr Creakle's school as 'the type of our ordinary middle class schools' (Walcott, 1970, p. 113). It was this kind of school with which Norwood was familiar through his own personal and family experience.

Norwood's father, the Revd Samuel Norwood, was the headmaster of Whalley Grammar School in Lancashire from 1864 until 1880. This school was founded in 1547 and endowed by King Edward VI, but had fallen into difficulties and disrepair. The school was caught in the social territory between the upper reaches of elementary education and the lower grades of middle-class secondary education that left it in a precarious position. Samuel Norwood was the only teacher at the school, had no local trustees to support him, and was solely responsible for the maintenance of the boarders and day boys in his care. In 1870, he wrote to the Endowed Schools Commissioners to appeal for financial support for renovations to the school. As he explained, 'The school room and premises are as ill-suited to the requirements of the present day as they can well be' (Norwood, S., 1870). Nevertheless, the Endowed Schools Commission was obliged to point out in its response that it had no funds at its disposal from which to make grants to schools (Endowed Schools Commission, 1870). After another ten years of struggling on his own, Norwood resigned from his position and the schools had to be closed before it was reorganised and reopened a decade later (Durnford, 1881).

A young assistant commissioner for the Taunton commission, James Bryce, later to lead his own enquiry into secondary education (Bryce, 1895), was highly critical of the rural grammar schools of Lancashire such as Whalley. They were, he commented, 'ugly without and dingy within; ugly and dingy to a degree which not even a photograph could faithfully represent'. According to Bryce, desks and benches were old, clumsy and inconvenient, and there was a general air of discomfort and neglect. They were unable to maintain a healthy warmth for the teacher and pupils, the floor might be made of stone or even mud rather than wood, the main schoolroom was generally dirty and untidy, and the children tended to bring 'the mud of the street into the room' (Bryce, 1869, p. 491). Even worse than all of these faults, in Bryce's opinion, was the lack of proper ventilation which made them uncomfortably malodorous. He found it difficult to convey, though he tried hard, 'the disgusting closeness and foulness of these small rooms packed full of boys'. Moreover, he pointed out, this situation was especially unacceptable in small country schools: 'In towns it is bad enough, but in country places, where a good deal of clay comes in upon boots and trousers, and where the standard of personal cleanliness is not high, the result is sometimes scarcely endurable' (Bryce, 1869, p. 493). Whalley Grammar School, in an advanced state of disrepair, may well have been among the worst offenders in all these respects.

After he resigned from his position at Whalley Grammar School, Samuel Norwood moved with his family to Essex and made his living through private tuition. This was an even more insecure occupation, and he began a slow decline into isolation and obscurity. He appears to have taken to drink, and lost the support of his family to such an extent that by 1901, when his son Cyril was married, Samuel was not invited to the wedding, and Samuel's wife, Elizabeth, left him and went to live with the newly-weds. He died alone and unmourned a few years later. There is more than a hint of family scandal in this story that spelled potential ruin in middle-class English society. Cyril Norwood avoided all reference to his own background during his later educational career, and was a lifelong teetotaller. Equally significant for his position, however, was that he was in a position to see at first hand the realities of middle-class secondary education and the insecurity that they engendered. He seems to have drawn from this personal experience the lesson that Matthew Arnold preached; that the State should become actively involved to transform the position and character of middle-class education (Arnold, 1869/1932).

Norwood was also able to escape from his family's troubles through outstanding academic success that enabled him to shine at Merchant Taylors' School in London, and then to gain a scholarship to Oxford. This presages his successful period as headmaster of Bristol Grammar School, and his significant role in promoting the academic ideals of the grammar school in the early 20th century. Nonetheless, it is clear that his family and childhood roots were in the hazardous domain of local middle-class educational provision, characterised by struggle, insecurity and status anxiety. Despite his later evocation of an English tradition based in the élite public school ideal, he himself was an outsider and late recruit to this tradition, more David Copperfield than Tom Brown.

3. An alien at Harrow

Norwood's position as Head of Harrow School, during which time he produced *The English tradition of education*, also reveals a great deal about the paradoxical nature of his relationship to this tradition. He found it very difficult to gain acceptance at the school from some of the boys and masters, and this was at least partly due to the high social status of the school which he could not himself claim. There is an interesting glimpse of this in Jonathan Gathorne-Hardy's book *The public school phenomenon, 1597–1977* (Gathorne-Hardy, 1977). He suggests that Norwood's earlier appointment as the head of a grammar school led him to be despised by 'snobbish pupils' and 'snobbish staff', and quotes an unnamed informant from Harrow in the 1920s who says that Norwood was brought in to 'clean Harrow up': '"But he failed," said my aged informant with considerable venom, "because he wasn't really a gentleman. His nickname here was "Boots"—not quite-quite. He never got Harrow into his grip. He retreated to write his ridiculous book, to sit on Whitehall committees and eventually to St John's College, where he made an even worse mess"' (Gathorne-Hardy, 1977, p. 302). The social gulf between Norwood and the élite public schools had not fully closed even now that he was Head of Harrow.

Norwood's attempt to reform Harrow exposed the bitterly contested nature of the 'English tradition'. After his death in March 1956, some lingering echoes of controversy could be discerned through the obituary columns of *The Times*. Norwood's obituary referred to the 'disillusionment' that he had experienced in his years at Harrow (*The Times*, 1956a), and in the days that followed other sympathisers added their own personal testimonies. One of these observed that a 'struggle' had taken place between Norwood's ideas and 'traditionalism' (*The Times*, 1956b). The obituary that appeared in Harrow's own magazine, *The Harrovian*, made a point of mentioning what it described as the 'not very creditable obstructiveness' that some of his staff had shown to his reforms at the school (*The Harrovian*, 1956).

More hostile voices, while they also recognised the difficulties of the time, tended to blame Norwood himself for exacerbating them. One former pupil, Giles Playfair, complained in his autobiography that Norwood was 'an excessively self-opinionated man' whose attitude was 'tyrannic', and that he 'never welcomed contradiction or allowed his will to be flouted' (Playfair, 1937, pp. 109, 113). A recent major history of Harrow School, by Christopher Tyerman, also reaches an uncharitable conclusion: 'Typical of self-confident and not unsuccessful self-publicists, Norwood was honoured less by those working closest to him than the outside world.... Privately affectionate and concerned, he was viewed by snobbish boys and masters as common, dictatorial, insensitive, a poor listener, and in his view on education, faintly absurd ...' (Tyerman, 2000, p. 512). Tyerman portrays Norwood's headmastership as an assault on Harrow's distinctive traditions. On his part, Norwood recognised that he was engaged in a 'fight for the soul of the school' (Norwood, 1931). It was a struggle that exhausted both him and his loyal wife, Catherine, who hated Harrow, on her own account being treated as a 'drone'. When he finally decided to leave and take up the presidency of his old Oxford college, he acknowledged: 'I too am an "alien" at Harrow. It has never been a part of me as Bristol and Marlborough were' (Norwood, 1933).

One example of the contestation of the English tradition that took place within Harrow during Norwood's headmastership concerned the role of the house system and the powers of housemasters. In the 19th century, Montagu Butler as Head of Harrow had encouraged a strong house system and consolidated a federal or balkanised structure for the school as a whole, which was dispersed geographically over a wide area (Tyerman, 2000, p. 315). This led in turn to housemasters becoming very powerful, even though technically they possessed very little security of tenure, while headmasters were highly constrained in their ability to enforce their authority over the school as a whole. The housemasters became increasingly powerful under Norwood's predecessor, Lionel Ford, and came to lead the resistance to Norwood's attempts to provide strong central leadership. Norwood himself remained wedded to the ideal personified by Thomas Arnold at Rugby, of the headmaster as the fount of authority. Thus was set in train a clash between two rival conceptions of the English tradition: Norwood's idealised view of the English public schools, and the particular set of arrangements that had been established at Harrow.

One housemaster who was especially fervent in his support for the established traditions of the school was Charles George Pope. A classics master at the school since 1900, and housemaster of The Grove since 1915, Pope insisted on a strict adherence to school and house traditions. An appreciation of his life in *The Times* would later describe him, affectionately, as a 'tory of tories' (*The Times*, 1959). He refused to compromise on his commitment to the customs of the house. Surviving former pupils of the school, looking back over seventy years, vividly recall Pope as an 'absolute traditionalist', who 'clung obstinately to old ways ... whether in school dress or the boys' comfort' (communications with the author, 2000). These cherished habits were evident in the everyday practices of Pope's house. For example, the boys in The Grove wore tail coats every day, while the rest of the school wore blazers.

When Norwood arrived at Harrow in 1926, Pope was unyielding in his opposition to reforms. He regarded Norwood as a menace to the traditions of his house and of the school as a whole, and took every opportunity to try to thwart him. One of his former pupils remembers him referring to the headmaster as the 'Yellow Peril' (communications with the author, 2000). Over the next few years, Norwood and Pope engaged in a number of battles relating to reform, often over relatively minor matters that assumed symbolic significance for what they appeared to represent. One of the most characteristic of these was over the unique form of football that was played at Harrow. This was well-suited to the heavy clay soil of Harrow, but it did not allow for inter-school competition, and so Norwood replaced it with rugby. Such changes were anathema to Pope as they symbolised the undermining of the unique traditions of the school.

An open feud developed between Norwood and Pope that continued for three years, until in 1929 Norwood decided finally to dismiss his fiercest tormentor from the school. He accused Pope of being disloyal and of fomenting opposition. Indeed, Norwood complained, 'since I have been Headmaster, you have claimed a position from which you are to be free to criticise, to foster opposition, and to work on the minds of boys so as in effect to make them disloyal' (Norwood, 1929b). He was now at the end of his patience: 'I can suffer no longer the continuance of the "imperium in imperio", nor can I tolerate longer the separatism and contemptuous independence, which is the subject of comment among parents, boys and masters' (Norwood, 1929b). This reflected not only his resentment at Pope's criticisms and disloyalty, but also his awareness of two rival traditions in conflict with each other.

Pope himself claimed that 'imperium in imperio', far from being a fault as Norwood argued, was in fact 'more or less the ideal for a House in a Public School', although he conceded that he would never assert 'imperium contra imperium' (Pope, 1929a). For his part, Norwood was insistent that:

> There is between us a conflict of traditions which are not to be reconciled, and so long as that which you call the tradition of freedom persists, so long is the H. M. without real authority—and after a certain period he is forced to forfeit respect as well. I do not say that you invented the system by any means, but I think you have whole heartedly maintained it. (Norwood, 1929c)

Pope claimed that all he had ever wanted was 'to do my best for School and House, and to assist in producing English gentlemen' (Pope, 1929b). Nevertheless, Norwood took his case to the board of governors, arguing that Pope represented a view of Harrow as 'not so much a school as a federation of independent boarding houses, which combined to receive lessons and to play games together', and concluding that 'Harrow can never be in my opinion what it should be, or what it will be, unless the tradition, for which Mr Pope stands, is openly and completely crushed' (Norwood, 1929d). Pope eventually agreed to resign from his post rather than be dismissed (Pope, 1929c).

This unhappy episode seems distant from the ideals proclaimed in Norwood's *English tradition of education* (Norwood, 1929a). Yet there is some echo of his conflict with Pope in this work. For example, he pointed out that the reforms of Thomas Arnold had been brought into Harrow school in the 19th century by Charles Vaughan, one of Arnold's pupils, 'and it was Arnold's masters and pupils who carried his method and his spirit into school after school, new foundations and old, schools for boarders and schools for day-boys' (Norwood, 1929a, p. 16). He made it clear that in his conception of the English tradition, schools should continue to absorb new ideas, so that the tradition did not become 'fixed or dead' (Norwood, 1929a, p. 19). He noted that there were schools 'where the House counts for more than the School—a thing which is not altogether healthy' (Norwood, 1929a, p. 148). He also took aim at some masters in public schools who 'do not study education, though it is nominally their life's work, but hand on a rule-of-thumb tradition'. These, he claimed, were:

> ... ignorant not only of other systems of education, but of other parts of the system of their own country: they have a dim idea that all other schools are some form of Board Schools, a term which they retain from the vague impressions of their youth. They may have seen no school but the one in which they are, nor had any other experience save three or four years at Oxford or Cambridge. For all the higher ends of the school ideal these develop into the 'defeatist' section of the staff, for the thing which has been, it is that which shall be, and after all, they say, it is a jolly good system. Games remain with them, what they always have been, their chief interest. (Norwood, 1929a, pp. 135–136)

Just beneath the surface of this celebratory work, that is to say, there is a bitter contest going on between rival ideals and practices for the English tradition of education, and the malevolent image of C. G. Pope.

4. Dazzling the eyes of moderate folk

A further aspect of Norwood's career that belies the received image of his contribution relates to his interactions with the educational policy community. He was a leading figure in policy circles for nearly three decades, from the end of the First World War until the conclusion of the Second, and historians have often criticised his influence during this period (see for example Simon, 1974; Hunt, 1991). Yet he was not fully trusted in such circles, and his views were often openly despised or derided. He had a reputation of being independent-minded and sometimes unpredictable or even unsound or dangerous in his opinions. Such opinions were often expressed not only in private but also in public, as he was fond of making his case in middlebrow publications with a national circulation such as the *Daily Mail*, the *Spectator*, and *Time and Tide*. This habit was sometimes viewed affectionately and with tolerance, as, for example, when one leading official at the Board of Education noted that 'Like other eminent public men C. N. enjoys striking matches to dazzle the eyes of moderate folk.' In this case, the official added quickly that, 'he is shrewd enough not to burn his own or any other responsible fingers' (Williams, 1941). Others were less kind and appreciative of Norwood's preference for public discussion.

Another leading figure in educational policy circles, for example, was Sir Will Spens, who chaired a major committee to consider the future of secondary education, reporting to the Board of Education in 1938 (Board of Education, 1938). When Norwood was asked to review the secondary school curriculum and examinations in 1941, Spens was perhaps understandably disturbed at the prospect that his own contribution would be usurped. His complaints, however, were directed in particular at the role of Norwood himself and his potential for disturbing accepted conventions. According to R. A. Butler, the president of the board of education in 1942, Spens expressed 'great alarm' at the activities of Norwood's committee, adding that 'it would amount to nothing less than a scandal if this Committee were to replough the whole ground of the curriculum'. For this, he blamed Norwood, and made clear his 'deep distrust' of him (Butler, 1942).

Another example of such tensions related to Norwood's attempts during the Second World War to find a way to bring the public schools under the auspices of the State. This was fiercely resisted by most public schools, and Lord Hugh Cecil, provost of Eton College, took it on himself to voice their outrage at such an idea. He complained that Norwood's proposals, circulated widely in the press, were 'pure Totalitarianism'. Such educational union was not to be contemplated: 'Our educational system should have the variety that belongs to human nature, and should, above all, be filled with the atmosphere of liberty, which is the very opposite of a unified standardized State system.' Then he turned his attention to Norwood himself, accusing him of dictatorial tendencies: 'It is not surprising that Sir Cyril Norwood's scheme culminated in compulsory Military Service. The Brown House at Munich is evidently his spiritual home' (Cecil, 1940). This criticism of Norwood's ideas again suggested a very different notion of the English tradition to those expressed by Norwood, to the extent that Norwood's views are rejected in no uncertain terms as un-English and hostile to the national tradition. It was equally significant that the then president of the Board of Education, Lord de la Warr, agreed with Cecil's comments, replying: 'I don't think we need attach too much importance to some of the matter which has appeared in the press, and, so far as Sir Cyril Norwood's articles are concerned, I gather that he speaks for no one but himself' (de la Warr, 1940).

One element in these antagonisms was that Norwood attempted to reconcile the potential of the emerging national system of education with the traditions of the élite public schools, with the result that he became regarded with suspicion from both sides. They also reflected Norwood's characteristic style of open debate through the public media. Secretive officials and heads of schools, accustomed to discreet and private policy discussions within their own élite circle, tended to be hostile to such methods, particularly when they proposed innovations that appeared dangerously unsound and radical. At its most extreme, when Norwood was openly challenging the existence of established institutions and conventions in the press, his approach could even be regarded as being out of line with an English tradition of educational policy making. This was the most ironical twist of all when applied to the most widely known celebrant of the English tradition of education.

5. Conclusions

This appraisal has sought to look beneath the familiar image and reputation of Cyril Norwood to find a rather different and more complex set of characteristics in his educational career. In doing so, it has touched on the subtleties of social class and status in English educational history. Norwood, undoubtedly the most prominent and eloquent supporter of the English tradition of education, was himself located uneasily and precariously in relation to it. He was as much an outsider to this tradition as he was an insider, and found himself a combatant in a continuing struggle to define and interpret it rather than its accepted heir. This has been demonstrated in three distinct aspects of his life and career: his family and childhood background in relation to his father, his embattled position at Harrow School, and his uneasy relationship with the élite educational policy community. The current work has also observed some of the complexities of power and influence in education. Even in his exalted positions at Harrow School and the Board of Education, Norwood was not always successful in exerting his authority, and encountered difficulty in addressing criticisms and dissent.

More broadly, the case of Cyril Norwood demonstrates, rather unexpectedly, the importance of insecurity, as opposed to security, as a dominant motif of the history of education in England. Fred Clarke, as we have seen, emphasised the impervious nature of English educational traditions, and explained this in terms of the nation's long years of security from outside attack or invasion. Despite this, and for all his own idealisations of England's underlying continuity, Norwood's life and educational career reflected social anxiety, with aspirations for respectability that were closely related to fear of social decline. This dimension of the history of education may well be best exposed through further research that highlights the connections between biography and social structure, and the tensions between private troubles and public issues. These are seen at their most acute as we witness Norwood struggling to climb the educational and social ladder, much more successfully than his father. He became the very image of an Oxford man and a formidable defender of educational tradition, but nevertheless remained 'not really a gentleman' and, in the still more deadly barb of his enemies at Harrow, 'not quite-quite'.

Acknowledgements

I am most grateful to the Leverhulme Trust for its support for the research project 'The life and educational career of Sir Cyril Norwood (1875–1956)' (F/118/AU) on which this paper is based; and to participants in the History of Education Society (UK) annual conference, 19–21 November 2004, for their helpful comments on an earlier version of the paper.

Notes on contributor

Professor Gary McCulloch is Brian Simon Professor of the History of Education at the Institute of Education, University of London. His recent publications include *Documentary research in education, history and the social sciences* (RoutledgeFalmer, 2004) and *The Routledge reader in the history of education* (Routledge, 2005). He is completing a full-length study of Cyril Norwood and the ideal of secondary education to be published by Palgrave Macmillan in 2006.

References

Arnold, M. (1864/1969) A French Eton, or middle-class education and the State, in: P. Smith & G. Summerfield (Eds) *Matthew Arnold and the education of a new order* (Cambridge, Cambridge University Press), 76–156.
Arnold, M. (1865/1964) *Schools and universities on the continent* (Ed. R. H. Super) (Ann Arbor, University of Michigan Press).
Arnold, M. (1869/1932) *Culture and anarchy* (edited with an introduction by J. Dover Wilson) (Cambridge, Cambridge University Press).
Bamford, T. W. (1960) *Thomas Arnold* (London, Cresset Press).
Board of Education (1938) *Secondary education* (Spens Report) (London, HMSO).
Board of Education (1943) *Curriculum and examinations in secondary schools* (Norwood Report) (London, HMSO).
Bryce, J. (1869) Report to Schools Inquiry Commission, vol. IX, general reports by Assistant Commissioners: Northern Counties.
Bryce Report (1895) Royal Commission on Secondary Education.
Butler, R. A. (1942) note, 20 March (National Archives, Kew, file ED.136/131).
Cecil, Lord Hugh (1940) Letter to Lord de la Warr, 21 March (National Archives, Kew, file ED.136/139).
Clarendon Report (1864) Royal Commission to Enquire into the Revenues and Management of Certain Colleges and Schools.
Clarke, F. (1940) *Education and social change: an English interpretation* (London, Sheldon Press).
Communications with the author (2000) from former pupils at Harrow School.
de la Warr, Lord (1940) Letter to Lord Hugh Cecil, 29 March (National Archives, Kew, file ED.136/139).
Dickens, C. (1850/1948) *The personal history of David Copperfield* (Oxford, Oxford University Press).
Durnford, R. (1881) Report to the Secretary, Endowed Schools Department, 3 January (National Archives, Kew, file ED.27/2318).
Endowed Schools Commission (1870) Letter to Revd Samuel Norwood, 16 October (National Archives, Kew, file ED.27/2318).
Gathorne-Hardy, J. (1977) *The public school phenomenon, 1597–1977* (London).
Honey, J. R. de S. (1977) *Tom Brown's universe: the development of the public school in the nineteenth century* (London, Millington).
Hughes, T. (1857/1949) *Tom Brown's schooldays* (London, Dent).
Hunt, F. (1991) *Gender and policy in English education: schooling for girls 1902–1944* (London, Harvester Wheatsheaf).
Martin, J. & Goodman, J. (2004) *Women and education, 1800–1980* (Basingstoke, Palgrave-Macmillan).
McCrum, M. (1989) *Thomas Arnold, Head Master: a reassessment* (Oxford, Oxford University Press).
McCulloch, G. (1991) *Philosophers and Kings: education for leadership in modern England* (Cambridge, Cambridge University Press).
McCulloch, G. (1994) *Educational reconstruction: the 1944 Education Act and the twenty-first century* (London, Woburn Press).
McCulloch, G. (2004) Norwood, Sir Cyril, in: *Oxford Dictionary of National Biography* (Oxford, Oxford University Press) 41, 203–205.
McCulloch, G. & McCaig, C. (2002) Reinventing the past: the case of the English tradition of education, *British Journal of Educational Studies*, 50(2), 238–253.
Mills, C. Wright (1959) *The sociological imagination* (London, Oxford University Press).
Newcastle Report (1861) Royal Commission to Enquire into the State of Popular Education in England.
Norwood, C. (1929a) *The English tradition of education* (London, John Murray).

Norwood, C. (1929b) Letter to C. G. Pope, 25 June (Norwood papers, University of Sheffield).
Norwood, C. (1929c) Letter to C. G. Pope, 13 July (Norwood papers, University of Sheffield).
Norwood, C. (1929d) Memorandum to Harrow School board of governors, August (Norwood papers, University of Sheffield).
Norwood, C. (1931) Letter to A. Benn, 4 August (Benn papers, private. I am most grateful to Mr Benn for making this letter available to me).
Norwood, Cyril & Catherine (1933) Note, 'For staying, for going' (Norwood papers, University of Sheffield).
Norwood Committee (1943) Final minutes of the Norwood Committee (unofficial), 23 June (National Archives, Kew, ED.12/479).
Norwood, S. (1870) Letter to the Endowed Schools Commission, 11 August (National Archives, Kew, ED.27/2318).
Playfair, G. (1937) *My father's son* (London, Geoffrey Bles).
Pope, C. G. (1929a) Letter to Cyril Norwood, 30 June (Norwood papers, University of Sheffield).
Pope, C. G. (1929b) Letter to Cyril Norwood, 29 July (Norwood papers, University of Sheffield).
Pope, C. G. (1929c) Letter to Cyril Norwood, 15 November (Norwood papers, University of Sheffield).
Selleck, R. J. W. (1994) *James Kay-Shuttleworth: journey of an outsider* (London, Woburn).
Simon, B. (1974) *The politics of educational reform, 1920–1940* (London, Lawrence & Wishart).
Taunton Report (1869) Schools Inquiry Commission.
The Harrovian (1956) Obituary of Sir Cyril Norwood, 3 May.
The Times (1956a) Obituary of Sir Cyril Norwood, 14 March.
The Times (1956b) 'Cyril Norwood: a courageous leader', 20 March.
The Times (1959) Obituary of C. G. Pope, 11 February.
Turner, G. C. (1971) 'Norwood, Sir Cyril', entry in *Dictionary of National Biography*.
Tyerman, C. (2000) *A history of Harrow School* (London, Oxford University Press).
Walcott, F. G. (1970) *The origins of culture and anarchy: Matthew Arnold and popular education in England* (Toronto, Toronto University Press).
Williams, G. G. (1941) note, 23 December (National Archives, Kew, file ED.12/48).

Anthony Crosland: intellectual and politician

Maurice Kogan

Anthony Crosland was one of the formative politicians of his generation. Yet there is a discernible gap between the power and impact of his writing, which effected mainly in the decade or so after leaving Oxford, his statement of policies, and then his ability or perhaps even his motivation to put precept into full policy practice. This may be a deficit to which all politicians, even the best, are heirs. We take note of it as we identify his conspicuous contributions to and achievements in policy-making.

He is rightly credited with providing the intellectual foundations of 'revisionism' (e.g. Lipsey, 1981; Crosland, S., 1982; Radice, 2002) which eventually emancipated the Labour Party from its traditional belief in nationalisation as the way to greater equality, and provided the theoretical foundations of a more participative and liberal society. He was an active party leader and highly successful minister within a wide range of departments, including Education and Science.

Educated as an economist, Crosland took a first in philosophy, politics and economics, although he had been admitted as a scholar to Trinity College, Oxford, to read Greats. For much of his political life he was engaged in economics as an intellectually active author, as a back bencher, or in the Shadow Cabinet, or as a Minister in the ill-fated Department of Economic Affairs and the Board of Trade. He was Secretary of State for Local Government and Regional Planning and later the Department of the Environment. At his death in February 1977 he was Foreign Secretary.

Although on becoming education minister in 1965,[1] he found, unsurprisingly, that his mind reverted at first to the DEA and economic policy, he soon established supremacy in his first Cabinet post. His time as Secretary of State for Education and Science was relatively short, from January 1965 to August 1967, but he had prepared himself for it both intellectually and in working through the underlying values issues.

Of the list of Oxonians who occupied education ministerial posts, hardly any had applied their minds to the issues they might face once in office. Crosland's written work contained many socially-committed statements about education. No other education minister within living memory put in that level of work.

His thinking was embedded in impressively analytic published books and articles which spared no pains in considering the philosophical, ethical and economic issues. They read fluently and well and combine argument—some of it inevitably partisan, to the point of historical imprecision—with reflective exploitation of current research. In particular, *The future of socialism* (1956) and *The Conservative enemy* (1962)—or in elegantly succinct form, *Social democracy in Europe* (1975)—were effective statements of the egalitarian case which, before the Blair regime swept all before it, led the field in revisionist Fabian social democratic thinking. These writings were widely admired, although one commentator has compared the key work, *The future of socialism*, disadvantageously to Jenkins' *The Labour case* (1959) 'which put forward many of the arguments with more style and in a much less self-consciously intellectual way' (Cannadine, 2004, p. 282). Some, however, might prefer their social philosophers to stand and argue the case from first principles; Jenkins left no lasting testimony in terms of social or political philosophy. Crosland's written work enables us to evaluate the extent to which his thinking fed into his actions as a politician and minister.

His arguments followed clear conceptual tracks which enabled him to eschew some of the more traditional canons of Labour policy. He had a positive dislike of policy packages which embodied faded and often unspoken value assumptions. He was thus able to explore several different paths to the ultimate objectives of a free and equal society. Susan Crosland summarised his views: '[He] saw values and ideals as central to politics. He separated these from the means of achieving them. Means change as society changes ... and the revisionist needs continually to examine the range of means available.' He could thus distinguish social democracy from communist doctrines which depended on nationalisation. He wrote: 'the ownership of the means of production is not now ... the key factor which imparts to a society its essential character' (Crosland, 1975).

He never let go of the intellectual approach, which he reinforced through the seminars held at his home. As a close observer (Cockerill, 2004) put it: 'how many intellectual Ministers had to contend with theories of education alongside egotistical colleagues like Vivian Bowden, an occasional C. P. Snow, a prima donna, Jennie Lee (Arts and OU and a direct line to No 10)—not to mention a football referee (Howell) bent on the World Cup ...'

Critic of the status quo

Although other leading members of the Labour Party have attempted to contribute to the party's stock of ideas—R. H. Tawney, John Strachey, as well as Roy Jenkins come to mind—Crosland stands out as one who operated as an intellectual of the highest calibre whilst playing a full part in the politics of the party and of the polity at large. He recounted how Marxism had been 'the dominant influence'—he cited John Strachey and Harold Laski as leading the field—of his time. But 'Marx has very little or nothing to offer the contemporary Socialist, either in respect of practical policy or the correct analysis of our society. ... His prophecies have been almost without exception falsified, and his conceptual tools are now quite inappropriate' (Crosland, CAR, 1956, pp. 2–3). He was going to follow Bernstein in becoming the leading revisionist of his time.

He published *The future of socialism* in October 1956 when Labour had just suffered its second defeat at the polls. He asked 'What is socialism now about?' The Marxist theory of the inevitable collapse of capitalism had been invalidated by cumulative democratic pressures. He knocked the ground from under the Marxists' feet by showing that there was no evidence of the gradual pauperisation of the masses or that capitalism as an economic system was at all near the point of collapse. Whilst still in the army he had exchanged letters with Philip Williams which anticipated themes that were to re-emerge in *The future of socialism*, summarised by Susan Crosland as 'the resilience of capitalist economy, the ability of a gradualist but determined reforming government to change the balance' (Crosland, S., 1982, p. 13). 'Nor was it any longer true that that society was effectively controlled by a capitalist ruling class. The pre-war capitalist class did hold this power. But today the capitalist business class has lost this commanding position' (p. 7)—perhaps one of his more quickly outdated judgements.

The traditional power of the capitalist had been broken, and ownership of industry was now irrelevant: 'what mattered was who managed it and how ... Industry was now in the hands of the professional managers ...' Business leaders were paid by wages and not by profit: 'The political authority now exerts control over a much higher proportion of economic decisions than before the war—they employ over 25% of the work force and are responsible for over 50% of total investment.'

There was no necessary link between class and power. The devotion to Clause 4 was misplaced: nationalisation was a means, not an end. He was a pluralist. He could envisage state ownership and the co-operative principle coexisting with private ownership. Greater equality in a democratic society could best be secured by economic growth, rather than nationalisation.

He enumerated socialist aspirations as co-operative, and related to welfare and equality. In laying out his blueprint he argued for far more than equality of opportunity, advocating the virtual destruction of the existing social hierarchy. Ability was a chance factor, not something earned; it should be rewarded only while it was useful to society, not for its own sake. 'No one deserves either so generous an award or so severe a penalty for a quality implanted from the outside and for which he can claim only a limited responsibility.'

The socialist must be committed to increased social expenditure. The economy was growing at a rapid pace, and there seemed every prospect of it continuing to do so. Beyond taxation changes, two main reforms were required to break down barriers in society. The first was education: the comprehensive principle needed to be propagated; entry into the public schools to be democratised. Education, not nationalisation, was to be the main engine in the creation of a more just society:

> If the state provides schools and hospitals, teachers and doctors, on a generous scale and of a really high quality... then the result will be, not indeed a greater equality of real incomes, but certainly a greater equality in manners and the texture of social life. (1980, p. 85)

His analysis was appropriate and powerful in its time. He could not foresee the effects of both the Thatcher and the Blair regimes in reducing the role of local authorities, through transfer of powers to quasi-market bodies, by reduction in resources and by plain derogation.

It would be appropriate to compare the two Labour leaders with whom revisionism might be associated. Both Blair and Crosland had views on equality as it might be achieved through education. Because Crosland could discern between means and ends he was able to discriminate between different degrees of equality—the hard and the soft, the weak and the strong. He saw clearly that in any world, whether that of his contemporary Britain or any future and more ideal world, there would not be absolute and pure equality. But one could at least set down principles by which degrees of discrimination would be applied. Getting a good education would not of itself lead to good social rewards, a view point certainly not shared by New Labour.

The second reform lay in the Blairite devotion to market-like devices. Crosland was not prissy about the market but would not have thought that main line public provision should be made for profit or subjected to its values and rewards.

He could not anticipate the extent to which business leaders were to enrich themselves by acquiring large share holdings as part of their pay packet, or the way in which even a Labour government was to reinforce their power by the award of titles, and to place them in key positions on governmental allocative bodies (higher education, research councils and cultural bodies come immediately to mind). (Would he have gone along with knighthoods for pop idols—his father, a distinguished civil servant, refused a knighthood—or millionaire pickings for footballers?) Nor could he predict the growth in social and educational cachet of the independent schools which have grown rather than diminished in competence and power and continue to reinforce the grip over social position of those who can afford places in them.

He was concerned with the style of life that might be entailed in a socialist future. The Left should turn to the question of restrictions already imposed by society on the individual's private life and liberty: 'divorce laws, licensing laws, pre-historic ... abortion laws, obsolete penalties for sexual abnormality, the illiterate censorship of books and plays, and the restrictions on equal rights for women' (Crosland, 1980, p. 355).

He wrote:

> We realise that we must guard against romantic or Utopian notions that hard work and research are virtues; that we must do nothing foolish or impulsive. ... Posthumously the Webbs have won their battle, and converted a generation to their standards. Now the time has come for a reaction: for a greater emphasis on private life, on freedom and dissent, on culture, beauty, leisure and even frivolity. Total abstinence and a good filing system are not now the right sign posts to the socialists.

His ability to think beyond conventional boundaries was displayed in *Britain's economic problem,* his first book. The price of coal was going up. He thought the price should be raised even further. Private industry should be charged what they could pay so that the coal industry became self-supporting. Later in *The future of socialism* (1980 edn.) he argued that 'we should now have a definite preference for the competitive public enterprise' approach, although there will still be cases where state monopoly still provides the right answer (p. 327). Later, whilst in opposition, he opposed the creation of a Capability Unit, and its associated programme budgeting as proposed in Heath's White Paper of 1970 (Kogan, p. 32). He became increasingly luke-warm about public spending as a way to greater equality. He cautioned against waste lest public spending be absorbed into self-sustaining bureaucracies (Lipsey, 1981, p. 34) and was sceptical of planning and industrial policy: 'He had no faith that civil servants at the Department of Industry would make a better job of running British industry than existing managers' (Lipsey, 1981, p. 30). 'A change from private control to state control is socialist only if that control is democratic. ... We should not be in the business of creating endless giant Leviathans manned by armies of bureaucrats' (Crosland, 1975, p. 5). He favoured equality of competition even if it meant inequality of outcome.

On education

The fundaments of his education thinking were brought to the test as he entered office. He had no doubts about where Labour policy should lead. He began with the assumption, in *The future of socialism* (1962), that 'the school system in Britain remains the most divisive, unjust and wasteful of all the social aspects of inequality' (p. 191)—a judgement that might not have been shared by many comparativists: many other systems at that time were selective and divisive. He contrasted our systems only with those of the USA and Sweden, which were examples favouring his case. The existing system had been primarily geared to educating the middle classes. Working-class children, with rare exception, were faced with overcrowding, a shortage of teachers, deteriorating buildings and were segregated into separate schools. He attacked the differences in opportunity offered to pupils selected to enter grammar schools and the conditions under which non-selected children were then taught in secondary modern schools. Nature ensures that an élite is always rising and asserting itself in a democracy, but the state should do its utmost, he said, 'to make it possible for those without money or position or a literate family background to have equal access to the opportunity that a decent education bestows.' Not only was it morally wrong for the state to determine which eleven-year-olds could go to the grammar school, which were deemed suited for the secondary mode: it was also wasteful of resources.

'More unjust and most wasteful were those public schools—Eton, Winchester—that provided the finest academic education to youths who would mostly disappear into the City or other parasitic occupations.' Again, one must wonder here at the sagacity of this judgement. The more valid objection to public schools might be that they were validating the elites that governed Britain.

Crosland 'could never understand why socialists could be so obsessed with the question of the grammar schools, and so indifferent to the much more glaring injustice of the independent schools' (1980, p. 191), a criticism which remains relevant to current policies. Of alternative ways of dealing with the private sector, he opted for that of integration, as on the lines of the Fleming Report (Fleming, 1944)—which was in part motivated by concern for the independent schools which were declining in pupil numbers in the 1930s—with perhaps 75% of places being made free of fees. 'By this solution the public schools, while retaining their distinctive character, teaching cadres, and genuine educational assets, would steadily grow more socially heterogeneous' (1980, p. 193). To that end they should not be open only to the ablest, but entry should be of mixed ability. He wrote in *The Conservative enemy* (1962) that the object of legislation would not be to prohibit all fee paying, 'which would be an intolerable restriction of personal liberty', but to regulate the conditions under which education is bought or sold, to secure a more equitable distribution of educational resources. His wife records that no one knew in 1965 how private education could be reformed. So in 1965 he set up the Public Schools Commission under the chairmanship of Sir John Newsom (succeeded by David Donnison in 1968) and then turned his mind to other things.

He accepted that a system still divided between private and state, selective and secondary modern would remain irretrievably divisive and unjust, and therefore ultimately opted for comprehensive education, nevertheless arguing that 'division into streams, according to ability, remains essential' (p. 202). Yet here, too, he could discern the difference between ultimate objectives and the operational provisions that might lead to them: 'The object of having comprehensive schools is not to abolish all competition and all envy ... but to avoid the extreme social division caused by physical segregation into schools of widely divergent status' (p. 202).

Not all of this could be done at once, but would take time and resources. To destroy good grammar schools in advance of providing effective replacements must be wrong. But the principles and intentions to act should be firmly established. And we must acknowledge the two major constraints on his actions: he had to plan for the second tranche of raising the school leaving age, and he had to provide for lengthening of the teacher training course to three years. And these against the economic malaise, that had begun to set in.

But here we stub our toes against the enigmatic nature of his radicalism. There is this lacuna between the radical, even fervent, writing that takes us up to the

1960s—with some effective reprises a little later on—and his unwillingness or perhaps, more fairly, his inability to follow through when in office. Anne Corbett has him on record as saying, 'I am not interested in public and direct grant schools any more' (Corbett, 2004), although this attitude was not evident in in-house conversations (Cockerill, 2004). Also we must note that the issue had no party political head of steam behind it; there was no fervour behind it equal to say, that pressing the current hunting issue. Nor did his successors pick it up. Later we will see that he became bored with universities too. These somewhat laconic remarks might have been casual chat at the end of the day but it may not be uncharitable to discern a neurotic caution that set in with the fatigue of office or the sheer difficulty of moving things along.

Moreover, although his analyses of the general social and economic scene were trenchant and held well together, many of his judgements of the educational status quo can be criticised as being distant from those who knew the schools at first hand. His detestation of the grammar schools (see later), based on *a priori* judgements of their divisive power, failed to acknowledge the opportunities they opened up to what was admittedly a minority from the lower socio-economic classes. There have been knowledgeable defenders of the pre-war senior elementary secondary schools, on much the same grounds (e.g. Elvin, 1969). The independent schools both instantiated privilege and produced working élites for the civil service, armed forces and business.

His denunciation of them would have carried more conviction if it had conveyed their merits as well as their faults. He failed to notice improvements taking place: educational expenditure per capita went up in the 1930s (Vaizey, 1958), new buildings were made available to denominational schools under the 1936 Act, and in the 1950s and 1960s conservatives complained about expenditure on secondary modern school buildings, described as 'glass palaces'.

Crosland had some strong hates which could have been mitigated by some awareness of the cross-grained reality of the institutions he attacked. One wonders how many schools he visited before becoming Secretary of State.

Crosland as minister

Crosland's principal achievements as minister of education included the restructuring of both secondary and higher education. He was not successful in his attempt to tackle the independent school 'problem'.

By the time he took office about 12% of secondary school places were in comprehensive schools. Although anxious to move policies fast, Crosland decided, in drafting Circular 10/65—which called attention to the government's declared objective to end selection at eleven-plus and to eliminate separation in secondary education—to 'request' rather than 'require' local authorities to introduce comprehensive schools. Susan Crosland recounts (p. 144) how he rejected 'require', the preference of his minister of state, Reg Prentice, as 'an empty toughness'. 'The Department could not cope with the pace already set. He didn't want the new system threatened by botching it.' He was glad, too, that in January 1965 the Cabinet had agreed not to enforce the comprehensive schools policy by legislation. It was fundamental to his view of democracy that reform would be more lasting if it could be achieved voluntarily.

Yet these cautions were not generated by lack of belief. His wife reports (Crosland, S., 1982, p.148) how in a conversation at home he said, 'If it is the last thing I do, I'm going to destroy every fucking grammar school in England ... And Wales. And Northern Ireland.'[2]

The working out of his policies was not wholly endorsed by those who had worked hard in the field to bring about comprehensive education. Whilst he was cautious about breaking up and merging existing structures, many people in, for example, the Young Teachers Committee of the National Union of Teachers hoped he would ordain a schools system for 11–18 year-olds in which former grammar schools would become sixth-form colleges. He was no doubt advised to be cautious by the lack of new resources and by the advice of such well regarded civil servants as Wilma Harte, who could warn him of the difficulties.

It is, however, important to recall that when Crosland was at Education, the school leaving age was 15. It was difficult to get resources to fund a meaningful, as opposed to tokenistic, comprehensive policy. School building was generally allowed only to secure roofs over heads and there was no resource for educational reform.

Yet to believe in consensus and voluntary action does not excuse policy-makers from attempting to predict and plan for consequences. Crosland can be criticised for relying on enacting major acts of state as the way to reform. The concept of the unintended consequences of policies was not then current. The schools in the 1960s were becoming better housed and equipped—one new school building a day was being opened. But it is doubtful whether the greatly expanded teacher force was well enough prepared to meet the huge professional challenges to which comprehensivisation gave rise. Both the Welfare State and the Opportunity State drew heavily on limited sources of talent as policies and the markets opened up new opportunities. There was inadequate preparation in terms of curriculum and providing support through social welfare and trained leadership. These obstacles to reform should have been made explicit and placed on the policy agenda.

Just as controversial was the decision to elevate 30 higher education institutions into polytechnics. There is a plausible case for arguing that the binary policy was justified by the natural and organic development of higher education. Many systems have started out with a 'noble' university sector whilst a vocational second level is allowed to emerge alongside it. Their ultimate elevation to university status is never contemplated at the beginning, but seems to be an inescapable trend.

The divided arrangement of higher education still obtains in Germany, Greece and Norway, and in an idiosyncratic form in France (not binary, but trinary), and until the 1990s was the pattern obtaining in Australia and New Zealand. The creation of a polytechnic sector has always been aimed at expanding higher education opportunities to a larger proportion of the population, enhancing the status of vocational and technical education and consolidating small and minor institutions into larger and stronger entities. In the UK, connections with schools were to be beneficially sustained by local education authority control over polytechnics.

Accordingly, Crosland (Woolwich, 1965) asserted a preference for the 'dual system as being fundamentally the right one, with each sector making its own contribution to the whole. We infinitely prefer it to the concept of a unitary system, hierarchically arranged on the ladder principle, with the Universities at the top and the other institutions down below'.

These arguments for a divided system might stand up on their own but not easily within the wider premises of an anti-divisive education policy that Crosland had so vehemently supported in the school phase. The hope that polytechnics would take care of the need for a technically and vocationally trained population ignored the fact that the bulk of non-university courses were in social sciences and the humanities and not in the 'useful' hard sciences or technologies. The hope that they would lead the country's technical and vocational advance was thus unlikely to be realised. The policy failed to anticipate the phenomenon of 'academic drift': higher education institutions almost all aim to acquire research reputations and to offer the award of doctoral and other post-graduate level qualifications. It failed to notice that to some extent the whole of the UK system was 'elitist' in that about 6% proceeded to university and another 9% to non-university higher education courses—in total well within Trow's characterisation of an elite system, recruiting 15% of the population (Trow, 1970).

The argument for division was thus weaker in the UK than in most countries. Finally, it blithely assumed that local authorities would allow the polytechnics the freedoms essential to high standing research and development. The polytechnic directors were able, a generation later, to feed Mrs Thatcher and her ministers with many stories of local authorities' narrow and restrictive attempts to control them (Kogan & Hanney, 2000).

Crosland's decision to opt for a binary system was all the more surprising in view of his own trenchant attacks on the divided secondary education system. Many have attributed Crosland's decision to opt for a binary rather than a unitary system to the persuasive arguments put forward by Toby Weaver, the then Deputy Secretary for Higher Education.[3] Weaver and the powerful and expert further education inspectorate were wholly in favour of a structure that would put a coping-stone onto further and technical education. So were a small group of polytechnic intellectuals, notably Eric Robinson and Tyrrell Burgess. So also were the further education teachers association, the ATTI, who 'had a great deal of influence on the development of the binary policy' (Crosland in Kogan, 1971).

Halsey (2005) notes, however, that 'like most Oxonians [Crosland] did not understand that nearly every respectable boy from the working class had a decent education through apprenticeship and night school. He himself went to Highgate and Trinity in total unawaresness of the fate of the majority of his compatriots. Hence he could easily be taken in by the clever arguments of Weaver in favour of the so-called binary system.'

The creation of the first Colleges of Advanced Technology in 1957, later to be renamed technological universities, to some extent weakened the status of the institutions that were left behind. This initial development preceded both Crosland and

Weaver, although it was they who determined the ultimate binary nature of the structure in the mid-1960s.

The decision to opt for a binary system must have been taken on high, between Crosland and Weaver. We know that quite senior officials were considering a range of alternatives—such as universities surrounded by a cluster of other institutions—the mode adopted in Australia. But these ideas were soon left behind.

Crosland's policy was not pleasing to all. Richard Crossman noted in his diary:

> When I was Shadow Science Minister I became more and more convinced that one of the biggest jobs for ... Labour... was to break down the rigid division between HE and FE and institute a unitary approach as opposed to the existing binary approach ... although I knew that officials in the Ministry were firmly committed to it. I was disappointed to hear that he had decided to maintain the binary system and I was greatly disconcerted when I learnt later on that he was by no means convinced in his own mind that it was right. (Crossman, 1975, vol. 1, p. 326)

It is difficult to imagine Crosland bending to arguments that he did not fully accept: he—if anyone—could have stood up to Weaver. But he certainly evinced no pro-university bias; it is worth recalling that it was under his ministry that universities were subjected to audit by the Comptroller and Auditor-General for the first time (Kogan, 1969), although this might have been seen as inevitable under any minister. His somewhat sniffy approach to universities as elitist and stuffy sat oddly with his own golden career at Oxford, although those close to him (e.g. Price, 2004) felt that he had not been impressed by his experience as a don; he had a positive disdain for the self-regard displayed by the ancient universities, and his own college, socially exclusive Trinity, was probably not at all to his taste.

Susan Crosland recounts how he found one of his days 'interminable. ... The Vice-Chancellors this evening went on and on and on as if their precious universities weren't already rich and successful. ... If one is to be truthful, I'm not frightfully interested in the universities ... tomorrow I shall tell the Vice-Chancellors they can stuff themselves. "Enough of this niggling and nagging", I shall say: "I have enough on my mind than your petty preoccupations. Away with you!"' (Crosland, S., 1982, p. 147). His decision to take the Weaver line still remains something of a mystery, although we might fairly credit him with a wholesome ambition to create a new set of institutions, which would both trump the university card and open up both social and economic opportunity. And the universities might have seemed immoveable on issues of wider access.

The establishment of the Public Schools Commission, which was to 'advise on the best ways of integrating the public schools with the state system of education', followed his own political philosophy:

> The public schools offend not only against the 'weak' let alone 'the strong' ideal of equal opportunity; they offend even more against an ideal of social cohesion of democracy. ... We might get the desired social mixture by the operation of free choice. But if we do not and the demand remains heavily slanted, the authorities must deliberately allocate free places in proportion either to certain broadly defined income brackets or to different types of state schools.

Thus Crosland favoured a directed form of Fleming reforms. His intentions were defeated by lack of resources, by the time available to enable a degree of acquiescence to develop in the public schools, and, perhaps, the scepticism of his own Public Schools Commission. The issue now remains buried under the current reluctance to remove incentives to educational divisiveness.

Crosland took up a theme first developed in the Plowden Report on primary education (Plowden, 1967), the creation of education priority areas. He called this the testing of the geographic theory of poverty (Halsey, 2005). He recruited Michael Young and A. H. Halsey to organise a nation-wide study of slum schools in a major collaborative effort to collect evidence-based theory for government and local government action to raise standards of schooling in deprived areas. And he solicited from the Treasury substantial funding for it.

Crosland evidently intended to make some mark on the planning capacity of the department. He established a Planning Branch but it did not have the mandate, and he did not hold office long enough to bring different kinds of planning to fruition. He did, however, decide to discontinue the Central Advisory Councils for England and Wales. These had produced several notable reports—*Early leaving*, Crowther on 15–18s, Newsom on non-selective secondary education. According to Halsey (Halsey & Sylva, 1987), this decision was based:

> on the instinct of an outstanding politician that the amiable reflections of an essentially amateur Establishment of the 'great and good' were too unwieldy and too slow to be of service to modern government. He already had the notion that planning backed by economic and sociological research could be internalised into DES administration in such a way as to enable an energetic Secretary of State to link social scientific knowledge to political and popular opinion.

The judgement of what was needed may have been sound—a stronger internal entity was certainly needed—but the verdict on Plowden and the other CACs was the product of lazy thinking, not untypical of the laconic and casual style that we have noted Crosland adopting in attacking other features of the system that he disliked. Were the members recruited from the great and the good? Hardly. Of the 25 members about half were well known and respected educationists. The other half included A. J. Ayer, J. M. Tanner, Ian Byatt, Tim Raison, Molly Brearley, David Donnison—all strong intellectuals who would hardly count as being of the great and the good, if by that is meant those who are placed on such bodies because of vague reputational connections (although Lady Plowden and John Newsom might have qualified by some such criteria). They were not essentially amateur, but included people well respected in their own fields. More fundamentally, Crosland had not thought through the functions performed or best performed by the CACs. They had two unstated functions: to produce analysis about the state of education—a technocratic task to be undertaken by social scientists and educationists, but also to offer normative statements of and models about education. They may have not performed these functions perfectly but their replacement provided none. The attempt at a new planning system could have at least taken these functions into account, and the whole area of what would constitute competent planning fully evaluated.

As a person

Much has been made of Crosland's family background and how he divested himself of the rigours of the Plymouth Brethren faith. Commentators have attributed his strong work ethic to his background.

Whilst officials welcomed his arrival at Curzon St House, *Education* (29 January 1965) commented 'With the arrival of Mr Anthony Crosland, the Department of Education and Science has exchanged the solid, professional, middle of the road qualities of Mr Stewart for a less predictable, more brilliant, more controversial personality.' He was 'highly intelligent and has the reputation of a wicked conversationalist with a gift for amusing and malicious disputation. He is accused by his enemies—of whom, within the Labour Party, he seems to have an unlimited number—of being merciless at tearing his opponents to shreds while himself being thin skinned and easily offended. ... he is impatient and intolerant, a man of words, who must find the slow and laborious business of negotiation and consultation tiresome and tedious'. That did not turn out to be the experience of him as a minister, and he left with golden opinions. He thought carefully before making moves. He consulted the main associations on large issues of policy and took the least extreme lines on the public schools and comprehensive education.

Yet, whilst deeply committed to equality and freedom and maximum participation in decision-making, he made little effort to stroke those who worked for him. *Education*'s estimate of him as 'a man of words' failed to acknowledge the able analyst who worked 14 hours a day on producing his major works. One close observer (Cockerill, 2004) noted that he seemed shaken by the sheer volume of work. He insisted on getting on with the business in hand and expected officials to do the same, without much benefit of emollient drink or chat, except with his own selected coterie of advisers. His wife recounts some rather tough treatment of a private secretary. He did not scruple to tick off a Permanent Secretary with others present for arriving late at a meeting. But he acquired respect and admiration for his ability to grasp and work through complex issues. On at least one occasion he sought the views of all the under-secretaries and above on the age of transfer to secondary education (Kogan, 1971, p. 184). And he did express appreciation of good work.

If his policies were radical he did not sponsor over-hasty or dramatic political behaviour. Following a well-worn statement by Arthur Henderson, he noted that 'a lot of incoming Ministers feel they must make some immediate dramatic gesture to impress the Department with their strong personality... I don't think this sort of thing much impresses civil servants; they see through it and give a smile of tolerant amusement' (Kogan, 1971, p. 155).

He hated the life of the back-bencher, and being out of office. He was still disconsolate when Willem van der Eyken and I took him to lunch in Islington—not yet the mythic centre of journalistic fables—to persuade him to be interviewed for *The Politics of Education* (1971). He grumbled at the newspapers littering the streets, but cheered up at Fredericks' restaurant which was bathed in sunlight. 'Positively Italianate', he said, 'there's even an old priest with a young man over there.' (I should add that he was a perfect interviewee—crisp and concise and expert in reviewing drafts.)

He found most Parliamentary debates boring and of low quality. Indeed, the life of the politician in general seemed to hold little appeal: 'he is constantly going to be attacked in Parliament and criticised in the press, badgered by endless and often hostile deputations ... If he becomes a minister he will suddenly lose his job because his party is chucked out of office ... If I look back on my life, insecurity has been a very marked characteristic ...' (Kogan, 1971, p. 151).

His family life comes out as a source of support and delight. He had a circle of well-prized friends. He was not however, a networker or mixer except with established friends. He could be intimidating to those he thought not performing well enough—his wife gives examples of this. My last vision of him was as minister at the NUT annual bash, surrounded by hand-licking journalists, morosely staring out to the festive room. He made no attempt to circulate or 'work' the room as others will do. And this refusal to play populist games must have counted against him in the leadership competitions which came towards the end of his life.

He was deeply loyal to the Labour Party throughout—a little odd for one who presented as so fastidious and sceptical—but who 'had moved early on and was bang in the middle of intellectual flux that started when my faith in the CP and 100% was shattered, and continued when my brief period of faith in the Left intellectuals and 85% marxism was shattered. Where I shall end Heaven knows ...' (Crosland, S., 1982, p. 18).

As for general social attitudes, in spite of the upper class accent, and star like good looks, 'he said he was an egalitarian and meant it' (p. 71). 'His tough mindedness made him impatient with the Right's caution.' His positive view of socialism was the way to widen free choice, not to narrow it. In the blood of the socialist, 'there should always run a trace of the anarchist and the libertarian, and not too much of the prig and prude.' A. H. Halsey (1997) writes of him as a libertarian socialist, 'passionately so'... 'He hated the "pool of ability" theorists, wanted many boys and girls to go to grammar/technical schools and thence believed that the Marxist line (Clause IV) was wrong and concluded that the way to a civilised socialism lay through education in interaction with economic growth' (Halsey, 2005).

A product of Oxford?

How, if at all, do the life and work of Crosland and his impact on educational policy relate to his 'experiences' at Oxford as student and don? What, in the first place, was the significance of that impact?

He stood out, both in his writing and in his ministerial programme, as a determined thinker and activist who caused change, particularly perhaps in the comprehensive schools policy and in the creation of the polytechnics. As noted above, the implementation of these policies was not fully thought through and perhaps we have become more accustomed now to look for the unintended consequences of policy change. We have also noted a kind of neurotic caution about going too fast, too soon. To each radical theme in his thinking, there was always some moderating qualification. He thought that a wholesale effort to suppress the motive of personal gain could have undesirable side effects as well as being unrealistic. He noted that: 'You can't solve anything. But start things moving in the right direction' (Crosland, S., 1982, p. 294). But his were major achievements made in a short period of office and backed by the intellectual assurance that he had earned through the eloquence and analysis of his written works.

An underlying question must be: To what extent has any minister or politician had any deep effect on the educational life of the country? In some areas of policy, for example those concerned with income distribution, major acts of state can quickly make differences. Such structural changes, too, as the creation of the polytechnics can radically change the landscapes of higher education and opportunity. But education in general, concerns complex processes of affect and structure that take time to come to fruition. To succeed, a minister must not only set the policy and find resources to implement it but put in place the processes that will make it work. For example, comprehensive schools only received building programme allocations if they could demonstrate a need for extra roofs over heads. No training systems helped their teachers acquire expertise in the particular problems—curricular, organisational and pastoral—of dealing with mixed ability groups. A minister cannot deal with all of these operational sequelae of policies, but can set them in motion or make sure that others do.

This does not dispose of the question of whether these were *Oxonian* contributions. The problem will be to find a competent definition of 'Oxonian'. The long list of Oxford-educated ministers of education—Edward Boyle, Hailsham, Keith Joseph, John Patten, Michael Stewart, Shirley Williams, William Waldegrave, Baroness Young, Anthony Crosland, Ruth Kelly—includes such variations in ability, style and ideology, and little in common, save perhaps, self-confidence, that it would be impossible to identify an Oxford factor.

Oxonians may see more than others. Thus Giles Radice, in his excellent biographies of Crosland, Healey and Jenkins (Radice, 2002), attributes long lasting disappointments to the fact that Crosland was ahead of Jenkins at Oxford but was yet unsuccessful in the race for the Chancellorship of the Exchequer. If so, and the argument does not ring as very convincing, that shows that Oxford recollections linger long. But they hardly account for any particular theme or strand in Crosland's mode of thinking. How could one weigh the effects of impressionable years at Highgate, or the tough war time experience, against the time at Oxford?

There is a tendency to believe in what one can call the co-terminosity of institutions. At one time, it was assumed that independent schools were not only good in themselves but also for the example they set to the public system, a belief apparently held by our present Prime Minister. Such an assumption fails to notice how the attraction of able parents, pupils and teachers away from the mainstream inevitably weakens the public system. Similarly, the presence of Oxford (and Cambridge) has presented targets and perhaps a beau ideal of learning to some schools. It certainly offered the tutorial model that many of us in less esteemed universities sought to emulate. But these influences were not mediated through politicians but by the acquired knowledge of school and university teachers. Where Oxonian ministers have had an effect on schools or universities it has not always been a mixed blessing. And at any rate, it is difficult to discern anything particularly Oxonian in, say, Joseph's attacks on the SSRC, or in the steadfast creation of a testing culture in the schools.

So if all these ministers have all been one-offs, Crosland was a supreme one-off—in the quality of his intellect, in his determination to put it to direct policy uses, in his ability to sustain an argument in long-haul works of distinction and analysis, in avowal of social and personal values that still present a challenge to our existing policy leaders. Current hagiology, however, may not make sufficient allowance for his caution and his propensity to make contestable judgements as the starting point for key decisions.

References and sources

For reasons beyond my control, I was unable to pursue a full research exercise for this article, and I have depended mainly on published sources, given below. In addition I have benefited greatly from discussion with knowledgeable observers of Crosland's scene. Anne Corbett, the most perceptive education journalist of her time, helped me sharpen and, to some extent, turn round my argument. Geoffrey Cockerill provided some invaluable close-up judgements, as did Chelly Halsey. Richard Cunningham, Mary Henkel, Harry Judge, David Kogan, Margaret Maden, Brian MacArthur, Chris Price, Clive and Kathleen Saville all contributed to my thinking and sources.

Notes

1. Roy Jenkins was offered Education before Crosland, but turned it down because he preferred to wait for the Home Office (Wilson, 1971, p. 66; Crossman, 1975, p. 136). Wilson followed George Wigg's suggestion: 'If we can't have Roy Jenkins, let's have Crosland. He's got a good brain, he's written well about education and he will be a positive addition to the Cabinet.'
2. Crosland referred to this conversation when being interviewed for *Politics of education*, but decided to cut it out of that text. Halsey (2005) describes it as made by a tired man after an exasperating day. Grammar schools seemed, however, to attract opprobrium from both sides. David Eccles once stated that farmers liked secondary modern schools and preferred them to the 'rat holes' of old-fashioned and small grammar schools (Kogan, 1975, p. 33).
3. Weaver was a powerful and highly intelligent official whose earlier career had been spent in local education authorities, and he may not have felt as uncomfortable as some with the notion of aldermanic control of higher education institutions, although his own report (Weaver, 1966) later sought to strengthen the autonomy of public sector institutions through the enhancement of the powers of Academic Boards. After a meeting with Weaver, Edward Boyle remarked: 'There is really no substitute for high intelligence.'

References

Cannadine, D. (2004) Writer and biographer, Ch. 17, in: A. Adonis & K. Thomas *Roy Jenkins. A retrospective* (Oxford, Oxford University Press).

Cockerill, G. F. (2004) Discussion and personal communication.
Corbett, A. (2004) Discussion and personal communication.
Crosland, C. A. R. (1962) *The Conservative enemy* (London, Cape).
Crosland, C. A. R. (1975) *Social democracy in Europe.* Fabian Tract 438.
Crosland C. A. R. (1980) (2nd edn) *The future of socialism* (London, Cape). This was first published in 1956. Page references are to the latest 1980 edition.
Crosland, S. (1982) *Tony Crosland* (London, Jonathan Cape).
Crossman, R. (1975) *The diaries of a cabinet minister, Vol I* (London, Hamish Hamilton and Jonathan Cape).
Department of Education and Science (1966) (Weaver Report) *Report of the Study Group on the Government of Colleges of Education.*
Elvin, L. (1969) Essay, in: R. S. Peters (Ed.) *Perspectives on Plowden* (London, Routledge).
Fleming Report (1944) *The public schools and the general educational system. Report on the Committee on Public Schools.*
Halsey, A. H. (1997) Politics and education, in: P. Mortimer & A. Little (Eds) *Living education. Essays in honour of John Tomlinson* (London, Paul Chapman), 182–192.
Halsey, A. H. (2005) Personal communication.
Halsey, A. H. & Sylva, K. (1987) Plowden: history and prospect, *Oxford Review of Education,* 13(1), 3–12.
Kogan, M. (1969) Audit, control and freedom, *Higher Education Review,* Spring.
Kogan, M. (1971) *The politics of education* (Harmondsworth, Penguin Books).
Kogan, M. (1975) *Educational policy-making. A study of interest groups and Parliament* (London, George Allen & Unwin).
Kogan, M. & Hanney, S. (2000) *Reforming higher education* (London, Jessica Kingsley Publishers).
Lipsey, D. (1981) Crosland's socialism, Ch. 3, in: D. Lipsey & D. Leonard *The socialist agenda* (London, Cape).
Price, C. (2004) Personal communication.
Plowden Report (1967) *Children and their primary schools.* Report of the Central Advisory Council for Education (England) (London, HMSO).
Radice, G. (2002) *Friends and rivals* (London, Little Brown).
Trow, M. (1970) Reflections on the transition from mass to universal higher education, *Daedalus,* 99, 1–42.
Vaizey, J. (1958) *The costs of education* (London, George Allen & Unwin).
Wilson, H. (1971) *The Labour Government 1964–1970. A personal record* (London, Weidenfeld & Nicholson and Michael Joseph).
Woolwich Speech (1965) Speech at Woolwich Polytechnic, 27 April, quoted in: J. Pratt & T. Burgess (1974) *Polytechnics: a report* (London, Pitman), 203–207.

Alan Bullock: historian, social democrat and chairman

Geoffrey Caston

Introduction

I worked very closely with Alan Bullock for several years in the late 1960s and early 1970s, at the Schools Council and in the Oxford University administration. The effect on me of his personality and style was immediate and enduring, as it was for so many others who were close to him. Consideration of any aspect of his life and work must take account of this magnetism. His personal presence was immense—he always seemed to be a much bigger man than physical size would suggest, and his voice much louder. His relationships with colleagues and others were coloured by what psychologists would call 'affect', emotion rather than (or as well as) rationality. In speaking of him, people would say that they loved, rather than just liked, him. It worked both ways: he was vulnerable to criticism, and I remember how wounded he was by the attacks from student rebels during his Vice-Chancellorship.[1]

This personal warmth contributed to his great gifts as a public speaker and fundraiser. He loved, as he admitted, to put on a good performance. It went along with the desire, all through his career, to make a difference in people's lives. It fitted with his decision to devote his remarkable scholarly talents as a historian to the then unfashionable field of 'contemporary' history, which he defended vigorously before an often sceptical profession. It fitted also with his commitment to popularising learning. In his 30s he was an eloquent member of the BBC's then pioneering *Brains Trust*, a radio panel of academics who squabbled about philosophical questions put to them by a lay audience. In his 60s he launched and edited the 'Dictionary of Modern Thought' (Bullock & Stallybrass, 1977) with the mission to make philosophy accessible to ordinary people. His concern for the immediate impact of policies on people is also perhaps related to the distaste for abstractions which permeates much of his life and work. As he put it: '*I am instinctively suspicious of all systems of thought and explanation and of that fascination in playing with abstract ideas which is the hallmark of the intellectual*' (Bullock, 1977).

This is the man whose relations with British education, particularly with schools, are considered here. His contacts with teachers and their pupils in schools were warm and abundant. Throughout his working life, he enjoyed nothing more than to visit and talk with them. Yet he wrote very little about 'education' and, by his own assertion, was not an 'educationalist' (*Guardian*, 1994). (In all the time I worked with him, I do not recall a single earnest discussion of the subject.) His thoughts and feelings therefore have to be gleaned from lectures and addresses, often mainly concerned with other matters. To discover any influence these might have had on educational policy and practice we have to search for indirect indicators. What was his part in the immense changes in Oxford University which took place between 1950 and 1980? What was the impact of those changes on the schools? What public role did he play in the bodies which affected educational policy? What were the personal views on education of a man who was, because of his position at Oxford and because of the force and warmth of his personality, close to many of those who played a more direct part in policy-making?

Autobiography

Alan left no memoirs or autobiography. In September 1977, however, he wrote a vivid synopsis for a book he intended to write. It was to be titled *Father and son: a double memoir* (Bullock, 1977). It was to be in three parts: a memoir of his father Frank, a memoir of his own activities, and a conclusion (of great importance to Alan) drawing together the other two. In the event, only the first part was written, and published in 2000 as the moving 'portrait' of his father, *Building Jerusalem* (Bullock, 2000). So we were deprived of the reflections on his own life which he had promised; as his wife said afterwards, he was too busy and, more importantly for him, they might have overshadowed the account of his father, to whom he was so deeply attached and by whom he was so profoundly influenced.

What clues does Alan offer in this 1977 autobiographical fragment? His father had left school at the age of 11, and abandoned a gardening apprenticeship to become a Unitarian Minister, first in Lancashire then in Bradford. Frank Bullock was entirely self-educated and vastly well-read. Alan wrote of him:

> *[He] read for several hours each day for the best part of fifty years. David Cecil once remarked to me that he was the best-read man he had ever met. [My father] was the best speaker I have ever heard—and this is not said lightly, for, as a speaker myself, I have always taken pleasure and interest in the performance of others. He enjoyed life enormously, had as great a passion for people as for literature and displayed a remarkable gift for communicating with and drawing into discussion men and women of the most diverse types and backgrounds. To be with him was to feel elated and excited by the possibilities of life and no man more completely expressed his teaching in his way of living. ... He made a deeper impression on me than any other of my teachers and the impression has proved to be indelible.* (Bullock, 1977)

This was the model which Alan took with him into his contrasting life, spent almost entirely at Oxford, where he went from Bradford Grammar School with a scholarship to read Greats and Modern History. In Oxford, he was '*very unhappy to begin with*', and there was always some lingering ambivalence about his own educational experience.

> *Thanks to [my father], I received the formal education he had missed. (We agreed, later, that it would probably have been fatal to the development of his gifts.) My energies have been dispersed over a wide range of activities, never leaving me time to carry out the sustained reading and reflection which were possible for my father.* (Bullock, 1977)

In the 1977 synopsis, Alan summarised his own career to that date as follows:

> *Returning to Oxford after the War, I became a Fellow and Tutor in Modern History at New College and was one of the generation of historians which established contemporary history in the universities. I published Hitler, A Study in Tyranny, in 1952 and in 1957 took the lead in founding a new Oxford college and raising the funds to build and endow it. St Catherine's was opened in 1964 and in 1969 I became the first elected full-time Vice-Chancellor of Oxford. I had in fact become a professional chairman and in this capacity presided over a variety of bodies from the Schools Council to the Trustees of the Tate Gallery and two controversial Government committees which produced 'Bullock Reports', the first on literacy, the second on industrial democracy. When the second was published amid much controversy, I was described by The Times as 'the quintessential meritocrat', and by The Observer as 'a clanking Victorian steam-engine'. I was knighted on the recommendation of a Conservative Prime Minister in 1972 and made a life peer on the recommendation of a Labour Prime Minister in 1976. I took my seat in the Lords as crossbencher, refusing to identify myself, as I have all my life, with any party, class or establishment and, like my father before me, valuing my independence more than anything else.* (Bullock, 1977)

In the Double Memoir, Alan describes the '*seven main areas of interest about which I should wish to write.*' The first is Education, including '*Merits and shortcomings of a traditional grammar school education*' and reflections on his experiences as chairman of various committees, and also '*the unrealistic demands on schools and why they fall short*'. In the event, he wrote very little about education, confessing (or boasting) to a Guardian correspondent in 1994 that '*I have never in my life read a book on education and I have not taught much.*' But in the same interview he added '*There was room for reform in education but in the last 15 years it has been done at such a cost. We have lost so many good teachers. I think it is a very sad story.*' He modestly disclaimed influence. '*My ideas did not play any part in English education, but the role which we [Alan and Ronald Dearing, another 'professional chairman'] have played is as facilitators and enablers*' (*Guardian*, 1994).

Chairmanship of educational bodies

However, he took much pride in his chairmanship of educational bodies, and many would credit him with considerable influence on English education as a consequence. His aim in the chair was always to secure consensus, but in a way which would have practical effect, and to advance acceptable, if not always radical, change. So we should look at how he handled each of these bodies, and whether in fact they had effect.

Alan's appointment to these jobs was no surprise. It was customary for the chairmanship of such advisory bodies to go to senior academics 'near enough to the educational world to know its problems and not frighten its practitioners, but distanced enough from the schools to be authoritative about them in dealing with the Government and with witnesses' (Kogan & Packwood, 1974), and Alan became, in John Grigg's words, 'a notable member of the Great and the Good' (Grigg, 1994).

As a relatively young but eloquent Oxford figure, he played a prominent role in the 1963 Campaign for Education, alongside such others as the Archbishop of Canterbury and Sir Ronald Gould, long-serving and highly respected leader of the National Union of Teachers. In a public address, Alan urged a substantial increase in the number of teachers and of students in higher education generally. He coupled this with a plea for a breakdown of hierarchies in higher education and of '*the traditional association of higher education with social class ... to break through the barriers which divide the great working class of this country from higher education ... to deal with the boy or girl coming very often with suspicion and doubts from a working class home*' (Bullock, 1963). Strong words from traditional Oxford, but entirely in keeping with the mission he had articulated for the new college (St Catherine's) just opened, of which he was, by 1963, the first Master.

National Advisory Council on the Training and Supply of Teachers

He himself ascribed his first public chairmanship to his work for this Campaign. He was invited to chair the National Advisory Council on the Training and Supply of Teachers (NACTST). After duly assessing the statistical evidence the Council, as expected, urged a large acceleration of teacher training. However, this was the occasion of his first brush with the educational establishment and its often quarrelsome politics. He was unable to secure a total consensus among a diverse body dealing with policy issues of critical importance to some, notably the unions and the local education authorities. While all agreed on the importance of rapid expansion, they fell apart over the more controversial questions of how and in what institutions the training was to take place. The differences proved irreconcilable, and led to a minority report signed by ten members and to notes of dissent from three. Alan was apologetic about this in his formal report to the Secretary of State, and resigned in 1965 because, he said, the Council behaved politically and therefore should be chaired by a Minister (Kogan & Packwood, 1974).

Schools Council

Nevertheless, he accepted appointment in the following year to succeed another great and good Oxford figure, John Maud, as Chairman of the Schools Council for Curriculum and Examinations. This was the body established in 1964, after prolonged negotiation between the Department, the Local Education Authorities and the teachers' unions, to deal with matters concerning the schools' curriculum and the system of public examinations. The Council was funded jointly, and generously, by the Government and the LEAs, but it had a majority of teacher representatives. It was committed to the principle that each school was responsible for its own curriculum. The Council therefore had no mandatory authority and had to exercise its influence over schools through persuasion and professional credibility. The full Council had 85 members, and was frequently described, not least by Alan himself, as a kind of parliament for schools.

The Council funded, especially in its early years, many research and development projects. Most of them have not, of course, survived in any recognisable form after 40 years, although the thinking behind the most important, such as the Stenhouse Humanities Curriculum Project and those in science and mathematics conducted jointly with the Nuffield Foundation, persists in the bloodstream of the teaching profession. Those of us who worked for the Council at the time thought that we were taking part in an immensely important and in some ways revolutionary enterprise, involving innovative response to social change which would be controlled by the educational profession, and free from the central control of the Government. As I wrote in 1969, it was a powerful force for pluralism; its importance was not just educational, but political, and it is in that context that its work should be judged (Caston, 1969).

All this appealed greatly to Alan. He was averse to the politics of party, power and government, but enjoyed the politics of pluralism, the search for compromises, the wooing of support from disparate groups. He was ready to stump the country, to address conferences of teachers and local government officials with his infectious preacher's oratory, to persuade them of the importance of this new process, and to mobilise the energies of the different elements of the profession behind it. The Council staff loved him for it. Especially, perhaps, because he showed no great wish to interfere in the educational substance of what we were doing.

The rise and fall of the Schools Council has been extensively chronicled elsewhere (see, for example, Bell & Prescott, 1975; Lawton, 1980; Plaskow, 1985; Lawton & Chitty, 1988). Here it is sufficient to say that from the mid-1970s onwards, Labour and Conservative Governments alike became increasingly determined to assert central power over education, at the cost of teacher organisations and LEAs alike. In this climate, heroic efforts by its two last chairmen, Alex Smith and John Tomlinson, could not stave off the inevitable. The dispersal of power became unacceptable to any Government, and the Council was finally abolished in 1984. Pluralism had become thoroughly unfashionable, and with it the enthusiasm for innovation. Alan's words in opening the international curriculum conference in Oxford (which, of course, he chaired) in 1967 had proved all too prophetic: *'Curriculum innovation is in some danger of becoming the latest intellectual fashion of the educational world. But no historian is ever likely to underrate the importance of fashion …'* (Bullock, 1967) or to be surprised at its evanescence.

The 'Bullock Committee'

In 1972, Alan accepted a chairmanship which was to prove an even greater challenge from the educational system, and a heavier load on him. The National Foundation for Educational Research had published research which suggested that reading standards had declined over the previous decade, and this fuelled public, and therefore political, anxiety—Michael Marland has called it 'a time of national near-panic' (Marland, 1977). Mrs Thatcher, then Secretary of State, appointed in response a Committee 'to consider in relation to schools … all aspects of teaching the use of English, including reading, writing and speech …' As the Committee itself ruefully noted, this was widely, but wrongly, interpreted as an inquiry solely into reading.

The Committee comprised 16 outspoken primary and secondary school teachers, six trainers of teachers, and five leading researchers; each group contained representatives of different factions or schools of thought. The Secretary of State chose in Alan, a 'neutral chairman, someone not already credited with views on the controversial issues … she called together a disparate crew and told them she fervently hoped for a unanimous report', as a prominent member of the Committee wrote (Britton, 1982). This was a tall order: the Committee proved to be a battleground for 'progressive' and 'traditionalist' educators, or, in the more precise terms of a professional critic of its report, 'those who believe in carefully constructed linear programmes, buttressed by claims for sequence, system and structure, and those who believe that development in language can only be achieved in by working in a much more flexible and open-ended way' (Rosen, 1975).

Alan relished this situation. He later reminisced that *'it was clear from the beginning that the committee was much divided. Some of the people would not speak to each other'* (*Guardian*, 1994). But he strove throughout its two years and 54 full sessions for compromise and unanimity, as committee members subsequently testified, often with irritation that their own view had not been able to prevail. According to Britton, the chairman 'repeatedly reminded members that they must resist the temptation to overstate their views for the sake of reducing the scope of wilful misrepresentation' (Britton, 1978). He was determined to get a report which was to be useful and practical and commanded some support from all factions.

The minutes of the Committee show examples of his methods. At the first meeting, he said: *'I hope that preconceptions will be disturbed, that recommendations will be practical.*

Expensive solutions will be of little value' (Minutes, 5/7/72). He constantly tried to prevent the 'progressives' from running away with the Committee: '*The Committee's Report would be discredited if it revealed that evidence received had been seriously biased towards what is termed 'progressive' practice. Witnesses are needed to challenge the assumptions and trends of the last decade*' (Minutes, 3/10/72). '*Between the best practice in 'traditional' and in 'progressive' education, there is far less difference than occurs when each side presents the worst examples of the other*' (Minutes, 30/10/72). In one place he revealed one of his own humanist prejudices: '*If there is some evidence in a situation that can be quantified, today's way of putting it says that this is the most important evidence, merely because it can be quantified*' (Minutes, 1/11/72).

After some epic wrangling about the final text, a virtually unanimous report was published under the title *A language for life* (DES, 1975), with only one dissenter, a primary school head from the traditionalist camp. It ran to 609 pages, with 333 conclusions and recommendations. The progressives, who for the most part won the skirmishes, were nevertheless disappointed with the consequences of compromise and the restraint they felt this had imposed upon them. Britton reflected that 'its establishment status, the size and diversity of its membership, the amount of data it was expected to handle, all militated against the production of a forthright and convincing document' (Britton, 1978). Rosen, in his editorial to one of the many volumes of discussion papers which followed publication, was more pungent: 'The Bullock Report is about language and its authors use vast quantities of it, or, more precisely, one variety of it. Yet there is a numbing deadness about its steady march through argument and evidence. Why? Because above all the very people whose language development is their constant theme have been almost totally gagged' (Rosen, 1975). Subsequent attempts to review progress showed little evidence that the recommendations had been widely implemented, and the Government (by this time Labour) was notably uninterested and gave it no boost and no funds, to Alan's particular annoyance. Yet there were those who predicted a long-term impact. Minovi (1978), from an urban secondary school perspective, commented sourly on 'the general belief, now apparently stronger than ever, that, no matter what Bullock said, standards are falling and it's time we did something about it', but concluded that 'in 25 years' time, I expect that Bullock will be seen as one of the important milestones in the progress towards real education in our schools.' Marland (1977), another Committee member, also gave it 25 years: 'from the perspective of 25 years hence, *A language for life* will be seen ... to have been one other necessary unifying force in secondary education.' Harry Judge, writing nine years after publication, found that 'it has had a profound effect upon teachers in schools, and generated a new awareness of the importance of language' (Judge, 1984).

What did Alan himself make of it? He was not one to revisit past achievements, and had no huge expectations. At the TES 'Bullock plus one' conference, he declared: '*We never thought we had gone up a mountain and come down with the 10 commandments. ... The report is just an incident in a long, long story*' (TES, 20 February 1976).

Perhaps more revealing were comments he included a few years later in his Foreword to the report of an international symposium (which he chaired) sponsored by the Aspen Institute for Humanistic Studies on 'What is an Educated Person?':

> Today we are so impressed by the need for planning in education, so overawed by the bureaucratic structures we have created, that it is easy to conclude that only through these means can new initiatives take effect. I am not convinced that this is so.
>
> While taking part in these [Aspen] discussions, I was also acting as chairman of a committee set up by the British Government to inquire into the level of literacy in England and Wales and to make recommendations for the improvement of language teaching. ... It became clear to us that there would be no funds available to carry out any of the reforms we wanted to propose, and that the government (which was by then in the hands of a different party) was not interested and would do nothing to implement any changes we recommended. We decided, therefore, to address our report not to ministers and civil servants, but to teachers, parents and local education authorities. To our surprise—and even more, I suspect, to the surprise of the Department of Education—the report not only survived the absence of official encouragement but was taken up with enthusiasm by local groups (especially teachers) throughout the country. The members of the committee found themselves overwhelmed with invitations to speak to meetings of people who were already proceeding to put our recommendations into practice without any official initiative. A year after the report was published the Times Educational Supplement ran three special numbers and organized a conference to report on the unexpected response that the report had elicited. The reason for this was not to be found in the virtues of the report itself, which was lengthy, full of detail, expensive to buy, and (thanks to the inadequate number printed by the government) difficult to obtain. No, the reason was the fortunate coincidence (far from being planned) between its publication and an accumulated anxiety among those on whom implementation depended. It made them receptive to the suggestions we put forward, whether they had official blessing or not.
>
> This experience leads me to ask whether, on other occasions than the one I have described, the decisive factor in bringing about educational change may be the dissatisfaction with accepted views felt by those most closely concerned—teachers, parents, students—and a consequent readiness to open their minds to new ideas. (Kaplan, 1980)

This is Alan Bullock the historian speaking, with the emphasis he always placed on the importance of specific events, people, circumstances and accidents, in determining history: 'History ... is interested in moving away from generalisation towards the particular, from abstraction toward the concrete. Historians justify doing so on the grounds that human experience—what you and I actually experience, whether as individuals or as members of a group—is always experienced in a particular context' (Bullock, 1990).

House of Lords

His experience in this Committee, and the apparent indifference of the Government to the painfully forged consensus and abundant documentation of the Report, added to his already growing distrust of governments, of officials and of formally powerful institutions. After 1976, he no longer engaged directly with the education policymakers, returning instead, in his 60s and 70s, to perhaps his most prolific period as a historian, completing the third volume of his biography of Ernest Bevin in 1983, and the remarkable 'Parallel Lives' of Hitler and Stalin in 1991. In 1976, he became a member of the House of Lords, but in nearly 30 years chose to make only three speeches of substance. The first was to urge better funding for universities, emphasising their national importance as centres of knowledge and research. The second (in 1980) was an intervention designed to ensure that the Government took full account of local views when considering the closure of a small school. The third (in 1993) was to urge the case for the establishment of a Humanities Research Council alongside those already funding the sciences. But he chose to remain silent in the debates of the 1980s and 1990s surrounding the steady accretion of power over school education to central governments, both Conservative and Labour.

Oxford University

It may well be, however, that Alan's most substantial contributions to British education lay in his regular, and powerful, role in the administration of Oxford University itself. Elected in 1953 as a member of the Hebdomadal Council, he served on it for 25 years. It was a period of transformation for the University, both socially and academically. By 1970, the proportions both of state school students and of science students had roughly doubled since 1938. Oxford had become what it remains today, a major science university, with a student body almost entirely composed of individuals who had been admitted on the basis of intensive academic competition, with a much increased proportion of post-graduate students and a huge commitment to research, much of it externally funded. What have been described as the 'Brideshead' and the 'anti-science' myths had become totally out-dated by the 1960s, although they survived damagingly in outside perceptions, as Joseph Soares has documented in his recent extensive and insightful analysis of the 'Modernization of Oxford University' (Soares, 1999).

This transformation, achieved without external intervention, came about only after many internal controversies, committees, working parties and debates concerning admissions policies and qualifications including the abolition in 1960 of compulsory Latin, seen by many as a 'symbolic turning point in the intellectual history of Oxford' (Harris, 1994) and long advocated by Alan in spite of his own impeccable Greats record. Academic and building policies and the allocation of resources also reflected the move towards science. On all these fronts, Alan was at, or near, the centre of the reformist group. In 1969, he became the first elected, full-time, four-year Vice Chancellor.

St Catherine's College

The transformation had been exemplified, and to some extent anticipated, by the new college for whose foundation Alan had worked indefatigably through the late 1950s and early 1960s. In 1952, he became Censor of St Catherine's Society, which he described as 'the poor man's gateway into Oxford'. In ten years of political manoeuvring and arduous fundraising, he transformed it into the new St Catherine's College. This work was part of a conscious strategy to meet what he perceived as the University's need to respond to changing social needs by building upon the traditions of the older college institutions, and using them to meet new social demands. Many years later, he wrote to Sir Alan Wilson, who had worked with him on the fundraising campaign as a close ally from industry:

> Our target [at St Catherine's] was two-thirds admission from maintained schools, one-third from independent schools. This was very much on my mind at the time because I was afraid that Oxford and Cambridge might shut themselves off from the mainstream of British education. ... In the expansion of science and of the intake from the state system of education, I think we helped to set a trend which has continued. We were thirty years ahead in a number of new approaches which are now being urged upon universities. (Bullock, 1989)

His creation—and there is no doubt that his colleagues acknowledged it to be his personal achievement—realised his aspirations for it. Soares saw it as an exemplar of the University's modernisation:

> The St Catherine's Society, previously a sort of low-status annex for underprivileged boys, became the college for lower-class, state-school, science undergraduates ... it campaigned vigorously for modernizing the whole of Oxford, from admissions practices to bridging the gap between the two cultures [arts and science], to full implementation of the Franks Commission's reforms. It was Oxford's first college to de-emphasize the humanities and focus on the sciences; it bypassed the public school network and recruited aggressively from state schools, thus increasing its already sizeable working class contingent; it was among the first men's colleges to admit women; and in recent years it has led other colleges in its vigorous relations with private business. (Soares, 1999)

Alan himself spent many tiring days on the road talking up the College to schools of all kinds, soliciting applications from state schools, something, as he wrote later '*that was just not done in the early 1960s*' (Bullock, 1989), however commonplace it has now become.

Department of Educational Studies

In keeping with Alan's commitment to the diversification of the University into science was his support for what were regarded by Oxford traditionalists as its fringe activities. Examples were his sustained enthusiasm for the social sciences and Barnett House, for the Ruskin School of Fine Art, for extra-mural work and continuing education, and, above all, for the Department of Educational Studies. He took a keen personal interest in the appointment, soon after he became Vice-Chancellor, of its new Director (the Editor of these pages, Harry Judge), and energetically backed the Department's pioneering work in the development of school-based teacher training, which in time became a new national orthodoxy. He was also the founding chairman of the Editorial Board of the *Oxford Review of Education*. I cannot do better here than to quote Judge himself, who was in a key position to make an assessment:

> Alan Bullock had clear opinions on how a major university should relate to educational policy and discourse. Lifelong ally of teachers that he was, he opposed undergraduate degrees in education in or conferred by this university. He believed passionately that the work of a university education department should be intimately linked to the daily lives of mainstream schools, and to producing for them effective and scholarly teachers. But he also believed, with equal and characteristic vehemence, that Education was too important to be left to Educationists, and that the resources of the whole university—and not only of

one professional department within it—should be directed towards research and scholarly discourse on the educational issues of the day. (Judge, 2004)

Alan's opposition to the proposal (eventually defeated) that the University award an external honours B.Ed. to those graduating from associated teacher training colleges came as a surprise to many of his friends in the educational establishment (including John Maud, his predecessor at the Schools Council), although he was supported by Harry Judge and myself. His reasoning was entirely consistent with his disrespect for 'Education' as an adequate disciplinary preparation for schoolteachers in itself. This was coupled with concern for the integrity of the University and its degrees, which he felt would be prejudiced by their award for work taught outside the University, even if examined within it.

Meritocracy

By the end of the 1970s, admission to Oxford had become almost entirely a reward for those who could best persuade college tutors of their potential for academic success. The result was a spectacular rise in admissions standards (see discussion in Thomas, 1994). Halsey has shown how the percentage of Oxford entries with top A-level grades rose from 43% in 1961 to 58.6% in 1970, and to 73.5% in 1980, compared with a fairly stable figure for all British universities of about 22% (Halsey, 1982). This 'Ultra-meritocracy', as it has been described, has had unexpected consequences. Alan had expected that the move towards admissions by academic merit, coupled with the emphasis on science, would be accompanied by a shift towards more lower-class entries, and this diversification had been one of his objectives. This was initially the case, but by the late 1980s the proportion of state-school entrants, having peaked, began to fall. Since admission to Oxbridge was, and continues to be, prized in almost all secondary schools, this has transformed incentives, and therefore, among other things, the structure of the sixth-form curriculum. But above all this process was seen in private schools, with their greater flexibility and, for the most part, greater resources. Soares has described what happened as follows:

> The race for a child to get into Oxford had been intensified, apparently requiring increased family investment, and ever younger preparation. ... From the 1970s forward, Oxford appeared to be less, not more, accessible to the lower classes. ... Those inside Oxford who hoped to open opportunities to the lower classes in the name of social justice very quickly got a narrow middle-class meritocracy of such high standards that the barriers between it and society were nearly as great as they had been when wealth determined a student's admissibility. (Soares, 1999, see also discussion in Brock, 1994)

The remedy prescribed by social democrats today for this situation is, of course, some form of positive discrimination, by which quantitative measures of merit (such as examination scores) are qualified by more subjective indicators of unequal opportunity (such as social deprivation or type of schooling, or even ethnicity). Whatever Alan's views might have been on such devices, it seems likely that he would have opposed any that risked dilution of the quality of performance at Oxford. He would probably have been prepared, in the interests of social justice, to contemplate new methods for determining the potential of a candidate for eventual academic success by Oxford's standards, but not, even in the interests of social justice, to compromise those standards themselves in any way.

But these were not the problems which exercised him in the 1960s and early 1970s. His immediate and, as he saw it, practical objective, was to promote merit in as broad a range of young people as possible, without damage to the standards of his University. At that time the University Grants Committee was concerned, partly in the interests of social justice, to promote greater equality in resources between universities. It was no doubt some argument with its Chairman, Kenneth Berrill, about the possible conflict between equality and excellence that was the occasion of one of Alan's favourite anecdotes: '*I entertained the whole [University Grants] Committee to dinner in [St Catherine's] Hall. There was one of those moments when suddenly there is a lull in the conversation, and the voice of the Vice-Chancellor was heard to ring out: "But I damned well believe in excellence." All I could say, as they roared with laughter at my misfortune, was that I would accept it as an epitaph*' (Bullock, 1988).

Personal views on education: The Two Cultures

Although, as we have seen, Alan had no particular wish to explore in any depth in his writings (or indeed his reading) the philosophical and theoretical issues surrounding education, he did reveal throughout his career some of his own attitudes.

He was always concerned about the achievement of a proper educational balance between the sciences and the humanities. In 1957, two years before C. P. Snow's famous lecture on 'The Two Cultures', he spoke of '*the deficiencies in my own education [which had left me with] ... complacency engendered by a classical and literary education ... ignorant of the sciences ... unable to form any judgment about the most important form of social change in the modern world, namely the sciences.*' He urged '*a new form of general education, a genuine hybrid, including courses in scientific method for arts graduates ... Science Greats*', and asserted that '*The most important intellectual task of our generation is to overcome the split between science and the humanities*' (1957). He so impressed Snow, the Cambridge scientist turned novelist, that he earned an exemption by name from Snow's strictures of the 'gulf of mutual incomprehension' in Oxbridge between literary intellectuals and scientists (Snow, 1964).

Twenty years later, he was still asserting: '*Science is the greatest intellectual achievement of modern man. It ought to occupy a corresponding place in the education of every young person as one of the most important ways in which man learns about himself. ... Non-scientists are at present deprived of what should be every man's and every woman's educational birthright in the modern world ... the need to develop scientific literacy*' (Bullock, 1976). But he sensed at that time that it might soon be the humanities which came under threat, and demanded in the same speech that '*Scientists must recognise the validity of other modes of thinking.*' A few years later, he was writing of the '*need for a humanistic revival, bringing science and the humanities together*' (Bullock, 1985).

The Humanities

He developed this theme extensively in his Aspen Lectures, published as *The humanist tradition in the West* (1985), relating Renaissance educational values to what he saw as our contemporary situation. By now he was turning away from his earlier preoccupations with the education of élites, and widening access to them. He perceived

> the real threat ... of a growing deterioration, already taking place, in human relations, in the way people treat each other, which is the substance behind the abstract term society. ... Whatever else humanists might disagree about, all, including Luther and Machiavelli as well as Erasmus, agreed on the importance of education. ... If a man lived in a society, especially in societies as small and intense as those of Italian cities, then his education had to develop his social as well as his mental qualities. In an age of violence he had to learn to control his passions; in an age when power was exercised brutally, to learn the art of courtesy; in a competitive age, to prefer the gamesmanship of the amateur to that of the professional. ... The central theme of humanism was the potentialities of man, his creative powers. These powers ... were latent; they had to be awoken, brought out, educed and the means to that end was education. (Bullock, 1985)

He was not particularly optimistic that the message would get through. '*If we [in the West], with our higher standards of living and well-established institutions, such as representative assemblies, responsible government, free elections, the rule of law, civil peace, public education, freedom of opinion, the welfare state—all of which derive from the humanist tradition—if we who owe so much to that tradition have lost faith in its relevance, the rest of the world is not likely to be convinced.*'

He saw a way forward through the development of social as well as mental qualities in all young people, not just the academically gifted. The right educational experiences to be offered were not only to be intellectual experiences, which he thought had been over-emphasised.

> *During the student troubles in the late 1960s and early 1970s ... I had to fight hard against becoming infected with a siege mentality, and alienated from the young. ... But I have learned, in a world in which older people are continually deploring the disappearance of values, the extent to which young people are trying to work out for themselves new values to live by, their own codes of behaviour, their own concepts of conscience and of the qualities they prize.*

> *At a time when the place of the humanities in education is under question, young people's search for values by which to live seems to me to define the role the humanities can play. It will require something of a revolution in the presentation of history, literature and the arts, to start not from the achievements of the past, but from the human needs of young people today. But it is the same role which the rediscovery of the ancient world played for the Renaissance, providing those who were young then with a strange and exciting world which they could explore and on which they could draw to work out their own answers to the questions and conflicts presented by their own experience. Today the material on which to draw ... includes the whole range of human experience, contemporary as well as historical, that of other cultures as well as our own Western tradition. This material, thanks to film, television and videos, is now accessible as never before.*

> *Here is a great opportunity to make available to young people in schools and colleges, not a traditional course in the humanities, but a direct encounter, taking advantage of the new media, with human experience of the questions that bother and fascinate them. It could focus in turn on questions such as conscience, conflicts of loyalty; rebellion and authority, the ambivalence of feelings, the search for identity, the power of art and myth, passions and compassion ...*

> *Any such encounter with the humanities is valuable not only for the results it can produce, but for the activity itself, engaging the imagination and the emotions in the penetration of other people's worlds and ideas. In an education which is all too inclined to fill students with information and limit itself to teaching them techniques, here is a way of fostering the emotional, subjective side of human nature which is of such importance to young people, and which needs to be developed as much as the intellectual if they are to acquire confidence and establish satisfying relationships with other human beings.* (Bullock, 1985)

This approach to the humanities—'the direct encounter with human experience'—preoccupied him in his later years. It is close to the 'alternative pedagogy' underlying Lawrence Stenhouse's Humanities Curriculum Project sponsored by the Schools Council and spread with missionary zeal in the 1970s and 1980s, although Alan had shown little active interest in that at the time. Then, as now, the intense competitive demands of the academic curriculum left little room in the school timetable for such encounters. Those demands arose in part from the very meritocratic values to which Alan had then been committed, and which Oxford advanced, and in part from popular demand for measurable educational achievement in useful skills.

But Alan had moved on from his meritocratic commitments to concern with the deeper needs of the young that might be met through education. In 1990, in a Memorial Lecture commemorating Edward Boyle, who had appointed him to the Schools Council 25 years earlier, he wrote:

> *I hope the day will never come when we take the view that, provided young people are taught enough to earn a living, to contribute to the economy, and understand something of the natural world in which they live, necessary as these are, it is no business of an educational system to help them form values, beliefs or tastes of their own ... they must not be denied the chance to share in the discussion of such questions with sympathetic teachers, to learn to discriminate in what they watch on television and to be brought up sharp against the range, the depth, the anguish and the courage of the choices men and women have made, in all the richness and the subtlety of history of drama and literature, the excitement of art, of intellectual debate and religious experience. ... I urge that in providing for this, we are contributing not only to the development of the individual but to the development and preservation of our society.* (Bullock, 1990)

Influence on education

It is hard to discern any significant or lasting impact of these ideas, or of his committees and their reports, upon educational policy today. But then Alan never had many illusions about 'policy', as laid down in national directives. A lifelong friend, asked about Alan's views on education, paused for a long moment before saying, 'It should be fair, and there should be more of it.' He believed in pluralism because it was more effective in bringing about change for individuals, and in pragmatism, because it permitted practical responses to changing circumstances. He was not very interested in the dogmas of his time about educational organisation, and took no part in the passionate debates about the merits of comprehensive schooling, social democrat though he was. He would not have been surprised at the vacillations of governments on these matters, but he would have been angered by the presumptuousness of those, on the left and right, who have progressively increased central control over educational institutions at all levels.

Alan Bullock was, for the 30 years or so following 1950, one of the two or three most prominent figures in Oxford life. Described as 'the quintessential meritocrat', he pushed through the reforms which led to the University becoming the 'ultra-meritocracy' of today, and the principal aspiration of most of the 'best' of the country's 17-year-olds. He fiercely defended 'excellence' as the essential attribute of the University, and criterion for admission to it, although he did have qualms about its definition in solely academic terms. He would have been concerned about the longer-term consequences for schools and their pupils of this intense competitiveness. Despite his profound conviction of the value of science as a major component of modern culture, he was a true humanist, and sceptical of those who rely upon quantifiable evidence of virtue: he would have intensely disliked the emergence of an educational hierarchy based upon measurable outcomes and league tables. He would have liked to see a much broader education emerge, with excellence defined in ways which would be accessible to far more of the country's young people.

For a true liberal, there was perhaps more than whimsy in his observation to the students of St Catherine's College: *'Education is like happiness. You sit and do all the things you have to do, but education, like happiness, comes of the things which supervene if you are lucky'* (Bullock, 1974).

Note

1. I have chosen, whenever possible, to express Alan's views in his own words rather than attempt a paraphrase. These words are italicised throughout. In writing their account of the creation of St Catherine's College, Alan's colleagues, Margaret and Derek Davies, say that they found it difficult to refer to Lord Bullock other than by his Christian name, and used that throughout (Davies & Davies, 1997). I have done the same.

Notes on contributor

Geoffrey Caston was Joint Secretary of the Schools Council for Curriculum and Examinations from 1966 to 1970, Under Secretary at the University Grants Committee from 1966 to 1972, Registrar of Oxford University and Fellow of Merton College from 1972 to 1979, Secretary-General of the Committee of Vice-Chancellors and Principals of UK Universities from 1979 to 1983, and Vice-Chancellor of the University of the South Pacific from 1983 to 1992. He also served as Vice Chairman of the SSRC Educational Research Board in the 1970s, and Chairman of the Libraries Advisory Council (England) in the same period. He chaired the Commonwealth Scholarships Commission from 1997 to 2002, and was awarded the Symons Medal for service to Commonwealth Universities in 2002. He is currently an Honorary Fellow in the Department of Education at Exeter University.

References

Bell, R. & Prescott, M. (Eds) (1975) *The Schools Council: a second look* (London, Ward Lock Educational).
Britton, J. (1978) In: F. R. A. Davis & R. P. Parker (Eds) *Teaching for literacy: reflections on the Bullock Report* (New York, Agathon Press), ix–xiii.
Britton, J. (1982) *Prospect and retrospect* (London, Heinemann Educational Books).
Brock, M. (1994) In: B. Harrison (Ed.) *The twentieth century,* vol.8 of *The History of the University of Oxford* (Oxford, Oxford University Press), 753–756.
Bullock, A. (1957) Science and the humanities, *Bulletin of the Institute of Physics,* 8, 380–387.
Bullock, A. (1963) *The case for advance* (London, Campaign for Education).
Bullock A. (1967) Foreword, in: S. Maclure (Ed.) *Curriculum innovation in practice* (London, HMSO), iii.
Bullock, A. (1974) Address to St Catherine's College students (private papers, St Catherine's College, Oxford.)
Bullock, A. (1976) Presidential address: science—a tarnished image? *Schools Science Review,* 621–627.
Bullock, A. (1977) *Father and son: a double memoir* (unpublished private papers, St Catherine's College, Oxford).
Bullock, A. (1978) The future of humanistic studies, *Teachers' College Record,* 82(2), 173–190.
Bullock, A. (1985) *The humanist tradition in the West* (New York, W. W. Norton).
Bullock, A. (1986) *Have the humanities ceased to be relevant?* (Inaugural Lecture, University of Warwick European Humanities Resource Centre).
Bullock, A. (1988) Reminiscences of a Vice-Chancellor, *Oxford Magazine,* 30, 3–5.
Bullock, A. (1989) Letter to Sir Alan Wilson, 9 March (unpublished private papers, St Catherine's College, Oxford).
Bullock, A. (1990) A case for the humanities: the third Edward Boyle Memorial Lecture, *RSA Journal,* cxxxviii, 5410, 664–675.
Bullock, A. (1993) Has history ceased to be relevant? *Manchester Memoirs,* 132, 5–12.
Bullock, A. (2000) *Building Jerusalem: a portrait of my father* (London, Allen Lane, Penguin Press).
Bullock, A. & Stallybrass, O. (Eds) (1977) *A dictionary of modern thought* (London, Fontana).
Caston, G. (1969) The Schools Council in context, *Journal of Curriculum Studies,* 3(1), 50–64.
Davies, M. & Davies, D. (1997) *Creating St Catherine's College* (Oxford, St Catherine's College).
Department of Education and Science (1975) *A language for life (the Bullock Report)* (London, HMSO).
Department of Education and Science (1982) *Bullock revisited: a discussion paper by HMI* (London, DES).
Grigg, J. (1994) *The Times,* 26 November.
The *Guardian* (1994) 26 July.
Halsey, A. H. (1982) The decline of donnish dominion? *Oxford Review of Education,* 8(3), 222.
Harris, J. (1994) The arts and social sciences, 1939–1970, in: B. Harrison (Ed.) *The twentieth century,* vol. 8 of *The History of the University of Oxford* (Oxford, Oxford University Press).
Hunter-Grundin, E. (1978) *Reading: implementing the Bullock Report* (London, Ward Lock Educational).
Judge, H. G. (1984) *A generation of schooling* (Oxford, Oxford University Press).
Judge, H. G. (2004) Lord Bullock of Leafield, *Oxford Review of Education,* 30(2), 163–164.
Kaplan, M. (Ed.) (1980) *What is an educated person?* (New York, Praeger).
Kogan, M. & Packwood, T. (1974) *Advisory councils and committees in education* (London, Routledge & Kegan Paul).
Lawton, D. (1980) *The politics of the school curriculum* (London, Routledge & Kegan Paul).
Lawton, D. & Chitty, C. (Eds) (1988) *The National Curriculum* (London, University of London Institute of Education).

Marland, M. (1977) *Language across the curriculum* (London, Heinemann Educational Books).
Minovi, R. (1978) In: F. R. A. Davis & R. P. Parker (Eds) *Teaching for literacy: reflections on the Bullock Report* (New York, Agathon Press), 158–172.
Minutes (1972) DES, Minutes of Committee on the Use of English (National Archives).
Plaskow, M. (1985) *The life and death of the Schools Council* (London, Falmer Press).
Rogers, R. (1980) *Crowther to Warnock* (London, Heinemann Educational Books).
Rosen, H. (Ed.) (1975) *Language and literacy in our schools: some appraisals of the Bullock Report* (London, University of London Institute of Education).
Snow, C. P. (1964) *The two cultures and a second look* (Cambridge, Cambridge University Press).
Soares, J. A. (1999) *The decline of privilege: the modernization of Oxford* (Stanford, Stanford University Press).
TES (1976) *Times Educational Supplement*, 20 February.
Thomas, K. (1994) In: B. Harrison (Ed.) *The twentieth century*, vol.8 of *The History of the University of Oxford* (Oxford, Oxford University Press), 193–195.

A. H. Halsey: Oxford as a base for social research and educational reform

George Smith and Teresa Smith

Introduction

Tourists arriving at Oxford by train since the new millennium have had to pass almost underneath the monumental new Said Business School with its token Oxford spire, past Blackwell's 1970s dark glass cliffs in Hythe Bridge Street, then to be faced by the city's 'cheerful' modern bus station complex. Their first glimpse of what appears to be a mediaeval college turns out to be Nuffield, with its Cotswold stone façade and impressive library tower. But Nuffield, too, is relatively modern, built in the late 1940s to the traditional inward-looking Oxford college pattern, but as the first explicitly social science research college at Oxford. While it is often bracketed as the social science equivalent of All Souls in terms of scholarly exclusivity, its founding motif was in part the contribution that such a concentration of social science talents in Oxford could make to the social and economic reconstruction of Britain in the post-war period.

A. H. Halsey has been a professorial fellow at Nuffield College since he was first appointed to Oxford in 1962 to head Barnett House, as Director of the university's recently created Department of Social and Administrative Studies. 'Barnett House', in comparison with Nuffield, had grown from an earlier (and slightly different) UK tradition of social service and social enquiry. Founded in 1914 in memory of Canon Barnett, the social reformer and first warden of Toynbee Hall, set up in London's East End thirty years earlier, Barnett House was not (until 1961) formally part of the university, though powerfully backed by its founding members who included several Oxford Heads of Houses and college fellows. It was to be a centre for the practical study of contemporary social and economic problems, and to provide training for young men and women to enter social work or social research (Halsey, 1967, 1976a). The University Department of Social and Administrative Studies was thus, in its origin as Barnett House, more of an intermediary institution, drawing on the resources of the university to address social issues and problems, and to prepare graduates from the university for practical work and research in areas where such problems were concentrated.[1]

Halsey,[2] throughout his working life at Oxford and before, has consciously drawn on both these traditions—of more detached scholarly study of social issues and of more engaged involvement with social and educational policy and practice. Indeed he would, no doubt, see them as part of a whole. As he wrote in 1970, 'the challenge is irresistible ... for the social scientist to become involved in the development of social policy, its definition of ends, its allocation and planning of means, and its measurement of results' (Halsey, 1970, p. 251). He did not resist—in a recent note, Wilensky describes Halsey as 'altogether a most impressive human being, scholar and activist'.[3] Symbolically, perhaps, for much of his working life before retirement, Halsey had a pattern of working in the department in the mornings and Nuffield College in the afternoons,[4] maybe in part recognition of these different traditions but also as a bridge between them. He also spent considerable energy trying to bring the rather fragmented social science effort in Oxford together on a single site in the mid 1970s,[5] and again to develop joint research programmes in the 1980s, but never fully succeeded.

These architectural and institutional traditions set the context for this paper. We explore Halsey's contribution to education, and schooling in particular, during his Oxford career as an academic and as a national (and international) policy advisor, and critically in the interface between these two settings. This interface includes what Halsey termed the 'political arithmetic' tradition, which:

> has a double intent; on the one hand it engages in the primary sociological task of describing and documenting the 'state of society'; on the other hand it addresses itself to central social and political issues. It has never, therefore, been a 'value free' academic discipline, if such in any event were possible. (Halsey, Heath and Ridge, 1980, p. 1)

And it also includes 'experimental social administration' (Halsey, 1970)—that is, the field testing of social innovation and social policy in advance of national implementation: 'to produce a theory of poverty and to test it in the very real world of the urban twilight zones' (Halsey, 1978, p. 144).

This paper is not a biography—Halsey has already written his own account (Halsey, 1996)[6]—nor is it an assessment of Halsey's wider contribution to sociology, though here we would underline Martin Trow's comment on Halsey's style of thought and 'breadth of vision', which he compared to Edward Shils. Drawing on his experience working with R. K. Merton at Columbia and later at Berkeley, Trow writes:

> a sociologist, we learned, had to be a social scientist, sensitive to historical forces, and something of a psychologist, ethnographer, economist, political scientist ... Chelly [Halsey] has been something of all those things, which kept his work always from being trivial or precious.[7]

In this paper we can only pick out a limited number of themes, some of which we follow through to demonstrate not necessarily Halsey's *direct* influence on later events, but the way that ideas—which he played a key role in pioneering—continue to be of central importance. We mainly focus on developments where Oxford was the base for initiatives elsewhere. We give less space to initiatives aimed at reform within Oxford. We ask whether Oxford, with its exclusive and elitist traditions, was an appropriate base for reforms that had an explicitly egalitarian purpose. Halsey has written extensively and elegantly about the changing role of academics and universities in the modern world (e.g. Halsey, 1971, 1992). But a core dilemma remains between the press for meritocratic excellence and wider social egalitarian concerns. High up on Halsey's list of recommendations to incoming sociology students was Michael Young's (1958) fable *The rise of the meritocracy*, set in the not too distant future where 'IQ plus effort' had become the basis for a new form of social and economic inequality.[8]

Before Oxford

Halsey has written fully on his own formative period (Halsey, 1996). Here we simply draw out some key features that are relevant to our theme. First, his working-class background, and his experience of growing up in both urban and rural areas are clear threads running through his continuing egalitarian concerns and anger against social injustice. But it is a respectable, orderly and stable setting that he portrays. Linked to that is a very strong sense of family and community, and—sometimes surprisingly to his more radical students—the idea of Christian fellowship (see Dennis & Halsey, 1988). As he makes clear in his comments on Peter Hennessy's version of the 'British ideology', the framework was a 'love of Englishness and conviction ... that social accord is necessary, and necessarily based on justice or at least accommodation between the classes' (Halsey, 1996, pp. 40–41). This consistently held position on social reform through some form of consensus certainly made the going much tougher in the later 1970s and 1980s with the decline of such consensus, not just in the wider political arena, but within universities and even within his own department.

Despite winning a scholarship to Grammar School, Halsey left school at 16 and became a sanitary inspector's boy. But war intervened. He joined the RAF, was selected to train as a fighter pilot, but after delays and extended training was only just finally qualifying when war ended. War, however, gave him the opportunity to return to education—first as a recruit to an emergency training scheme for school teachers and then to take up an undergraduate course for those whose higher education had been interrupted by the war. Halsey's later advocacy of 'second chance' higher education always drew on his own experience and that of his peers for whom the war had delivered this opportunity. So it was first to Westminster College and then to the London School of Economics and Political Science (LSE) to specialise in the sociology of education, in survey research and the use of official statistics (Halsey, 2004a). The early part of Halsey's autobiography contains several references to rugby and cricket at school, in the RAF and at university. While his skills on the games field are hardly relevant to our concerns, we note that he always played 'stand off half' in rugby. While rugby is a team game, the stand off half[9] is the 'playmaker'—an individualist who has to read the game quickly, seize openings and opportunities and then link with other players who can take these forward. Halsey has always been an extraordinarily good and rapid 'reader' of many different settings. One colleague commented[10] that he somehow seemed to have read books before they were published, or when arriving as speaker at a conference seemed to have absorbed what had already been covered by other speakers. He was also, in the best sense, an opportunist. But good fly halves are also heavily dependent on good possession. Without it they have to scratch around for openings. This works too, as in the tougher climate of the late 1970s onwards, Halsey admitted to much more difficulty in running a university department, as expansion turned to contraction and new opportunities dried up.

After a brief stay at Liverpool University as a researcher, Halsey moved to Birmingham University as lecturer in 1954. His period there was punctuated by two spells in the USA, as Fellow at the Center for the Advanced Study of the Behavioral Studies at Palo Alto and later as visiting Professor of Sociology at the University of Chicago. What we can draw from this period is, first, the developing network of contacts that built on his LSE years and made him a personal bridge with an earlier generation of sociologists (Parsons, Merton, Shils); second, the expansion of this network well beyond sociology and academia;[11] third, an extraordinary facility with the US setting, which meant that throughout his life he was treated not as some visiting 'British academic', but a sociologist with the same background and language, who 'knew American society and its higher education system as few Englishmen do';[12] fourth, a highly articulate and productive lecturing and writing style. These were closely linked and key factors in his growing influence. Following, he claims, Arthur Lewis's recommendation, Halsey learnt to lecture without using any notes or other aids.[13] This meant that he was able to engage the audience in ways that few academics achieve; the style was not to 'lecture at' them but to draw them in like an actor, relying on his personal magnetism and timing. Like the best 'touch' players, this nearly always worked—though there were lapses.[14]

At his peak he was undoubtedly among the very best lecturers in post-war Oxford. This skill was not limited to academic audiences or students, but worked across the board, with local groups in Sunderland or Liverpool, with mothers of preschool children, or senior civil servants. Often there seemed to be no evidence, and sometimes no chance, of preparation.[15] His style in managing meetings also used a similar mode, seeking to generate a shared understanding at the outset. Yet unlike many other noteless and impromptu speakers, Halsey typically spoke in wholly connected and structured prose. One reason may have been that his writing was increasingly dictated (at a time when British academics still had secretaries). So written and spoken forms were not far removed, and Halsey's writing style often had the same quality of direct engagement with its readers. 'To find a strategy for educational roads to equality! That has been a central theme of educational discussion from the beginning of the twentieth century' is the opening to *Educational priority* (Halsey, 1972a, p. 3). Finally, this period laid down the foundations for Halsey's major contributions to education—his work with Jean Floud on social class and educational opportunity (Floud *et al.*, 1956), the sociology of education (Floud & Halsey, 1958) and education, the economy and class structure (Halsey, Floud & Anderson, 1961; OECD, 1961), which in combination defined the direction of educational sociology until the 1970s.

Why Oxford?

In one sense the answer is easy. Halsey came to Oxford because he had been 'recruited' in the traditional Oxford way through a series of informal contacts. He mentions Evans-Pritchard who was at Palo Alto with him, Isaiah Berlin and Alan Bullock and no doubt others who encouraged him to apply. Oxford (or rather some individuals in Oxford) clearly wanted to get its hands on a rising world-class talent. But it was a 'two way street'. Halsey wanted to come. Having decided to turn down offers to move to the USA, being invited to apply to Oxford was attractive. And in addition to the plans he was developing for Oxford in terms of sociology, there was no doubt he saw Oxford as potentially a better base for his wider concerns with social reform; bluntly, that he would be taken more seriously and get better access.

Oxford as a base for wider educational reform

Halsey's working life at Oxford now spans more than 40 years. In that time, Oxford has changed relatively slowly until recently (and Nuffield College hardly at all), but in the world outside there has been rapid social change, much of which Halsey has charted in the UK (Halsey, 1995; Halsey & Webb, 2000). Here we pull out some key changes that set the background to our examples. First is the sheer change in the scale of policy-related research. At the outset in the 1960s there were a mere handful of academic sociologists, and even fewer concerned with policy; and there was very little large-scale empirical social research. Most major committees of enquiry in education in the 1950s and 1960s had to begin by undertaking their own studies. In arguing for the spread of 'experimental social administration' Halsey (1970) described the 'trend away from advisory virtuosos like Professor Lindemann towards councils and committees ...' But it did not stop with the rapid expansion of sociology and social policy from the 1960s and the subsequent growth of social research. Government departments, too, changed. When Halsey worked as advisor to Tony Crosland at the Department of Education and Science (DES) in the 1960s he would have been the only practising social researcher in that department, certainly the only sociologist. That would have remained more or less true until the 1990s.[16] While the DES may have been a special case, even the celebrated Home Office Research Unit, which was the largest social research group within central government (after the OPCS Social Survey Division), had about 40 professional staff in 1979 (Blume, 1982); the Home Office RDS now has approximately 300 researchers, statisticians and economists. Thus the picture that Keith Banting (1979), for example, draws of the way that a small number of social science academics—Halsey among them—was able to influence social policy during the Labour government of the 1960s, had been transformed. The civil service's guard against this new form of intervention, which Banting argues did not really exist in the 1960s, was now fully in place, staffed by a phalanx of in-house researchers and policy analysts.

The social policy-making process in the UK has also been transformed. No longer is it a case of three year commissions, extended discussions, parliamentary and party debate before proposals are put forward, but rather tight-knit groups working within government to generate more or less definitive policies that are then put out to very time-limited consultation (Smith & Smith, 1992). These changes severely restrict the direct influence of researchers or academics who are independent of government or outside this loop. And even if Oxford weekends and 'high table' discussions over port between policy makers, civil servants and academics were ever an effective method of influencing policy, it is clear that the balance has shifted significantly to London, through pressures of time and the sheer density of academics, policy makers and social researchers in the London area. Even though Oxford was always his base, Halsey, we should underline, expected to travel. Indeed the most likely place to find him was on the way to (or back from) somewhere else.

The OECD and educational reform

Halsey was drawn into the OECD through his contact with Ron Gass and was selected to act as the 'rapporteur' of a major OECD conference in Sweden in 1961. The published report, *Ability and educational opportunity* (OECD, 1961), shows the way that Halsey seized this opportunity to lay down or draw out key messages for education and the OECD. Lionel Elvin, who chaired the conference, notes diplomatically that the publication 'is neither a statement of his [Halsey's] own views, nor a mere précis of our debates, but ... a personal formulation of the "sense of the meeting"' (OECD, 1961, p. 9).

The three themes that stand out, welded together in Halsey's contribution, are first, the increasingly central role of education in economic development (a theme also developed by Floud and Halsey in the opening section of their reader published in the same year). Here, Halsey draws on the emerging work of Schultz (1960) and others on the economic returns from education. Second, is the argument about the 'pool of ability' which was critical to the issue of educational expansion, and was at the core of the Robbins proposals for the expansion of higher education in the UK in the early 1960s. And third is the concern with 'equality of opportunity' presented in terms of social background and access. Halsey was able to draw on his own work and that of others to present an optimistic conclusion, one that was linked to untapped ability, the unacceptable levels of educational inequality based on social background, and access to the higher and more selective levels of education. In combination these three sets of ideas, articulated by Halsey and others, underlie the gradual shift in the OECD from 'the somewhat narrow macro-economic and trade organisation of the 1960s' where the primary focus on education was restricted to 'manpower planning', 'to the multi-disciplinary policy institution of today'. This laid down the agenda for OECD's major expansion into education and later into social policy more generally.[17]

If the early 1960s set the agenda, then the middle to late 1960s focused on actively developing the OECD programme in education. This, for Halsey, included securing backing from Crosland (then Secretary of State for Education in the UK) for the OECD role in education, and flying with the Secretary General of the OECD to persuade the Ford Foundation to make a major grant to set up the OECD Centre of Educational Research and Innovation (CERI—of which Halsey was the first chairman), and then to Tokyo to charm the leaders of the Japanese ministry of education into support. Interspersed with these trips were international conferences and meetings to draw on the experience of US researchers and innovators and link them with other OECD countries. Thus a conference hosted by the Ford Foundation in New York drew together US experience in the 'war on poverty' for a largely European audience, just beginning to take the first small steps in this direction (Little & Smith, 1971). Halsey refers to the 'buccaneering' style of these developments:[18] there was a strong sense that opportunities were opening up, doors opening, policies shifting and resources available, if only the package or proposals could be pitched in the right place and time. Yet the number of people involved was still small, and the weight of OECD work in this area limited and therefore heavily dependent on a favourable national and international climate of educational expansion and reform.

The OECD Manpower, Social Affairs and Education Directorate headed by Ron Gass began developing 'country reports' on education, following the parallel of the highly influential OECD reviews of national economies. The form was a visiting review panel that assembled and commented on material provided by national governments, drawing on research, data and evidence for other systems. The outcome was a report containing the examiners' judgments and national response debated in the OECD education committee in Paris. Halsey lists six such national studies in which he took part, concluding with his review *Higher Education in California* (OECD, 1990). These reports often have a distinctive flavour, which, on one or two occasions, deeply offended the country in question. They were midway between the examiners' own assessments and a more objective account. Halsey's reports certainly carried their own individual stamp. This was perhaps inevitable given the lack of comparative data and the relatively short time and resources available. Such studies remained relatively intermittent affairs, perhaps because there were relatively few academics or researchers able or willing to take on the assessment of a whole country's education system.

Yet if we roll the clock forward, the position has been transformed. With the major initiatives within the OECD to develop better comparative international educational statistics (in *Education at a Glance* from 1992 onwards) and the incorporation of international educational performance measurement into the OECD programme (under the PISA label[19]) from 2000, the latest OECD country studies are able to draw on much more robust and comparable data, including educational outcomes.[20] They have moved much closer to their economic counterparts in the OECD. Thus the so-called 'PISA shock' (where countries face up to their relative educational results in mathematics, science and literacy in the OECD reports) may have a major impact on education systems. The latest country report on Denmark (2004) shows this new reliance on data but also the traditional OECD concerns with social and educational equity. Its principal examiner, Peter Mortimore, sees himself explicitly working within the agenda set during the Halsey/Gass era and the 'political arithmetic' tradition,[21] but with a much more robust set of information to draw on. What began as a limited venture in Halsey's day has since become a very major part of the OECD programme.

Research advisor at the Department of Education and Science (DES)

Halsey was appointed as advisor to Tony Crosland when the latter became Secretary of State for Education in 1965. It was technically a two-days-a-week secondment from the university. Halsey had in fact first met Crosland in Birmingham through their mutual interest in the cooperative movement (Ostergaard & Halsey, 1965) rather than education. Philip Williams at Nuffield College was also a key go-between in making the link. Crosland's era at the DES (1965–1967) is indelibly linked with the move to comprehensive secondary education and the end of selection at 11+, with circular 10/65. This set out six possible models of comprehensive reorganisation to which local education authorities were 'requested' to respond with their plans. But 'going comprehensive' was already official Labour policy: the previous Secretary of State, Michael Stewart, had gained cabinet approval in 1964, and the circular was already in preparation when Crosland arrived in January 1965 (Kogan, 1971; Kerckhoff *et al.*, 1996). Between 1960 and 1965, too, the educational tide was running strongly in favour of comprehensives, with increasing proportions of secondary age pupils in these schools (up from 4.7% to 8.5%).[22] Halsey's arrival at Curzon Street later in 1965 would have made little direct impact on these developments, as is clear from his own and others' accounts (Kogan, 1971; Halsey, 1996, p. 124). It is also highly unlikely at this point that civil servants would have allowed a part-time advisor anywhere near the detailed drafting of circulars and guidance, and Halsey was never a 'detail man', going instead for the broader picture and the underlying arguments. As he makes clear, his role was with the DES research programme. His influence on this major development in secondary education was indirect, through his earlier research and writing on the relationship between selective secondary education and social class, on the 'pool of ability' and the waste inherent in terminating the majority of secondary schooling at age 15 without qualifications. This was allied with the growing volume of educational research on testing children at 11+, and the consequences of such selection both on primary and secondary schools. Unusually at this time, there was a sufficient body of research coming together to form a powerful case on several fronts against selective education. Halsey's appointment as advisor perhaps reflected that shift; for Crosland, it was significant that he was a sociologist (Kogan, 1971, p. 185) rather than a mainstream educational researcher or from the economics of education, which his successors tended to be.

Most of this research, it should be underlined, was on the failings of the selective system. There was very little research on comprehensives. Empirical research has to focus on what is the case, not what might be. The positive examples came largely from other countries, from the US and Husen's conclusions from the Swedish case (Husen, 1961). And while a research study of comprehensives was commissioned by the DES at this period, the policy development went ahead. The effects of these national changes in secondary education could only be assessed after the event, over the next twenty years.

With hindsight, what is striking about this change of policy was the relative lack of detail on the content of these new forms of secondary education. The concern was with reorganising structures, as if this alone would produce the desired result (and without significant increases in funding). Clearly at this point the role of the DES was far removed from any notion of determining the detail of what went on in schools, particularly the curriculum. It was another ten years before serious discussion on the 'core curriculum' at national level, and a further ten before the 1988 legislation for a national curriculum reached the statute book. But there was a vacuum, where the growing clamour over standards in schooling from the first Black Paper in 1969 (Cox & Dyson, 1969), and the focus by researchers on what went on in the classroom, increasingly made the running. From the mid-1970s Halsey recognised the challenge of this 'new sociology of education' and admitted to 'selective inattention' to what went on within the 'black box' of schooling (Karabel & Halsey, 1977). But by then the agenda had shifted, the majority of secondary pupils were in comprehensives and comprehensives were increasingly under attack.

Halsey's own assessment of his role at the DES (1965–1968) was that it had been 'less successful in practice than in theory' (Halsey, 1996, p. 124). Certainly he made little long-term impact on the way DES research was organised,[23] though he was able to promote specific research studies. He put this lack of impact down, in part, to his unfamiliarity with the anthropology of the 'strange tribe' of the civil service. Ironically perhaps, it is his social survey (with Ivor Crewe) of the civil service, as part of the Fulton Commission in 1969, that is now the most widely listed of Halsey's publications in the official files in the National Archives, as each government department responded to this first systematic study of their customs and practices. But the contacts he had established at the DES led on to further developments, often through civil servants who had been influenced by the climate of ideas he had articulated in a language that they found appealing. This lasted through a change of government. Thus when the Conservatives took over in 1970 and Mrs Thatcher became Secretary of State, Halsey still had considerable input into her 1972 White Paper *Education: a framework for expansion*, but this was on the importance of preschool, and not secondary, education.

In the more recent controversy over comprehensives, Halsey has, on occasions, been cited as one of the founding fathers of the reform who has now had second thoughts (most recently in his appearance on the radio programme, *Desert Island Discs*, in 2003). His stated position (Halsey, 1996, p. 130) is that his idea of comprehensive reform, which he claims was also that of Crosland, was 'of taking grammar schools plus technical schools to all our children'. But this ideal has not as yet been realised. One conclusion to draw is that while he now classifies himself as a 'naïve supporter' of the original reforms, the focus at that time was primarily on the reorganisation itself with the 1960s optimism that this would, on its own, bring the desired result. We should also underline that while Halsey worked energetically and supportively with local comprehensives as parent and governor,[24] his research focus was never on the detail of their internal organisation. The nearest he came to advocacy here was in his support for the community schools movement in the 1970s, and the idea of a core curriculum.

Government against poverty in school and community[25]

The Educational Priority Areas (EPA) programme (1968–1972) grew directly from the Plowden Report on Primary Education[26] and Halsey's role as advisor to Crosland. The key ingredient was Michael Young,[27] who was both a member of the Plowden Committee and first chairman of the newly created UK Social Science Research Council (SSRC). The origins of the EPA programme are well documented.[28] Our focus here is more on the way it happened and how these small networks operated in and around central government at that time. Michael Young had been put forward for the Plowden Committee by Kogan,[29] though this was in the final stages of the Conservative administration. Having played a key role in drafting the Labour Party's manifesto in 1945, by the 1960s Young was already the leading 'social entrepreneur' in the UK with a string of ideas and institutions[30] on the go. As he wrote in a brief memoir to Halsey, 'I wanted to push for more 'equality' of course and was impressed with what I saw ... on my trip around the USA for Plowden. ... I tied it up in a parcel and thought of the label 'Educational Priority Area' and wrote Chapters 4 [Participation by Parents] and 5 [Educational Priority Areas] of Plowden'.[31]

When the Plowden Report was published in 1967, it listed 197 recommendations, but stated unequivocally 'we have given absolute priority to only one of our proposals—the creation of educational priority areas' (Plowden, para. 1185). The aim was initially to reach the schools containing the two per cent most deprived in the first year, rising to ten per cent over five years. The committee also proposed research 'to discover which of the developments in educational priority areas have the most constructive effects ...' (para. 177). The national reception and debates in both Houses of Parliament were positive—Crosland in the Commons concluding that EPAs were 'a most radical recommendation—utterly convincing and striking illustration of what Professor Titmuss and others have recently been saying—that we cannot rely on economic growth alone to even out gross social inequalities' (HoC, 16 March 1967). Yet little action followed—the state of the economy was, as usual, the reason. At the so-called 'Plowden seminar' at Crosland's house, shortly after the Report had been published, Halsey, supported by Young, argued that a small start should be made and the possibility of using research money was raised. Young and Halsey worked increasingly in tandem over the next few months, scaling down their original request for £10m, then £5m and finally a much lower sum from the SSRC and DES research budget. As the government began to respond to the Plowden proposals for EPAs, encouraging LEAs to identify their priority areas and allocating additional money for new school building, and later salary supplements to teachers in designated EPA schools, Young laid out more or less the full EPA proposal in a letter to Crosland (August 1967), arguing that money for school buildings was one of the least imaginative of the Plowden proposals for EPAs. What was needed was 'experimental action' at the local level to implement and test out innovation. Young had indeed already done something like this as a demonstration for the Plowden Committee on the effects of parental involvement (Young & McGeeney, 1968). The idea was of small teams working for selected LEAs, backed by research from the local university, to implement the more imaginative proposals for EPAs. Young contrasted the sluggishness in education to pilot field test new ideas with the position in health.

But by now Crosland had moved to the Board of Trade. The response by his successor, Patrick Gordon Walker, while broadly positive, raised a fundamental problem, endorsed by civil service comment. It was not legally possible for DES money to be used in this way to support specific developments in selected areas. While this is a detail in the overall story, in part it explains why Halsey's department in Oxford became the route. It was a way round this blockage. The next few months were taken up with attempts to get local areas signed up, in addition to 'the ghastly drawn out negotiating and keeping-sweet of SSRC, DES and SED people. We wanted the five biggest cities—London, Birmingham, Manchester, Liverpool, Glasgow ... Manchester ran out and we put in the West Riding because of Clegg. Birmingham ran out ...'.[32] This took place more or less at the same time as the negotiations with the Ford Foundation for support of the OECD centre, and from time to time the possibility of OECD funding for EPAs was dangled. But by the end of 1967 there was a draft of the full proposals for an action-research programme which gained formal support from the DES and SSRC by April 1968. Funding was modest with £100,000 from the DES and £75,000 for the SSRC—though this was the largest grant given up to that point.[33] It was for a three-year programme in four selected areas in England and one linked Scottish study in Dundee. Joint action-research teams were to be employed in each area, for the four English EPAs employed directly by Oxford, with Halsey as the national director and Young as chair of the national steering committee.

One result was effectively to double the size of the Oxford department,[34] though all the new staff were based elsewhere.[35]

Though there had been local experimental projects before EPA, it was the first 'action-research' programme in the UK explicitly designed to test out national policies, but run through a university department. Young had clearly initiated the idea and mapped out the detailed proposals; Halsey had added his own distinctive stamp; his conception of 'experimental social administration' was broad enough to cover everything from randomised experiments at preschool level in the West Riding to the Liverpool project's emphasis on research as an adjunct to action-generating support for ideas such as increased parental participation, locally and nationally. Halsey's style as director, having set things going at the start, was to provide an umbrella of general support and regular visits to each project, but never detailed management, though there were standard data collection exercises run from Oxford, and a centrally-designed preschool intervention programme (Payne, 1974). This style of management meant that the successful projects were able to develop their own distinctive programmes, but some struggled to carve out a coherent strategy, given the terrifyingly wide objectives[36] and the competing groups and pressures. As Midwinter recalls, one of the most forceful lessons conveyed by the US 'poverty warriors' at Ditchley Park in 1969 was that the worst thing to do in an action-research project was to involve a university. 'Oxford was the rule proving the exception, almost entirely because [Halsey] had the clarity of mind and the firmness of purpose to transcend all that nonsense.'

The EPA projects began in autumn 1968 and ran for three years, ending with five HMSO published reports (*Educational priority*, vols 1–5, 1972–1975) and a linked Penguin Education Special (*Priority education*, Midwinter, 1972). Here we can only summarise their impact. During the period of the programme, support for area-based targeting of social need increased, with further programmes. Nationally, the EPA programme gathered speed and coherence, as the new Urban Programme after 1969 removed the bar on the expansion of nursery education. And by luck of timing, Mrs Thatcher's White Paper in 1972 was able to draw on the EPA findings on preschool. The programme also made a substantial impact on teacher training colleges, which increasingly began to develop options for students wanting to teach in EPA areas. Overall the balance sheet in 1972 indicated that a very small project, even if with national backing and standing, had made very considerable national impact, and apparently laid the foundations with a series of successor organisations to continue work both nationally and locally.

But from then on the going proved much tougher. We have charted elsewhere the main reasons (Smith, 1987). The social and economic climate shifted dramatically away from education as the key ingredient in tackling social deprivation. One of the key messages from EPA, that education alone could not resolve major social and economic inequalities, contributed to its own marginalisation. New projects and programmes sprang up that attempted to address these issues directly. And worse, the very analysis that had underpinned EPAs, of a few areas that had missed out on economic growth, was overtaken by the growing realisation in the 1970s that these problems were spreading to all areas, as industries declined and unemployment rose.

By the late 1980s, while there were still some traces of the EPA programme (teachers in designated schools continued to be paid an extra allowance), what was depressing on visiting schools in such areas was to find little evidence of the enthusiasm that the EPA programme had generated. But the EPA idea certainly took root in other countries, with visitors seeking advice from Halsey. These included the French team developing their national *Zones d'Education Prioritaire* (ZEP), which were introduced in France in 1981/2. With the revival of concern about educational disadvantage in the 1990s, demonstrated by the 1993 Ofsted report *Access and achievement in urban areas*, there has been a major swing back to many of the ideas in EPA, including the increased importance given to the role of education. The incoming Labour administration in 1997 announced Educational Action Zones (EAZ), and later the Education in Cities (EiC) programme. Designating areas of high social need formed a central plank of the 'Area-Based Initiatives' programme with initiatives on a very much larger scale than in the 1960s. The original EPA programme has proved not a dead-end but rather a precursor for this much larger enterprise.

Halsey was also a principal player in the early stages of the Home Office Community Development Programme (CDP), which in conception predated EPA but was much slower to get off the ground. Though based in the Home Office, CDP was designed as an inter-departmental programme involving the main social ministries. Its principal architect, the senior civil servant Derek Morrell, had been at the DES and clearly drew on the EPA ideas and model for the CDP enterprise. Enoch Powell's 'rivers of blood' speech in 1968, and the hastily cobbled together Home Office Urban Programme, gave Morrell the chance to launch CDP (Mayo, 1975). Halsey became the national research director for CDP in its early phase, much to the relief of some cabinet members who were uneasy at Morrell's almost mystical views on the power of 'community'. While CDP was seen effectively as the successor programme to EPA in the early 1970s, relatively little of its programme focused on schools. It was also much larger and more complex, with twelve local authorities, other central government departments and university research teams in each area. Much of the early effort went into making these complex structures work (Lees & Smith, 1975), and while the Oxford department provided the research teams for three of the CDP areas, Halsey dropped back to an advisory role.[37]

If these local programmes were precursors to the later area-based initiatives, then Halsey's ideas of 'experimental social administration', the field-testing of new social policies, might be seen as a precursor to the emphasis on the 'evidence-based' interventions, RCTs and 'systematic research' reviews of the 1990s. But, as Halsey argues:

> The laboratory is, by definition, natural and not experimental. ... The desired outcomes of action are often imprecisely defined and in any case resistant to clear measurement. The inputs are not completely controlled and the relation between input and output is to that extent indeterminate. ... Nevertheless, the challenge is irresistible. (Halsey, 1978, p. 143)

Academic and activist

In this paper we have primarily focused on Halsey's 'activist' role in policy development across the UK and elsewhere that directly affected schooling and related areas of social policy. We have given much less attention to Halsey's role as one of the leading sociologists of education in the second half of the 20th century. We have covered the period in the 1950s and early 1960s when Halsey and Floud effectively laid down the agenda for the sociology of education; but there were also the three major 'readers' (Halsey, Floud & Anderson, 1961; Karabel & Halsey, 1976; and Halsey, Lauder, Brown & Wells, 1997) that have influenced generations of students (and tutors); major research studies on British academics (Halsey & Trow, 1971 and Halsey, 1992), and above all there is the series of studies linked to the major Oxford Social Mobility project from the mid-1970s onwards, where Halsey, as ever, played the central role of holding together over many years a highly distinguished, but at times fractious, group of academic sociologists particularly taking the lead on the role in education and social mobility. All these contributions may have had effects on schools and educational systems that were far more significant than any direct impact that he may have made as a 'policy activist', but we are not in a position to assess these impacts here.

We have noted the way that Halsey's academic work on social mobility rose, as the conditions for social reform deteriorated in the 1970s and the necessary consensus began to break down. But it is important to stress the continuity of purpose with his activist phase. 'We have set ourselves a question in this book which in its most general and deceptively simple form is whether education can change society' (Halsey, Heath & Ridge, 1980, p. 1). The answer, as with the EPA programme, is complex and mixed: 'We must avoid the error of generalising from a particular history to some supposed universal imperative of social policy. The record gives no warranty to easy optimism: but neither does it endorse defeatism' (Halsey, Heath & Ridge, 1980, p. 216).

Halsey notes that Morris Ginsburg, head of the Sociology Department at LSE, had assumed that he (Halsey) might make an 'adequate WEA [Workers' Educational Association] tutor' (Halsey, 1996, p. 51). In fact, Halsey took his broader educational and dissemination role very seriously, speaking to a very large number of groups of all types across the country on the EPA programme and acting as a missionary for its ideas and recommendations. But this always extended to a wider educational role. Between 1972 and 1994, he published regular columns in the *Times Higher Education Supplement* (Dennis (1994) records 63 articles). In 1977 there came his delivery of the BBC Reith Lectures, at that time still the most prestigious series of public lectures in the UK (delivered in 1977, and published as *Change in British society*, currently in its fourth edition, 1995). There are also the three editions of *British social trends* (Halsey, 1972b, 1988; Halsey & Webb, 2000) which clearly fit into the political arithmetic tradition of 'documenting the state of society'. The goal of local dissemination also lay behind Halsey's involvement with Professor Jerry Bruner in the Oxford Preschool Research Group (OPRG), and with Harry Judge's Oxford Educational Research Group (OERG) in the late 1970s.

★★★

What was the role of Oxford in these developments, particularly the activist phase? While it may have been the case that Oxford added something, it would be hard to argue that it could not also have been possible from Birmingham. After all, it was the timing, content and articulation of the message that contributed to the main impact. But this is not the whole story. What was striking about these developments for those closely involved was that it often proved much easier to carry out this kind of initiative from Oxford at this time. This was underlined by the (sometimes very extensive and convoluted) negotiations to involve other universities in the EPA or CDP programme. Oxford was as yet much less institutionally bound, and heads of department more or less autocratically able to determine what they would do. Funds flowing through the University Chest to play schemes in Liverpool, or for a market stall rent in the West Riding, were rarely, if ever, challenged. Halsey was expert in working with the system, and had the right contacts in both Oxford and outside to make it work. But, as he himself charts in *Decline of donnish dominion*, the window has been closing. By the mid-1970s, the tightening financial climate and increasing oversight from the centre gradually reeled in the high level of autonomy that had existed. Such activities may still be possible, but require disproportionate time and effort.

But the critical counterpoint to this autonomy was the lack of institutional follow up. Why, asked US academics, as Halsey was a world-class sociologist, so successful in creating these ventures that affected national and local policy, did not resources and support flow from the university? In fact the reverse was almost the case. Once the resource climate tightened from the mid-1970s onwards, and Halsey moved increasingly to more conventional academic research as the Oxford Social Mobility project gathered way, this part of his enterprise fell back. He never managed to secure long term research funding, though this was increasingly the pattern of support in other major social policy research centres. By 1980 or so, what had been a major programme of social intervention and research in the 1970s was reduced to a single project or two.

Reform within Oxford

We should remember that during the time he was most active outside Oxford—his 'activist phase' was perhaps 1965–1975—Halsey successfully built up a medium-sized university department from a backwater on the periphery of the university. He taught and lectured well beyond his formal 'stint'. Indeed 'wheeling out Chelly' to meet visitors who needed to be impressed, give a lecture at short notice, or represent the department with external bodies where progress had stalled, was an effective and widely used device. Expansion of the department came not just through the policy-related research, but with the University's agreement to expand and refashion the graduate social work training in the mid-1960s, demonstrating the traditional link between sociology and other disciplines and the applied study of social problems (Halsey, 1967). The two-year MSc social work course in the department became the largest Masters course in the social studies faculty and one of the best regarded training programmes in the country, and had produced over a thousand graduates by 2000, many in senior positions in social services departments and local and central government policy organisations, as well as in professorial posts. Moves in the 1980s to parallel this in social policy and social research (including education)[38] by training prospective social policy researchers on a two year programme, while well conceived, never developed to the same level, though the relatively small numbers of students who went through this course included several who have made their mark in this field. The result by the mid-1980s was a department that increasingly focused on professional social work training.

Beyond the department, sociology had been introduced into the PPE undergraduate degree in 1962 and, together with Julia Parker, Halsey later introduced social policy. He was also a key figure in the new Human Science degree initiated in 1971, which combined the social and biological sciences (Halsey, 1969; Pringle, 1972). Most recently he has undertaken a series of studies to assess the relative 'fairness' of the university's admissions from the private and state school sector. Drawing on this research in evidence to the House of Commons Select Committee on Education and Employment in 2000, Halsey produces a classic restatement of the persistence and origin of class inequalities,[39] as applied to higher education and society's needs.

Conclusion

Halsey has spent more than 40 years working as a senior academic at Oxford.[40] Unlike most of the other figures in this collection, he was neither an Oxford product himself nor a national politician or administrator. He defines himself explicitly as an 'academic', but one we should add that has never placed a tight boundary round his field of work—sociology was about 'understanding society'—'what we had at LSE was an education that was *not* a training for sociology but a course in the understanding of society' (Halsey, 2004a, p. vi). Nor does he see the ends, means and outcomes of social policy to be illegitimate concerns for an academic. Halsey's extraordinarily wide range of interests and activities and his prodigious written output means that an overall assessment of his contribution to education and schooling would have to take account of both direct and indirect effects on policy. As has been argued by Weiss and others (see Smith & Smith, 1992), the most important effect of research and academics on policy may be this indirect route of 'illumination', setting agendas, redefining problems and proposing solutions. We have tried to indicate the ways that Halsey contributed to this set of effects.

But there are other routes that are much harder to measure—for instance, by individual example through the influence of teaching or writing on the next generation. We have not attempted to capture this aspect, though it could be the most important of all. Almost at random, we discovered students of Halsey's in the 1970s who commented 30 years later that his lectures on community and fraternity had influenced their life's work, and Barney Pityana's[41] 2002 address as Principal and Vice-Chancellor of the University of South Africa (UNISA) invokes Halsey's conception of the role of universities.

Our focus has rather been on Halsey's direct involvement, particularly during his 'activist' phase (1965–1975), where it is slightly less difficult to measure the effects on policy. Here the results in the short term were impressive. Halsey brought together ideas, not always ones he had originated, which he turned into powerful arguments and prescriptions for practice, for positive discrimination, area-based policy development, preschool, parental involvement, the community school, all of which received a very significant lift up the policy agenda by well-timed interventions, reports and skilled advocacy. But for much of this period the tide was moving in the same direction, and even Mrs Thatcher as Secretary of State for Education in the 1970s was anxious to enlist Halsey's backing for the expansion of pre-schooling. The idea of 'experimental social administration' was also a major refinement on what had gone before—the idea of field-testing innovations and EPA demonstrated the manifold ways that this could be done.

From the mid-1970s the tide turned and the going got much tougher. Halsey spent more time on research studies such as social mobility and higher education. Doors were no longer opening, and even the ideas that had made the activism possible were no longer in place. In the mid-1980s, Halsey played a major part in the Archbishop of Canterbury's Commission on Urban Priority Areas. The thrust of this study was to recreate the earlier agenda and draw attention to widening inequalities. But this bounced off a government that was not only unwilling to accept that there was a problem of urban poverty but formally ruled out the use of the word 'poverty' to cover conditions in the UK. It was not until the 1990s with the publication of the Joseph Rowntree Foundation's *Inquiry into income and wealth* (Barclay & Hills, 1995) that the tide turned.

We have also charted the way that many of the ideas current in the activist period have returned to the central agenda from the mid-1990s onwards. The HMI report *Access and achievement in urban education* (OfSTED, 1993) echoes, perhaps unconsciously, Crosland's arguments for the EPA programme in the Commons in 1967, adapting J. F. Kennedy's phrase to conclude 'the rising tide of educational change is not lifting these boats'. Since 1997 we have had a raft of policies to boost education in disadvantaged areas, and the development of a far more extensive and well-funded set of area-based programmes, not just in education, but across the social policy spectrum, through the work of the Social Exclusion Unit and later the Neighbourhood Renewal Unit. Resources are allocated in a far more systematic way than in the 1970s.[42] The national moves to evidence-based policy making, though part rhetoric, also fit with the moves to a central state that plans and regulates, rather than directly provides, services. We have noted, too, the way that the OECD country reports draw directly on the approach developed in the Halsey era, though again with much better comparative data. And many initiatives hailed as new ideas—such as the commitment to preschool intervention as even more important than higher education, and the role of parents as 'amplifiers' of their children's educational development—are revivals of the ideas that were developed in the EPA and CDP programmes, now resurfacing in the post-1997 policy climate.

Much of this is an indirect legacy, though some of the current players still provide a direct link. Halsey's direct contacts with Blair (Halsey, 1996), and later Blunkett, when Secretary of State for Education, are unlikely to be key factors in this transmission. Will it last? Here, we should simply note than many of the same issues that lead to the relative collapse of this approach in the 1970s remain; this is not just the perennial question of targeting versus universal welfare polices, but much bigger issues. As Halsey commented in 1969:

> what we have to consider is the development of government inspired and financed programmes, posited on the assumption that the welfare society may be attained through the legitimate use of the existing political structures ... which may turn out to have been nothing more than a shibboleth of liberal society in decline. (Halsey, 1974)

And it was the collapse of the consensus that this was both possible and legitimate that undermined such interventions. In education, Halsey reminds us that the effects of formal schooling may be limited:

> Schooling goes far beyond schools; it is fashioned in the kitchen and in the street and it is influenced by the media and the peer group. Much of it is beyond politics in a free society.[43]

Acknowledgements

Our thanks go to a large number of people who have provided suggestions and comments and allowed us to draw on material; these include Tim Brighouse, Geoffrey Caston, Juliet Cheetham, Norman Dennis, Jean Floud, Ron Gass, Harry Judge, Maurice Kogan, Kenneth Macdonald, Eric Midwinter, Peter Mortimore, Julia Parker, Martin Trow, Hal Wilensky, two anonymous reviewers and A. H. Halsey himself.

Notes

1. For a direct comparison, see Alan Fox's autobiography *A very late development* (1990). Alan resigned his fellowship at Nuffield College and moved to Barnett House as lecturer in industrial sociology.
2. Halsey is very widely and affectionately known by his nickname, 'Chelly', used by family, colleagues and students alike. But in the interests of lexicographers and Google-searchers we have used his official name throughout this paper.
3. Professor Hal Wilensky, *personal communication*, 16 January 2005.
4. Since his retirement in 1990, after 28 years as head of department, Halsey has continued to work at Nuffield College on a formidable number of studies (Halsey, 1995, 1997, 2000 and 2004a)—and there is more to come.
5. This has only (partially) come about in the new millennium with the opening of the Social Sciences Centre in Manor Road in 2004.
6. See also Dennis (1994) for a biography and a full list of publications up to 1994.
7. Professor Martin Trow, *personal communication*, 25 January 2005. For the links between Halsey and Shils, see Halsey (1996), and his assessment of Shils in the new Oxford Dictionary of National Biography (Halsey, 2004b).

8. Michael Young's trajectory as a social reformer offers an instructive comparison with Halsey's. Despite being the first chair of the UK Social Science Research Council (1965), Young largely operated outside higher education in his own self-created institutions. Halsey has always been an academic.
9. The stand off or fly half (or 5/8ths) in rugby has some affinities with the quarterback in American football, though the rules are very different.
10. Halsey attributed this to Peter Collinson.
11. For example, Halsey's links with the politician Tony Crosland and with Ron Gass at OECD.
12. Professor Martin Trow, *personal communication*, 25 January 2005.
13. He kept to this, with few exceptions.
14. Notably, his review of E. G. West's *Education and the state* in the *New Statesman* (24 December 1965) which led to a published retraction in the *New Statesman*, action and legal costs in favour of West and the Institute of Economics Affairs (IEA).
15. At a major Anglo-American conference at Ditchley Park in 1969 on anti-poverty programmes, the non-appearance of Patrick Moynihan to give a keynote address meant that, with general agreement, Halsey was asked to stand in. He began straight away without notes: 'I want to make 14 points ...' and proceeded to do so.
16. DES (and later DfEE) statisticians were always keen to distinguish their activities from 'research'.
17. Ron Gass, *personal communication*, 1 February 2005.
18. For example, suggesting to an OECD consultant on an official mission to the US that he hid money in his shoes to evade UK exchange controls.
19. PISA is the OECD's Programme for International Student Assessment.
20. See the foreword by Barry McGaw to the *Denmark* report, *Denmark: lessons from PISA 2000* (OECD, 2004).
21. Professor Peter Mortimore, *personal communication*, 14 February 2005.
22. Figures from Kerckhoff *et al.* (1996, p. 27).
23. It was only at the end of the 1970s that Kay could claim a shift (in DES research) away from 'a series of isolated research projects spread thinly across the whole range of Departmental interests' (Kay, 1979, p. 25).
24. Mrs Julia Parker, *personal communication*, 1 March 2005; Professor Tim Brighouse, *personal communication*, summer 2004.
25. Title of a paper given at Ditchley Park, 1969, published as Halsey, 1974.
26. Central Advisory Council for Education (England) (1967) *Children and their primary schools* (London, HMSO); now reproduced in full at http://www.dg.dial.pipex.com/plowden.shtml
27. Later Lord Young of Dartington.
28. See, for example, Halsey, 1972a, and Smith, 1987.
29. Interview with Edward Boyle, Secretary of State for Education (1962-4) by David Dodds (1975).
30. See Michael Young's obituary in the *Guardian*, 16 January 2002, and the biography by Asa Briggs (2001).
31. Letter from Michael Young to A. H. Halsey, October 1970.
32. Letter from Michael Young to A. H. Halsey, October 1970.
33. More like £1.8m at 2004 prices, with at least as much again added from local and other sources.
34. Halsey claimed the numbers (including researchers) expanded from seven to something like 35 posts.
35. Dr Eric Midwinter, *personal communication*, 20 January 2005: 'I often reflected on the anomaly of treading the streets of Liverpool 7 and 8 under the aegis of Oxford University, receiving project money from the Oxford University Chest and being paid the same rate (if not allowed the same holidays) as university staff'.
36. These were to i) raise pupil achievement, ii) raise teacher morale, and iii) involve parents and the community more closely in education. As Eric Midwinter asked, 'What do you do on the second day?'

37. At the same time as the national CDP, Halsey supported the development of a local community development project, linked to the University department, based in the Barton estate, one of the most disadvantaged areas in Oxford. This combined a welfare rights centre, a 'fieldwork base' for professional community work and social work training, and research into disadvantage and the effectiveness of preventive intervention projects. 30 years later, the project survives in the form of a local welfare rights centre and a student unit, based in Ruskin College, which plays a key role in local community activity and in regional social work training.
38. Mrs Julia Parker, *personal communication*, 1 March 2005.
39. Memorandum from Professor A. H. Halsey to the House of Commons Select Committee on Education and Employment, July 2000, minutes of evidence (HE57). See www.parliament.the-stationery-office.co.uk/pa/cm199900/cmselect/cmeduemp/400/
40. In more formal roles, Halsey chaired the Social Studies Board in the 1970s, and was later on a member of the University's General Board and of Council. Active in Nuffield College throughout this period, he himself recounts (Halsey, 1996, pp. 89–91) how close he came to being elected college warden in 1978.
41. His wife, Dimza Pityana, took the social work course in the department in the 1970s. See also Halsey, 1976b.
42. Researchers in the department have been centrally involved in these developments, for example, the local area studies in the 1995 Joseph Rowntree Foundation report, work on the Indices of Multiple Deprivation to create the local measures of deprivation that are used to allocate resources across the UK (e.g. Noble *et al.*, 2004), and evaluations of some of the major neighbourhood programmes.
43. Memorandum from Professor A. H. Halsey to the House of Commons Select Committee on Education and Employment, July 2000, minutes of evidence (HE57). See www.parliament.the-stationery-office.co.uk/pa/cm199900/cmselect/cmeduemp/400/

Notes on contributors

George Smith was Professor Halsey's graduate student in the 1960s. He worked as a consultant for the OECD, and as researcher on the Educational Priority Areas (EPA) and Community Development Programmes (CDP). He was both a lecturer and researcher in Halsey's Oxford Department from the mid-1970s. Later he served as research advisor to HM Inspectorate of Schools from 1981. His research interests are in educational disadvantage, the measurement of deprivation at the local level and the evaluation of local anti-poverty programmes. He is currently Reader in Social Policy at the Department of Social Policy and Social Work at Oxford and in October 2005 took over as Head of Department.

Teresa Smith was a graduate student in Professor Halsey's department in the 1960s, and worked in the West Riding Educational Priority Area Project 1969–1972. She returned to Halsey's Department as a University Lecturer in the 1970s. Her main research interests are community, disadvantage, pre-schooling and the family. She currently leads the national evaluation of the government's Neighbourhood Nursery Initiative and acts as advisor to the House of Commons Select Committee on Education and Skills. Since 1997 she has been Head of Department of Social Policy and Social Work at Oxford, one of the two successors to Halsey's Department of Social and Administrative Studies.

References

Banting, K. G. (1979) *Poverty, politics and policy* (London, Macmillan).
Barclay, P. M. & Hills, J. (1995) *Joseph Rowntree Foundation inquiry into income and wealth* (York, Joseph Rowntree Foundation).
Blume, S. S. (1982) *The commissioning of social research by central government* (London, SSRC).
Briggs, A. (2001) *Michael Young: social entrepreneur* (Basingstoke, Palgrave).
Cox, C. B. & Dyson, A. E. (Eds) (1969) *Fight for education* (London, Critical Quarterly Society).
Dennis, N. (1994) Data and decency: understanding A. H. Halsey, in: R. Page & J. Baldock (Eds) *Social policy review 6* (Canterbury, Social Policy Association).
Dennis, N. & Halsey, A. H. (1988) *English ethical socialism: Thomas More to R. H. Tawney* (Oxford, Clarendon Press).
Dodds, D. H. (1975) *The origins of the EPA at Denaby: the anatomy of a decision* (unpublished MA thesis, University of Leeds).
Floud, J. E. & Halsey, A. H. (1958) The sociology of education—a trend report and bibliography, *Current Sociology*, 7(3).
Floud, J. E., Halsey, A. H. & Martin, F. M. (1956) *Social class and educational opportunity* (London, Heinemann).
Fox, A. (1990) *A very late development: an autobiography* (University of Warwick, Industrial Relations Research Unit).
Halsey, A. H. (1967) The new graduate diploma in Social and Administrative Studies, *The Oxford Magazine*, Trinity 7, 380–381.
Halsey, A. H. (1969) A human sciences degree, *The Oxford Magazine*, 2 Michaelmas 24 October, 25–26.
Halsey, A. H. (1970) Social scientists and governments, *Times Literary Supplement*, 5 March, 249–251.
Halsey, A. H. (Ed., 1972a) *Educational priority: EPA problems and policies, Vol. 1* (London, HMSO).
Halsey, A. H. (1972b) *British social trends since 1900* (London, Macmillan).
Halsey, A. H. (1974) Government against poverty in school and community, in: D. Wedderburn (Ed.) *Poverty, inequality and class structure* (Cambridge, Cambridge University Press), 123–139. Reprinted in M. Bulmer (Ed.) (1978) *Social policy research* (London & Basingstoke, Macmillan), 139–159.
Halsey, A. H. (Ed.) (1976a) *Traditions of social policy: essays in honour of Violet Butler* (Oxford, Basil Blackwell).
Halsey, A. H. (1976b) *Academic freedom and the idea of a university: the 17th T. B. Davie Memorial Lecture delivered in the University of Cape Town on 8 June 1976* (Cape Town, University of Cape Town).
Halsey, A. H. (1978) Government against poverty in school and community, in: M. Bulmer (Ed.) *Social policy research* (London and Basingstoke, Macmillan), 139–159.
Halsey, A. H. (1988) *British social trends since 1900, 2nd edn.* (Basingstoke, Macmillan).
Halsey, A. H. (1992) *Decline of donnish dominion: the British academic professions in the twentieth century* (Oxford, Clarendon Press).
Halsey, A. H. (1995) *Change in British society, 4th edn.* (Oxford, Oxford University Press).
Halsey, A. H. (1996) *No discouragement: an autobiography* (Basingstoke, Macmillan).
Halsey, A. H. (2004a) *A history of sociology in Britain: science, literature, and society* (Oxford, Oxford University Press).
Halsey, A. H. (2004b) Shils, Edward Albert, in: *Oxford Dictionary of National Biography* (Oxford, Oxford University Press).
Halsey, A. H. (Ed.) (1997) *Education, economy and society* (Oxford, Oxford University Press).
Halsey, A. H. & Trow, M. A. (1971) *The British academics* (London, Faber & Faber).
Halsey, A. H. & Webb, J. (Ed, 2000) *Twentieth-century British social trends* (Basingstoke, Macmillan).

Halsey, A. H., Floud, J. & Anderson, C. A. (Eds) (1961) *Education, economy and society: a reader in the sociology of education* (New York, Free Press & London, Collier-Macmillan).
Halsey, A. H., Heath, A. F. & Ridge, J. M. (1980) *Origins and destinations: family, class and education in modern Britain* (Oxford, Clarendon Press).
Halsey, A. H., Lauder, H., Brown, P. & Wells, A. S. (1997) *Education, culture and society* (Oxford, Oxford University Press).
Husen, T. (1961) Educational structure and the development of ability, in: OECD (1961) *Ability and educational opportunity* (OECD), 113–134.
Karabel, J. & Halsey, A. H. (Eds) (1977) *Power and ideology in education* (New York, Oxford University Press).
Kay, B. (1979) The DES and national educational research, *Trends in Education*, 3, 22–26.
Kerckhoff, A. C., Fogelman, K., Crook, D. & Reeder, D. (1996) *Going comprehensive in England and Wales: a study of uneven change* (London, Woburn Press).
Kogan, M. (1971) *The politics of education: Edward Boyle and Anthony Crosland in conversation with Maurice Kogan* (Harmondsworth, Penguin Books).
Lees, R. & Smith, G. (1975) *Action-research in community development* (London, Routledge and Kegan Paul).
Little, A. & Smith, G. A. N. (1971) *Strategies of compensation: a review of educational projects for the disadvantaged in the United States* (Paris, Centre for Educational Research and Innovation, OECD).
Mayo, M. (1975) The history and early development of CDP, in: R. Lees & G. Smith *Action-research in community development* (London, Routledge and Kegan Paul), 6–18.
Noble, M., Wright, G., Dibben, C., Smith, G. *et al.* (2004) *The English indices of deprivation 2004* (London, Office of the Deputy Prime Minister).
OECD (1961) *Ability and educational opportunity* (OECD).
OECD (1990) *Higher education in California* (Paris, OECD).
OECD (2004) *Denmark: lessons from PISA 2000* (Paris, OECD).
Ofsted (1993) *Access and achievement in urban education* (London, HMSO).
Ostergaard, G. N. & Halsey, A. H. (1965) *Power in co-operatives* (Oxford, Basil Blackwell).
Payne, J. (1974) *Educational priority, Vol. 2: EPA surveys and statistics* (London, HMSO).
Pringle, J. W. S. (1972) Preface, in J. W. S. Pringle (Ed.) *Biology and the human sciences: the Herbert Spencer Lectures 1970* (Oxford, Clarendon Press), vii–viii.
Schultz, T. W. (1960) Capital formation by education, *Journal of Political Economy*, 68(6).
Smith, G. (1987) Plowden twenty years on. Whatever happened to Educational Priority Areas? *Oxford Review of Education*, 13(1), 23–38.
Smith, G. & Smith, T. (1992) From social research to educational policy: 10/65 to the Education Reform Act 1988, in: C. Crouch & A. Heath (Eds) *Social research and social reform* (Oxford, Clarendon Press), 245–269.
Young, M. & Halsey, A. H. (1995) *Family and community socialism* (London, Institute for Public Policy Research).
Young, M. & McGeeney, P. (1968) *Learning begins at home* (London, Routledge and Kegan Paul).

How élite?

Sheldon Rothblatt

I. Oxford: a story of success

In the remarks that follow, under the editor's bidding, I plan to examine the structures and circumstances, as well as the historical factors, which contributed to Oxford's apparently disproportionate success in creating an ethic of public service. The contributions of the seven personalities discussed in these pages to the making of educational policy have been clearly laid out. My purpose is broader. I intend to place their lives in the context of British culture and university history and speculate on the extent to which we can conclude that their achievements were seminally determined by association with Oxford University and its colleges. All seven were at least students, fellows, professors or college heads, and several combined these roles. I have also gone one step further in the broader approach to ask whether certain types of institutions, denominated as 'élite', have a structural or cultural capacity to imbue their members with a particular social or moral mission, or even ideology.

Of Oxford's prominence in the story of the university as a distinct type of educational and service institution there is no question. It has long been admired, in company with its younger sister Cambridge, abroad as well as at home. Important Americans have been educated there, including a recent president, who was a Rhodes Scholar. The names of graduates decorate the histories of British empire and government. Oxford's pride in itself is long and lasting. College and university histories are abundant, and certainly no more than today as we peruse a shelf loaded with handsome volumes containing details that few histories of universities possess (Bill, 1973; Brock & Curthoys, 1997, 2000). In the United States, Harvard comes closest to the Oxford track record of self-examination through history (Keller & Keller, 2001). On the global rating charts compiled by magazines and the academic press, Oxford remains in a strong position, although down a bit from Harvard, and I dare say Berkeley. Although such ratings are of doubtful value, their popularity reflects the broad interest today in celebrity prestige and the entitlements such standing may bring.

The histories of legacy institutions read like a Homeric script of heroic legions summoned together to fulfil great destinies. Merely reciting the names of paragons who have passed through quadrangles and courts leaves the impression that a university that can produce such a roll call of famous names must possess some rare educational quality. It was John Henry Newman in *Loss and Gain* (1848) who first thought about writing a university novel in which the institution—in this case also, Oxford—was hypostatised into an actual character in the story, a composite of dons greater than any single one. A similar touch appears in *Zuleika Dobson,* a bewitching tale of Edwardian Oxford by Max Beerbohm. In one sequence he floats above the university, having been assigned by the Olympians the task of narrating its fate. He eulogises Oxford as a living entity. This is the manner in which universities and colleges (and also particular cities) inspiring affection and loyalty are usually presented. The cumulative effect is irresistible. If Oxford has given so many graduates of distinction to the nation, and to the world, drawing to its colleges outstanding ability from other countries, then surely Oxford is itself a person with magical, transforming powers? Those who enter its portals do so with an air of excited expectation. Less flattering depictions appear in other, generally later novels, especially mystery and detective novels now brought to the small screen, wherein dons are invariably depicted as superior, snobbish, arrogant, sometimes secretive and frequently hypocritical (Carter, 1990). But the attention bestowed upon the place by disgruntled writers is in itself a form of high flattery.

The reasons for Oxford's general appeal are hardly arcane. It long enjoyed a position of monopoly (or with Cambridge, duopoly) and over centuries educated the graduates who populated church, state and the liberal professions. Oxford men (there were no women before the 1860s) were amongst the celebrated 'statesmen in disguise' of the Victorian era. Oxford and Cambridge simply had no major competitors. Until the third decade of the 19th century, England possessed only two universities, outnumbered in this regard by its neighbour, Scotland.

Membership in an Oxbridge college was conferred only on those who secured admission to one of more than half a hundred foundations. The benefits included proximity to the scions of the landed and clerical classes, holding out the lure of patronage and preferment, election to various royal societies, such as medicine, and a strong nudge into political or bureaucratic positions. Academic careers were as yet undemanding; and while sojourns in the two institutions encouraged indolence and also boredom, the conversations were sufficiently distracting and the food intermittently satisfying if starchy. Friendships were made. Excellent libraries, beautiful grounds and mellow buildings, art and music in abundance—spacious and gracious were and are the attributes of the two senior universities of England.

The unprecedented expansion of the higher education system in the 19th century produced the London University federation, other regional federations, Durham (unfortunately first patterned on Christ Church, a model quite out of place in the north), and a system of state-supported colleges in Ireland. The newer institutions were indifferently funded. Except for London, they were primarily located in industrial or trading communities and lacked the greenfields cachet that a century later became a prominent feature of campus planning. Because mass secondary education at public expense was as yet many years away, the regional and civic university colleges, as well as the London University in its earliest years, could not rely on a steady stream of qualified entrants. University College London and King's College London created their own secondary preparatory divisions, as did many American universities such as Berkeley (founded in 1869). Even the Scottish universities, stung by criticisms that their standards were more like a school than a university, for a time sent their abler graduates to Oxford and Cambridge to read for Honours Schools and the Tripos. Until the second half of the Victorian age, lower standards were a price that the Scots were willing to pay in order to support more egalitarian admissions criteria. In this respect, they were similar to American colleges and universities of the same period. In short, exactly as we might expect, Victorian regionalism and market discipline created institutional differentiation from which a pecking order of universities resulted.

Expanding the provision for post-secondary education—it was not always clear whether the newer institutions were in fact 'higher' education—certainly strengthened Oxford's standing, its historical advantages becoming even more pronounced. The newer institutions had no connections with the social classes that had attended Oxford and uniquely dominated England's past. Consequently they could not provide easy entrance into the higher civil service, the upper reaches of the Church of England or the most prestigious of the liberal professions. However, they provided some of the essentials of a mass higher education system: a greater element of democratic opportunity and the technical skills and competences needed for an advancing industrial economy. With newer institutions able to meet the rising, if as yet limited, demand for higher education, Oxford and Cambridge could concentrate on recruiting the higher-achieving students. This was done gradually but surely. They became more demanding educational institutions than at any earlier point, with a much broader commitment to pathfinding scholarship and science.

Parliamentary intervention in the middle decades of the century helped. Legislation facilitated the legal invasion of ancient trusts. This in turn provided a necessary realignment of endowments to encourage greater educational flexibility in their employment and for the removal of burdensome subscription to the Thirty-nine Articles of the established church. Dissenters and Jews were freer to enter (with some carry-over of former prejudices), and eventually the Roman Catholic hierarchy removed its own ban on universities that one of its members, the convert John Henry Newman, regarded as seductive and dangerous to the truer faith. Celibacy was eliminated as a requirement for holding college fellowships (most professorships and headships were free of such restrictions), allowing for the growth of a professional academic class (Rothblatt, 1968).

The movement to repair the inherited deficiencies of endowed secondary schools in England occurred early enough in the 19th century to guarantee that Oxford and Cambridge would have their pick of the available qualified cohorts. By sending their own graduates back into those schools as teachers and headmasters, the ancient universities cemented their connections to a system of high-quality feeder schools. The closeness of those ties remains a subject of widespread discussion in our own age of 'diversity' politics. That Oxford today is even more openly meritocratic is not arguable (Soares, 1999). But as in the United States, and as predicted by Michael Young in his celebrated satire mentioned elsewhere in these pages, in societies where life chances are already maldistributed merit-based admissions create problems of their own, which continue to baffle American and British élite universities struggling to compensate for difficulties arising from social and familial causes well beyond their control (Lemann, 1999; *Diversity Prospectus*, 2002; Guhr, 2002).

In summary—by all comparative measurements of scholarship, science, research and dedication to instruction—Oxford, since about 1870 or 1880, became a far more important national and international centre than it had ever been, wider in its social reach and more closely connected to the numerous activities and energies of an advanced industrial or high tech economy. That legacy has been successfully bequeathed to the present century. However, multiple involvements on the current scale inevitably create massive funding and organisational problems, leading to frequent mission reassessments and discussions of educational priorities. The viability of an expensive and famous collegiate system and the relation of college to university are constantly under review. External political intervention contributes to an air of crisis and uncertainty, leading to discussions of institutional autonomy and academic freedom. Yet apart from the collegiate aspects, these issues are common to all of today's public sector research universities. If the past of élite institutions is any guide to the future, the historian might suggest that their chances of weathering crises should never be underestimated.

II. School, college and curricula

Four of the seven personalities selected for this volume were born in the 19th century when Oxford's inherited role as an élite preparation institution was particularly strong. T. H. Green, Michael Sadler, H. A. L. Fisher and Sir Cyril Norwood were all late Victorians by birth, educated in an Oxford that was transformed in the second half of that century, from a university that recruited mainly from landed and clerical society to one more responsive to professional norms. Although very different one from the other, many of the educational experiences of the seven are in several respects broadly similar. Intra-family connections form an important part of their story. Only one of the seven, A. H. Halsey, followed a completely different path into Oxford. He is unique and remarkable, as George and Teresa Smith so well explain, but his own special kind of success may well be a hint of Oxford's different élite situation as we move into the 21st century.

Six of the seven were undergraduates at Oxford and stayed on, or returned after spending time outside academia. Most had been to Clarendon or 'minor' independent schools. Sadler came to Trinity College from Rugby, as did Green, who spent his life in Balliol as undergraduate and fellow. The Rugby that its great headmaster, Dr Thomas Arnold, had earlier reformed became a quintessential source of Victorian rectitude, sending graduates into the world to perform acts of virtue and altruism. Norwood went to St John's College from Merchant Taylor's. H. A. L. Fisher advanced from Winchester to New College. Alan Bullock was at Bradford Grammar School, a well-established northern school with a good track record at Oxford. He then entered Wadham. Anthony Crosland was admitted to Trinity College, having come there from Highgate School. Halsey was a grammar school boy at Kettering, an example of the type of excellent pupil of working-class origins for whom the Education Act of 1902 provided free places (scholarships). His destination afterwards was Westminster College followed by the London School of Economics, just as he desired. While Sadler may have been a major figure in establishing comparative educational research as a university field of inquiry, Halsey is the only one in the group to have prepared himself as a specialist in education and social mobility by studying sociology and acquiring the skills of social survey research. Green, Fisher and Sadler read Literae Humaniores, popularly 'Greats', a mix of classics, philosophy and history. Bullock did that and also Modern History. Political history in particular was the new training ground for statesmen (Collini *et al.*, 1983; Soffer, 1994). Crosland entered Oxford to study Greats but shifted to Philosophy, Political Science and Economics or 'Modern Greats', a more social science curriculum that seems, from Maurice Kogan's account, to have served him well in his political career.

'Greats', classics generally or modern political history—the liberal arts, shall we say?—were praised as precisely the kind of education that produced leaders, administrators and proconsuls, or what H. G. Wells, in *A modern utopia*, called 'samurai', an Edwardian version of Plato's guardian class. The person of liberal learning, the generalist (to beg use of the word), was supremely able to rule empires precisely because he was not a specialist. The best preparation for a position of leadership, it once was said, was an education broad enough to encourage large views and a solid understanding of men and manners. All other subjects were narrow and servile, useful for technicians but hardly a manual for comprehending human nature. The apparent justification for such attitudes lay in the plethora of graduates who read the requisite subjects and moved forward into leadership positions in church, state and empire. Our line-up of the personalities of yesteryear seems to fit the pattern. If Halsey himself did not read Greats but the once suspect social science—well, the exception never truly disproves the rule. In any case, who would dare omit a man of such enviable cultivation from any pantheon of Oxford worthies?

For a dozen reasons, I am hugely partial to whatever can be scraped together today to fit some creaky historical definition of a liberal education, but the test of the Greats hypothesis is not in the examples provided here but in the substantial list of Honours Schools recipients who read the classical, historical and philosophical subjects and never made any mark on society whatsoever. Furthermore, it was the Victorian historian and India civil servant, Thomas Babington Macaulay, who once made the apt point that there is no perfect subject for preparing statesmen. (His famous 'Minute' argued for the use of English as the official language of British India.) Every society, he said in discussing the importance of examinations, decides which subjects are relevant to some purpose. It could be Latin, it could be English, but it could also be the Cherokee. And whoever translated the Cherokee best, or turned the best phrases in it, or wrote sonnets of supreme beauty in that tongue took the laurels. If undergraduates are told that they need Greats in order to enter the civil service and achieve distinction, or that ecclesiastical preferment is impossible without it, or that a fellowship in the Royal College of Physicians depends upon Greek, then they will study those subjects. Make it economics, business administration or chemistry, and the results are similar. And if such destinations are held out to them when at school, they will surely prepare themselves for the apotheosis to come. If they can't wing it, that is the end of the story. So it was in the traditions inherited from Victorian and Edwardian Britain. Ambitious students studied the subjects that were said to provide career advantages, gain entrance to a relatively close circle of influential people and allow them in turn to assume positions of wide responsibility.

Attendance at an independent or famous grammar school and an Oxford background notwithstanding, the biographical or prosopographical approach does not reveal common personality traits among the seven. We cannot expect that in any case. The variations in human temperament are far too great and volatile for anything so simplistic. But neither are shared characterological traits particularly discernible. No matter what they read, or what type of secondary education they underwent, the biographies of the seven are highly individual. I mention 'character' as distinguished from personality because for centuries one definition of an élite university was its character-forming or modelling capability. The pursuit of this objective required residence at the institution so that the distractions of home and community did not interfere with the socialisation process. The dons stood *in loco parentis* to students and exercised the authority expected of a parent. Yet perhaps it is better to introduce a nuance and merely say that residence establishes the conditions under which students and teachers are able to influence one another. In the Anglo-American traditions of university and collegiate education, residence is also expected to create the loyalties that result in well-established alumni networks.

By contrast, higher education institutions where residence is not featured lack the means to systematically influence young lives through intense daily interactions and hence cannot transform undergraduates into some semblance of a common type. Students come and go. Their universities recede in recollection as the years pass.

Time is not available for the cultivation of close relationships. Part-time commuting students, in particular, are not realistically expected single-mindedly to devote their attention to the formation of university-centred communities. Often working during the day, such students frequently lack stamina for their evening classes. But residence is costly and to insist upon it weakens a commitment to educational opportunity. Americans, struggling to pay heed to a democratic and populist inheritance, once dismissed the importance of place and its expensive correlates. It was enough, said the 19th-century advocates of the Log Cabin theory of learning, to think of education as a seesaw, a student at one end of the plank and a distinguished educator at the other.

III. The importance of place

Crucial to any conception of undergraduate élite education, residence in and of itself is necessary but not sufficient. Another step needs to be taken to complete the story of how institutions influence their members. If character formation is an essential element in the élite theory of education, the shaping of the learning environment is equally required. Oxford and Cambridge, through historical evolution, established the model that was subsequently developed into the American tradition of campus planning, elaborated first in the late 18th century. An attractive physical environment systematically moulded to careful ideals of place conveys a sense of personal privilege, enhancing the communication implicit in the residential idea. Frank Lloyd Wright, I have heard, once opined that a liberal education could only happen in liberal buildings. Newman spoke about the importance of 'place' in forming character, attitudes and values. A French interpreter of Newman turned his word 'place' into *milieu*, and that is surely correct. In the Romantic era in both England and America, the physical environment of a university—its buildings and gardens, their styles and the iconography and symbolism associated with places—were possibly as important in forming undergraduate sensibilities as the instruction received in classrooms. That is probably why Newman, who grew up in the Romantic period, concluded that a university was alive (Rothblatt, 1997, chapter 2). One sociologist has used the term 'totemic' to describe styles and spaces that encourage the development of a corporate spirit, or the formation of institutional 'clans'. It follows that the wrong kind of spatial treatments and the absence of institutional reminders of advantages disturb the expected outcomes (Abbot, 1971, pp. 104–105).

In the 19th century and thereafter the arrangement of territory to enhance learning became a major architectural activity in the United States, aided by plentiful land, a certain distrust of the city as a competitor for student attention, and the need for private colleges and universities to secure the devotion of alumni. Until the 20th century, the 'campus' could be considered a correlate of coming of age, appealing to undergraduates in their most impressionable years as they made the transition to adulthood. The contrast with the continent could not be greater, since across the Channel the mere fact of entering a university was an emblem of maturity, while in the English-speaking world attendance was a prolonged and closely supervised rite of passage.

How influential would Oxford have been if its handsome buildings, gardens, chapels and dreaming spires had been incapable of casting a spell? Yet we need to emphasise that the campus was created for undergraduates as part of an historical inheritance of liberal education. Most Anglo-American novels are also written about the youngest members of universities whose life destinations are assumed to be as yet undecided. The character-shaping formula operates differently for professional and research activities where careers are in the making and specialised competence is the aim. High-level intellectual and scientific work does not appear to depend upon the historic aestheticism of the campus idea. On the continent, the typical university environment has been coterminous with the city. The continental, as opposed to the generic Anglo-American university, has not been a self-contained campus, often sharply demarcated from circumjacent activities, but a collection of buildings, scattered throughout the urban fabric, often indistinguishable from banks or offices. Urban life provides its own distinct codes and values.

The campus planning model is now popular in countries where it has a weak history. In Sweden, for example, considerable effort has gone into making new regional universities attractive on the rationale that students from non-traditional homes should be given the same advantages of milieu possessed by privileged institutions such as Uppsala. For similar reasons, New York City educators wanted some of its municipal colleges to appear welcoming to the children of immigrants and made use of the neoclassical form with its long-standing symbolism of American civic virtue. Furthermore, use of the campus model by high-technology industries situated in suburbs also suggests a desire to appropriate some of its physical and symbolic benefits.

IV. Self-confidence

How often are we able to prove outright that the élite model of residence and learning is the decisive variable in creating the particular attitudes and viewpoints later converted into public policy recommendations? Kogan raises the necessary qualification in writing about Anthony Crosland. To what extent, or in what ways, he asks, were Crosland's unique views on education derived from his experiences at Oxford? Kogan goes on to observe that the undeniably impressive list of graduates who became civil servants and ministers of education 'includes such variations in ability, style and ideology' that a common 'Oxford factor' is impossible to identify, except perhaps for one trait, namely self-confidence, although the reader cannot be perfectly certain even there.

Yet the observation is worth exploring. Reading through the accounts of the luminaries, I would agree that self-confidence is one of the defining attributes of residence at an élite university. Simply getting in is a step in the direction of confidence building. Staying the course and obtaining an exemplary degree can hardly damage *amour-propre*.

Self-confidence has a long and interesting educational history, bound up with conceptions of a 'gentleman' inherited from ancient Greek and later Renaissance

Italian sources. While not restricted to English-speaking countries, the *beau idéal* of a gentleman, fascinatingly elaborated by Newman in *The idea of a university*, is especially English but also American. It has been largely overthrown for different but related reasons on both sides of the Atlantic. In England an ideal once theoretically meant to be universal, applicable to anyone with the requisite education, came to be closely associated with birth, class and exclusion. Instead of being universal, the ideal was more or less restricted to those who, by upbringing or means, were qualified to become gentlemen. In the USA class-specific dimensions were never irrelevant, but merit became a larger factor in the 1920s and 1930s owing to the earlier expansion of secondary education opportunities. Brand-name colleges and universities benefited from the changes that increased their pool of better-prepared students and made entry more competitive and selective. This led to the curious conclusion that an outstanding university was measured by the percentage of candidates it could exclude. Yet for A. Lawrence Lowell, the president of Harvard (and a man who scarcely concealed his anti-semitic prejudices), the rub was that the children of Jewish immigrants—more of them from the poorer Eastern European backgrounds—were proving to be outstanding candidates for merit-based admissions (Keller & Keller, 2001, pp. 46–48).

An interesting slant on self-confidence and the gentlemanly tradition is found in the history of the civil service in Edwardian Britain. The graduates of Scottish universities were said to be lacking in the poise and style of English candidates. They certainly performed as well on written examinations, but faltered during the interviews (Anderson, 1983, p. 327). If such results were frequent enough to solicit comment, one conclusion is that self-confidence may also be the result of other factors—prior schooling, for example, a stress on verbal communication, upbringing, or national and class cultures. By 1900, the Scottish universities had become more elitist and selective than earlier, conforming more to the English pattern of higher education, but the independent boarding schools, old or new versions, from which Edwardian Oxbridge heavily recruited undergraduates were a barely visible segment of Scotland's educational fabric. And the independent schools were also intended to be confidence-building institutions (whether or not they actually were). One innovation in this regard was a greater emphasis in them in the late 18th century on public speaking and debating, a foretaste of the famous Unions that would soon after become a conspicuous part of Oxford and Cambridge student history. Debating provided the style and address required for a political or administrative role. We cannot dismiss the possibility that instilling the kind of self-confidence required of public life was as much a product of school as of university, or even a product originating in the home—a theme that has always intrigued Halsey, who has often remarked upon the anthropology of dining in the kitchen.

However, there is also a sense in which attendance at an élite institution can shake one's confidence. Élite institutions increase the stakes for success: by heightening competition they make fine distinctions between abilities. No matter how successful in one's studies, or in one's career, disappointments are possible. Kogan perceptively makes this point. Crosland was 'ahead of [Roy] Jenkins at Oxford but was yet unsuccessful in the race for the Chancellorship of the Exchequer'.

V. Centre and periphery

The theme that self-confidence in general is a gift that élite institutions are customarily capable of bestowing upon their junior or senior members deserves to be developed further. In an essay first published in 1961, the American sociologist, Edward Shils, argued that élite institutions even at their most parochial and inward-looking have a special capacity to inspire their members with the self-assurance of being at the right place. He drew a distinction between centres and peripheries in intellectual life at just about the same time that he himself was moving between various centres, spending half the year at the University of Chicago on the Committee on Social Thought, which he helped found, and the other half at Cambridge. I have thought often of him since first we met at King's College Cambridge in 1961 when I was a research student and he a fellow, brought there to establish sociology. It was also whispered that he moved in circles that the Cambridge novelist of the day, C. P. Snow, called the 'corridors of power'. He was said to be the *eminence grise* behind *Encounter*, then in its heyday at the height of the Cold War. The magazine had a certain prominence, sponsored by an organisation that gave Paris, certainly another centre, as its address, and was widely reported as receiving financial support from the Central Intelligence Agency.

In a series of essays exploring the 'location' of intellectuals in Britain, Shils remarked upon the centrality of academia there as against the peripherality of Americans. He noted that while historically, especially and particularly in the early 20th-century expansion of Washington DC, intellectuals were widely distributed throughout government in various agencies and departments, feelings of marginality persisted in the federal capital itself. Not until Franklin Roosevelt's Administration were these feelings partially dissipated. Yet it was unlikely that a university-based class of humanists and scientists could in the United States experience the particular centrality that an Oxbridge college bestowed upon its members, drawing upon its historic ties to class and class-associated culture (Shils, 1972, chapter 7). Shils had his own version of C. P. Snow's two cultures, or Benjamin Disraeli's two nations. He wrote about the 'persisting traces of the barrier between the two nations within the intellectual class—the nation of London, Cambridge, Oxford, of the higher civil service, of the genteel and sophisticated; and the nation of the provinces, of petit-bourgeois and upper working-class origin, of bourgeois environment, studious, diligent, and specialized' (Shils, 1972, p. 150). We have a touch of that in H. A. L. Fisher's discomfort with the local manufacturers with whom he dealt when vice-chancellor at Sheffield. Shils sardonically remarked upon the self-satisfaction that resulted when an outsider became an insider. He mentioned the instance of 'a brilliant young university lecturer' coming of age in a privileged ecology and learning the codes and styles. Whereas once he could not 'tell grape juice from wine except by the after-effects', he could now 'tell the difference between the wines produced on two neighboring California hillsides' (Shils, 1972, p.150). We can wonder whether Shils could write so confidently (or enviously) about the centrality of Oxford and Cambridge after the Thatcher Revolution and the disappearance of the sometime friendly University Grants Committee—which was, however, showing its teeth in its final days.

For an intellectual (if so uncertain and contentious a term may be used) being at the centre is to be in touch with the sacred, with the preeminent values of a culture which Shils described as 'irreducible'. Those at the centre feel particularly responsible for safeguarding a treasury of core values. In accepting a position at the centre, an oath of fidelity is taken to a fundamental obligation. A centre can be perceived as a gathering point for mutually reinforcing ideas, and therefore as requiring a certain density—of culture, resources, and audiences—of the kind typically found in a city.[1]

Like such cities, universities are dense places for the intersection of ideas. However, they have not always been centres of advanced or cutting-edge thought. As we move through the long history of universities we can identify periods in which some of them are preeminent and others rather dormant. Various factors account for the flatter periods, particularly the brutal destruction of universities and their traditions by totalitarian regimes. Yet for the past 100 years the élite universities of Britain and the United States have managed to retain their reputations, as judged by peer review and alumni support, and have proved adept in attracting the students and scholars essential to their continuity. And increasingly they are in fact judged as centres of innovation and synergies, which have not always been the measures of success in the past. They are also centres of activities normally associated with other venues, being connected with political and economic elites, literary coteries, museums and galleries.

But a centre cannot be defined purely in terms of geographical position. Centrality is also a mental construct, an emotional location, as it were, an inscription of how and where one regards oneself. One can be at a place considered to be significant and instrumental and still feel out of sorts and unconnected to the wider zones of influences and activities organic to the centre. One may be at the centre but feel ostracised to a periphery. Shils' intellectuals who were based in Washington nevertheless thought of themselves as outside the Beltway. Cyril Norwood, as Gary McCulloch tells the tale, was at a centre but retained a sense of being outside because he was of the wrong class. He was also embarrassed by his father, an unsuccessful schoolmaster who had difficulties making a living and drifted into drink. Norwood's sense of being an outsider and unaccepted was sharpened by his experience at Harrow when he was headmaster there.

Erich Fromm singled out members of the lower middle classes as occupying a particularly vulnerable social location. They aspired to the self-assurance of the more successful middle classes but felt alarmingly close to the world of blue-collar workers, but without their solid communal traditions. The absence of cooperative institutions caused or exacerbated feelings of distance and isolation. Fromm's analysis may have some relevance for Norwood. He was an insider who was in effect an outsider. Yet variables such as social class origins are not always pertinent. Halsey, whose concern with the social problems of educational mobility is obviously connected to his working-class upbringing, has never professed to feeling marginal at any point in my long association with him.

Still, if location at a centre does not always provide the self-assurance of being in touch with the sacred parts of a culture, the converse is also true. Being part of the periphery may still allow for a sense of communication with the cultural mainstream.

Is that sense even stronger and more likely today when electronic communication and jet aircraft facilitate the creation of networks well outside one's home institution? Tony Becher's interviews with academics in Britain and America reveal the extra-institutional alignments of scholars and scientists whose closest associates and friends are not necessarily their immediate colleagues (Becher, 1989). Established academics are today taking positions in less prestigious but upwardly bound institutions because the remuneration may be enticing and because in the age of instant communications they are not out of touch, not necessarily any longer on the periphery. David Lodge's whiz-bang protagonist, Maurice Zapp, goes transatlantic from Berkeley, a US centre, to Birmingham in the UK in *Changing places* and finds that his new stodgy academic residence nevertheless provides him with easy airline connections to Paris and a local power base in his friendship with the Vice Chancellor. I am not suggesting that the distinction between centre and periphery has wholly evaporated or that it will—only that the circumstances historically separating them may be undergoing subtle revisions because of technology.

We must also allow for the fact that in certain nations, or at certain times in the history of a nation, there may be more than one centre. The centre for mid-Victorian England was the London-Oxford-Cambridge triangle. Shils was thinking of that configuration when he wrote. But in 1850 or 1860 there was also a second centre, a second source of cultural and intellectual influence in the midlands and the north from which George Eliot and Herbert Spencer drew their inspiration. And would the Scots of the time be happy if we described the centres as always lying south of the Tweed? It is difficult to identify a centre in the vast United States. With a few notable exceptions, the brand-name universities are on the east and west coasts. Washington DC is a latecomer to the world of centres, having been a relatively somnolent place before the enormous concentration of resources occurring during the New Deal of the 1930s. While there are excellent thinkers and academics in the universities and in the numerous think-tanks in the Washington area, no Capitol-based university enjoys the overall esteem of the major research universities elsewhere in America.

VI. Size

The size of an institution can be a factor in its capacity to stimulate an attitude of public service, although size is also a function of how a university is internally constituted. Smaller-scale units have the advantage of concentrating resources on discrete objectives. The London School of Economics and Political Science, a 20th-century *grande école*, long possessed such an advantage. Nevertheless, identifying mission objectives can be a drawn-out process. Debates occurred at the LSE over whether the institutional bias was to be in favour of social engineering or scholarship, social amelioration or contributions to the relevant republics of learning. Given the origins of the School and the leading role played by Fabian socialists, ideological issues were also continuous (Dahrendorf, 1995, 4, 20, 367–368). Halsey inherited both parts of the competing missions and drew no sharp distinction between them as he moved between Barnett House in Wellington Square and Nuffield College, uniting applied research and the training of social workers with core scholarship.

Presumably a collegiate university structure such as Oxford's, once common to many European universities, possesses advantages of size for the shaping of particular views. Colleges were, or are usually, small enough to facilitate the close fellowship necessary to guarantee a certain flow of influences. (But the history of some of the smaller colleges also reveals the degree to which a fellowship can be paralysed by quarrels and personality conflicts.) The collegiate structure allows separate or subordinate units to orient themselves to particular missions without engaging the entire university. It can and has been reinterpreted to include postgraduate institutions like Nuffield, almost a mini-LSE. Although colleges go back well into the medieval period, historians speak about the 'rise of the collegiate university' in England in the 16th century because it was then that monarchs, wishing to safeguard the as yet vulnerable Anglican identity of the established church, poured resources into colleges to make them reliable guardians of a new religious inheritance. Tutorial teaching deepened and strengthened the personal ties.

Although not commonly spoken of as a multiversity, as defined by Clark Kerr in his famous Godkin Lectures given at Harvard in 1963, a collegiate university system fits that definition in certain respects. Multiversities are composed of innumerable separate interior units with their own administration, lines of exterior communication, funding and core values (Kerr, 1963). In recent decades some of Oxford's sub-units, the laboratories and research units in particular, have risen in importance. Accompanying the change is a shift towards more postgraduate instruction, central governance and applied science and social science. Halsey and Martin Trow noticed this trend as early as the 1960s. Nearly half of the academics in their surveys were in natural or social science-based technology (Halsey & Trow, 1971, p. 157). In the view of several informed observers, the non-collegiate units are becoming stronger and more significant, and the colleges thereby weaker (Tapper & Salter, 1992, pp. 171–172). The implications of these changes for the issues of character formation and the inculcation of particular values of social commitment are anyone's guess.

I have no firm conclusions as to the optimal size required for the transmission of special educational influences, except to state the obvious. Unless greatly partitioned internally into smaller, quasi-independent satellite organisations, mass higher education institutions lack the means to create the type of personal bonds intrinsic to tutorial-based instruction. It is not merely the likelihood that ideas are best taught in this way (which I believe), but that the creation of relationships as much as the acquisition of knowledge is the key to the transmission of values. It is the open secret of Oxford's success. We can also see this occurring within the sometime German or *soi-disant* Humboldtian tradition of discipleship. Advanced students met in the library or laboratory of the chairholder, surrounded by the symbols of his intellectual eminence and authority. In this example, aimed not at a role in public life but in the maintenance of disciplines, the institution is less important than the professor. The conditions of authoritarian Germany ruled out any active political role for graduates in any case and certainly forbade any role that involved criticism of government. It is hard to imagine policy-making that does not in some sense, however mitigated, require re-assessment of existing social programmes.

Studies of Victorian and Edwardian Oxbridge indicate the primary importance of colleges as gathering places for the exchange of ideas (Rothblatt, 1968, chapter 7). In the 1830s Oriel College had a circle of 'Noetics' that included Thomas Arnold, and their liberal ideas frightened Newman, then a fellow of the College, into opposition. King's College Cambridge developed a reputation as an aesthetic incubator for artists and writers and along with neighbouring Trinity College helped create the literary coterie known as Bloomsbury—a label from the district in London where many of its members lived. In the present volume Balliol figures greatly, but then again, Balliol always does. It is one of the best examples of how an élite college with the right leadership can produce an environment conducive to public work, but the formula is hardly foolproof. Most Oxbridge colleges, I suspect, never achieved the intensity of late Victorian Balliol, although for physics, Trinity College Cambridge could not be improved upon. T. H. Green was a great and unusually influential figure in the Balliol that Benjamin Jowett oriented towards public service. Green, combining native British sources of thought with German idealism, infused Jowett's ethic of public commitment with a philosophic justification. He was extraordinarily successful in inspiring the generations that came after his early death, but he also functioned within an established system with clear-cut objectives with which he was in accord. When many decades earlier Newman tried to alter the way in which tutorial classes were taught at Oriel College in an attempt to advance certain pastoral views about education, he was ruled out of order by the Provost and roundly defeated.

Jowett himself, we learn, was uneasy about Green's approach, preferring a less abstract treatment of the subject of public activity. Other and different Oxford loci were also important, corresponding more closely to structures such as salons, intellectual drawing rooms or atheneums. Participation in this kind of activity can happen almost anywhere, customarily in metropolitan communities. Michael Sadler, impressed by the lectures of John Ruskin and Arnold Toynbee, was nevertheless more influenced by the circle that met in North Oxford at the home of Arthur Acland, who was educated at Rugby and Christ Church. The close and immediate environment of an 'Inner Ring' led Sadler into the University Extra-mural movement which had actually begun at Cambridge. Acland enjoyed a career in parliament and government.

VII. Multiple influences

Our biographies indicate that many other influences have acted upon Oxonians, or other participants in the life of élite universities. It is not possible, as Kogan observes, to precisely calibrate Oxford's independent intellectual or emotional contribution to the making of public men and women. It cannot be said—it can hardly ever be said—that the Oxfords of this world were the sole influences acting upon their members. Did Halsey receive his profound dedication to public morality, to sociology as the instrument of social policy and to Aristotle's notion of a life of virtue from Oxford?

The answer appears to be that he brought much more to Oxford than Oxford gave to him.

The origins and influences on him are well-detailed in his autobiography with its title taken from John Bunyan, *No discouragement*, and in his history of the English social moralists written with Norman Dennis. Christian socialism—traceable in a sense to Sir Thomas More in the 16th century, but more immediately to the great Victorians—and the LSE (where sociology was taught before it was taken seriously at either Oxford or Cambridge) both had much more influence upon Halsey than Oxford itself. Doubtless, Nuffield College, as the first graduate social science college in the University, was a suitable place for someone with his social and educational interests. And the Smiths state openly that Halsey's decision to accept an appointment at Oxford was related to his appreciation, or his hope, that an historic university, with innumerable associations to the great and the good, would facilitate his own efforts to improve the understanding of social mobility in Britain, giving him the ear of those in high places. For some decades this was indeed the case.

We can elaborate the multiple influences acting upon the formation of an ideology of service by turning to Noël Annan's famous essay on the formation of an intellectual 'aristocracy' or class in Britain, unique or possibly not unique in the longevity of the class and the propensity of its members to intermarry (Annan, 1999). Cambridge University has a dominant role in that 19th-century story. But so does Oxford. Annan's intellectual aristocracy began its mental and emotional journey in the evangelical movement of the pre-Victorian era—in low church, Quaker and dissenting families, some landed, others in business or in church or chapel. These origins account for several of the salient characteristics of the Victorian intelligentsia: reformist, earnest, moral instead of aesthetic, and establishment-minded rather than *déraciné* (as we might expect of continental intellectuals). One might venture to say that social origins not withstanding, Halsey's own Christian socialist spirit owes something to this Victorian heritage, and so do the Balliol connections—with R. H. Tawney as the outstanding representative (and Halsey sometimes referred to as Tawney's intellectual successor). Education was a foremost concern of the Victorian intellectual aristocracy. Many of its members were schoolmasters, dons, heads of colleges, prominent clergy or, like Matthew Arnold, civil servants in the government's department of education. Adult education was an interest and extended to the Workers Educational Association. H. A. L. Fisher was thoroughly a product of the intellectual aristocracy. Oxford, we read in his autobiography, was his 'destiny from the first'. His father and grandfather had both been fellows of Oxford colleges. His sisters married into other branches of the Victorian intellectual aristocracy. Bloomsbury contained his cousins, and his mother's family was related to William Gladstone. Green was the grandson of the Vaughans, another of the family branches, and grew up in an evangelical environment.

The necessary connections were all there for a reasonably clever young man. There were reasonably clever young men (and women) everywhere in the UK, but without these extraordinary family advantages and endowed school connections. In 1866 Jowett complained that Oxford was attracting only a small percentage of the kingdom's talent. Another Oxford eminence, Mark Pattison, the Rector of Lincoln College, agreed with him (Annan, 1999, p. 28).

Independent schools, resurrected grammar schools and Oxbridge colleges firmed up the networks of the children of the evangelicals who, through marriages within their religious communities, created the large cousinhood whose names can be found everywhere in British life well into and through the past century. Over time, for most of the descendants of the Victorian intelligentsia, religious commitments softened or became secularised. When religion is removed from morality, said Matthew Arnold, the result is the metonym 'culture' or, for some of the heirs, 'high culture'. For the others, what had once been a tradition of service suffused with a sense of religious obligation became a secular tradition of social engineering.

Fisher's personal history illustrates another factor in our pursuit of the structures and means at the disposal of élite universities for producing a reformist or public service ethic: the importance of self-selection. Thus far we have mostly named personalities who chose to attend Oxford, were steered there by family, friends and school, or accepted an invitation to join the community of dons. When this occurs, universities can reasonably be confident that most of whom they admit are willing to more or less adopt the institution's dominant values. But there are also those who pass through élite institutions without ever absorbing very much of its presumed dominant ethos. An occasional *enfant terrible* actually takes up arms against the institution. Fortunately for élite institutions, not every potential undergraduate or postgraduate aspires to enter them. Were it so, élite colleges and universities would be hard put to maintain their legitimacy, or their standards in the face of charges of wilful exclusion. Those charges are certainly being made today even as Oxford colleges make far greater efforts to recruit more widely than in Jowett's day. For élite institutions to maintain their reputation and position within democratic polities, numerous other types of higher education institutions need to provide alternatives and choices. The existence of so many different types of higher education institutions makes the educational task of élite universities much easier. Their students do not require remedial instruction nor do they need to be taught how to study.

Arguably, self-selection for Oxford was probably truer of the past than of today. Before the new system of admissions was introduced not too long ago, allowing colleges to group together to make choices, self-selection was in a sense more fine-tuned. Further back in the past, the networks of recruitment were likely to be clearer and more certain. Prospective matriculants applied to individual colleges knowing something of their particular style and inclinations. Some decades ago—I have in mind Alan Bennett's recent West End hit, *The History Boys*, about a northern England grammar school with a poor record in sending candidates forward into the ancient universities—Oxford and Cambridge were simply considered by many to be inaccessible. But headmasters of the leading secondary schools knew how to prime their best students for entrance to the colleges.

It is entirely possible that at certain moments the influences and tone of Oxford have been greater than at others, both because the student body was more homogeneous than later—I would not, however, overdo this likelihood—and because Oxford was less of a multiversity despite its collegiate structure, less fragmented educationally or culturally than now, with less of a commitment to postgraduate students. The college ethos was primary. Oxford was smaller in overall size, not yet fully devoted to a research mission and still dominated by Victorian assumptions about duty and responsibility. Scepticism and relativism, while present and especially noticeable in *avant-garde* movements, had not yet assumed the levels apparent a century later. Dons were shapers of character. Prior socialisation through family and school—I think of the Etonians who monopolised entrance to King's College Cambridge for much of the 19th century—meant that newcomers had older friends in college and already knew what to expect. Current efforts to widen selection, to include non-traditional groups, means that some undergraduates are essentially unacquainted with the anthropology of the place, its tribal totems and taboos. The Oxford Access Scheme and its publications are a fair indication of the hesitations and uncertainties of students from non-traditional families who need to be reassured that Oxford indeed welcomes them. New university support centres are appearing in élite universities where such special arrangements had never before been deemed necessary.

In sum, the American experience is happening elsewhere. American colleges and universities, anticipating or experiencing the effects of mass-access higher education, created counselling and advising centres, especially after 1945 when the federal government encouraged their formation in order to protect its investment in the large numbers of veterans attending universities under servicemen's entitlement schemes.

VIII. Useful questions?

I have explored several structural and historical factors that account for the possible influence that a particular institution exercises over its junior and senior members. I have tried to provide some understanding of the sources of that influence and how they are transmitted. I have also stressed that historical conditions account in part for Oxford's outside influence, and that we have entered a century where altered conditions may well affect what had been past expectations. I will now also add that notwithstanding those expectations, the vast majority of Oxford students took their degrees—when it was seen as necessary to complete Schools to have a good career—and subsequently disappeared, more or less, from history. Similarly, the vast majority of Oxford dons have not been contributors to social policy, do not choose that path and are, as academics elsewhere, primarily occupied with professional careers. Furthermore, academic styles and models change. The dons of one age do not necessarily share the aims of another. Most of the seven personalities studied in this volume came of age when Oxford fellows retained a Victorian commitment to the old liberal educational ideal of character formation, and all of them attended institutions where messages about social amelioration or improvement were conspicuously available. Can the same be said of the present?

I have been at some trouble to explain how unpredictable are the flow of educational influences into specific arenas of public life, and yet I must now admit that I still believe that élite colleges and universities are better able, or more likely, to place their members into significant public activity than the non-élites. They are adept at using heritage to fashion alumni loyalty. The famous institutions have a saga to tell, as Burton R. Clark has shown in his fascinating studies of the American liberal arts college (Clark, 1992), and that saga remains part of the educational gift that graduates acquire when they leave. Whether it is always expressed and how it is absorbed remains a question for study. But we also know very little about the lives of the graduates of non-élite institutions. Books are not written about them. If they compose memoirs and autobiographies, historians do not commonly mine them as they do the biographies of the known achievers. Few scholars sing their praises, or the praises of their institutions. The subway colleges of New York City—important to that city and as avenues of ascent for the descendants of Jewish immigrants—have as great a legacy as almost any other type of higher education institution, yet historians are usually attracted to their more glamorous cousins.

Clio rarely supplies concrete solutions to difficult problems, but the goddess does enjoy whiling away the time by asking questions, some of which are even occasionally useful.

Note

1. The Swedish geographers Torsten Hägerstrand and Gunnar Törnqvist have developed theories about centrality using the expression 'creative milieux', gathering points for mutually-reinforcing ideas. One essential requirement is a certain density, which usually means a city of culture, resources and audiences. Adding to the discussion, another scholar has classified creative urban milieux by their dominance at various historical moments. One drawback is a certain instability and impermanence. These centres retain their intellectual and cultural supremacy for only limited periods, succeeded in time by other successful gathering points (Hall, 1999, pp. 18-19).
   The notion of creative milieux as developed by Swedish professors has been adopted by the curators of the newly-established Nobel Museum in Gamla Stan, Stockholm. One display depicts the concentration of twentieth-century scientists in environments where work of Nobel Prize quality was likely. Michael Frayn's play *Copenhagen* captures this quite explicitly as Nils Bohr and Werner Heisenberg, now ghostly shades, recall their exciting days of scientific discovery in Denmark's capital.

Notes on contributor

Sheldon Rothblatt is Professor Emeritus of History at the University of California, Berkeley. He was educated at Berkeley and King's College, Cambridge University and holds an honorary doctorate from Gothenburg University in Sweden. He is a Fellow of the Royal Historical Society, a Member of the National Academy of Education (US) and a Foreign member of the Royal Swedish Academy of Sciences. He has been a Visitor at Nuffield College and has held fellowships from the Guggenheim Foundation, the Social Science Research Council (US) and the American Council of Learned Societies. His specialties are the comparative history of universities and the history of liberal education.

References

Abbot, J. (1971) *Student life in a class society* (Oxford, Toronto and New York, Pergamon Press).
Anderson, R. D. (1983) *Education and opportunity in Victorian Scotland, schools and universities* (Oxford, Clarendon Press).
Annan, N. G. (1999) *The dons, mentors, eccentrics and geniuses* (London, HarperCollins).
Becher, A. (1989) *Academic tribes and territories, intellectual inquiry and the culture of disciplines* (Milton Keynes and Bristol, Society for Research into Higher Education and Open University Press).
Bill, E. G. W. (1973) *University reform in nineteenth-century Oxford, a study of Henry Halford Vaughan, 1811–1885* (Oxford, Clarendon Press).
Brock, M. G. & Curthoys, M. C. (1997 & 2000) *The history of the University of Oxford*, Vol. VII (parts 1 and 2) (Oxford, Clarendon Press).
Carter, I. (1990) *Ancient cultures of conceit, British university fiction in the post-war years* (London and New York, Routledge).
Clark, B. R. (1992) *The distinctive college* (New Brunswick, NJ and London, Transactions Publishers).
Collini, S., Winch, D. & Burrow, J. (1983) *That noble science of politics, a study in nineteenth-century intellectual history* (Cambridge, Cambridge University Press).
Dahrendorf, R. (1995) *LSE, a history of the London School of Economics and Political Science, 1895–1995* (Oxford, Oxford University Press).
Diversity Prospectus, Oxford University (Oxford Access Scheme, 2002).
Guhr, D. J. (2002) *Access to higher education in Germany and California* (Frankfurt am Main, Peter Lang).
Hall, P. (1999) *Cities in civilization* (London, Orion Books).
Halsey, A. H. & Trow, M. (1971) *The British academics* (London, Faber & Faber).
Keller, M. & Keller, P. (2001) *Making Harvard modern, the rise of America's university* (Oxford, Oxford University Press).
Kerr, C. (1963) *The uses of the university* (New York, Harper & Row).
Lemann, N. (1999) *The big test, the secret history of the American meritocracy* (New York, Farrar, Straus & Giroux).
Rothblatt, S. (1968) *The Revolution of the dons. Cambridge and society in the nineteenth century* (London, Faber & Faber/New York, Basic Books).
Rothblatt, S. (1997) *The modern university and its discontents. The fate of Newman's legacies in Britain and America* (Cambridge, Cambridge University Press).
Shils, E. (1972) *The intellectuals and the powers and other essays* (Chicago & London, University of Chicago Press).
Shils, E. (1975) *Center and periphery. Essays in macrosociology* (Chicago & London, University of Chicago Press).
Soares, J. A. (1999) *The decline of privilege, the modernization of Oxford University* (Stanford, Stanford University Press).
Soffer, R. N. (1994) *Discipline and power. The university, history, and the making of an English élite, 1870–1930* (Stanford, Stanford University Press).
Tapper, E. & Salter, B. (1992) *Oxford, Cambridge and the changing idea of a university* (Society for Research into Higher Education and Open University Press).

Oxford and the mandarin culture: the past that is gone

Vernon Bogdanor

I

This compilation charts a vanished era, the era of the Oxford mandarin. Why should Oxford have been the home of the mandarin, and why has the era of the mandarin come to an end? The answers to these questions cast light not only on the changing relationship between Oxford and government, but also upon the evolution of British society and intellectual life in the 20th century.

It was T. H. Green who inaugurated the era of the mandarin in Oxford by giving it a creed. The *Oxford Magazine* of May 1883 noticed in the university the existence of 'a new faith with Professor Green for its founder, Arnold Toynbee, for its martyr and various socialists for its propaganda'.[1] That new faith was the gospel of citizenship.

Green's appeal was directed at those who found it difficult to accept the supernatural, transcendental or miraculous elements of Christianity. He sought to redefine Christianity as an ethical doctrine whose fundamental notions were those of duty and service. By contrast with the utilitarians, Green believed, with Aristotle, that man was essentially a social being, and that the state, far from being a necessary evil, was a means towards achieving the good life. The good life involved active citizenship—the willing acceptance of civic duties and responsibilities. 'True citizenship', Green told his friend, Henry Scott Holland, in 1868, '"as unto the Lord" (which includes all morality) I reckon higher than saintliness in the technical sense'.[2] Reform in this world was more important than saintliness in the next. This was an approach which fitted the spirit of the age. For, as Beatrice Webb had noticed, it was 'during the middle decades of the nineteenth century that, in England, the impulse of self-subordinating service was transferred, consciously and overtly, from God to man'.[3]

The gospel of citizenship was to be preached at all levels of government, from the Imperial to the local. Green's 'new faith' was similar to the municipal gospel of Joseph Chamberlain's Birmingham which 'urged service to the local community as a Christian and municipal duty, the corporation being seen as the contemporary expression in this regard not simply of the general interest of the town and its citizens but as much more, the embodiment of God's will and purpose and a means of giving them practical effect'.[4] Green thought the same. For him, 'civil duty, rightly regarded' was 'nothing less than a spiritual function—the life of citizenship is a mode of divine service'.[5]

> It is no time [Green declared in his *Prolegomena to Ethics*, published posthumously in 1883] to enjoy the pleasures of eye and ear, of search for knowledge, of friendly intercourse, of applauded speech or writing, while the mass of men whom we call our brethren ... are left without the chance, which only the help of others can gain for them, of making themselves in act what in possibility we believe them to be. ... Interest in the problem of social deliverance ... forbids a surrender to enjoyments which are not incidental to the work of deliverance.[6]

What Green offered was, in Ian Bradley's words, a 'call to seriousness'.[7] In his seminal book on Green, *The politics of conscience*, published in 1964, Melvin Richter writes, 'From aristocratic Oxford, which Matthew Arnold could still describe as "whispering from her towers the last enchantments of the Middle Age", there came a stream of serious young men dedicated to reform in politics, social work and the civil service. Many of them were to spend their lives in improving the school system, establishing settlement houses, reorganizing charity and the Poor Law, and working in adult education'.[8] R. G. Collingwood, in his autobiography, traces Green's influence as lasting from 'about 1880 to about 1910'.[9] But in fact Green's influence was felt well beyond 1910. It lasted at least until the 1960s, when a social scientific approach began to be applied to the problems of education. It is not quite dead even now, as the career of A. H. Halsey, perhaps the last disciple of Green, as mediated through Tawney and the English ethical socialist tradition, shows.

Recent research has tended to qualify earlier judgments concerning the far-reaching influence of Green, and to suggest that his impact was far less than had previously been thought.[10] Perhaps, however, the reaction has gone too far. For there can be little doubt that the language of 'self-realisation', 'citizenship' and 'community' greatly affected both popular and intellectual discourse even amongst those such as, for example, Hobhouse and Beveridge who were in no sense Idealists. Green's influence on politicians and civil servants was immense. The future Prime Minister, H. H. Asquith, according to his first biographers, retained, throughout his life, an 'ardent admiration' for him.[11] Indeed, one writer on British government believes that

Asquith, as Prime Minister, remembered all too well Green's message of the common good, of consensus, and found himself, as a result, ill-equipped to deal with movements which were very far from being products of consensus—trade union and suffragette militants, and the intransigent Ulster Unionists. For, on issues involving class conflict or the competing claims of Irish Nationalists and Unionists, it seemed that no common good could be found.[12] Green's philosophy was the philosophy of a homogeneous society. It was well-suited, therefore, to the pre-1914 world of the New Liberals. Its relevance was less clear to those who, influenced by socialist doctrines between the wars, believed that society was riven by class conflict, and that politics was a matter of determining who got what—'Who, Whom' in Lenin's famous phrase. Green's philosophy, therefore, seemed less well-suited to the conflict-ridden world of the inter-war years than to the pre-war era. But it was to have an unexpected renaissance in the 1940s, when community solidarity and citizenship became once again the watchwords; when so it seemed, all were for the common good and none for themselves.

Asquith, of course, was by no means the only undergraduate from Jowett's Oxford to have fallen under the sway of Green's teaching. For Green also influenced, amongst others, the educational reformer, R. B. Haldane, and the young men who undertook social work at Toynbee Hall in East London, men such as William Beveridge, Hubert Llewellyn Smith and R. H. Tawney. Sadler wrote in his diary in 1940, that from Green's *Prolegomena to ethics*, 'I got my religion'.[13] Bernard Allen, in his biography of Robert Morant, testifies to the influence of Green upon that most influential civil servant.[14] Green's influence extends even to the youngest of those celebrated here, A. H. Halsey, the only one of the seven mandarins who is still alive. Halsey indeed felt himself to be consciously working in the footsteps of R. H. Tawney, another Balliol man influenced by Green; as Halsey has noticed, Tawney, although spending much of his working life at the LSE, stayed faithful to the assumptions of Green throughout his life, and in particular the assumption 'that the state could act as a liberal force'.[15] The influence of Green thus survived until late into the 20th century. Halsey noticed it when arriving in Oxford in 1962 to the Department of Social and Administrative Studies, then located in Barnett House. 'Barnett House people', Halsey remarks in his autobiography, *No discouragement* (1996), 'whether or not they read him, were natural descendants of T. H. Green, collectivist rather than individualist in their outlook'.[16] As late as 1987, Roy Hattersley, Deputy Leader of the Labour Party, when asked during the election campaign for the philosophical foundations of his socialism, replied 'T. H. Green'.[17]

Green argued that the traditional liberal view of freedom—'negative' freedom, freedom from restraint, had been too restrictive. Liberals had neglected 'positive' freedom, the freedom to make the most of oneself. From Rousseau and Hegel, Green derived the notion that state action to remove 'obstacles' to self-realisation, ignorance for example, would enhance rather than restrict freedom. For the state to be able to fulfil its functions, however, it needed the support of public-spirited citizens. Thus education, and in particular humanistic education, played a vital role in creating the good society. Green's ideal was, in the words of a German professor, the *Erziehungsstaat*, the 'Educative State'.[18] He may be regarded, as Raymond Plant argues, as an ideological precursor of the comprehensive school. He would have applauded one of the aims of the comprehensive school, to create a common culture and sense of citizenship.

> Common education [he declared in his speech, opening Oxford High School in 1881] is the true social leveler. Men and women who have been at school together or who have been at schools of the same sort, will always understand each other, will always be at their ease together, will be free from social jealousies and animosities, however different their circumstances in life may be.[19]

It is a creed which Crosland or Halsey could have accepted. Education, Green believed, should help to realise the common good; it should seek to unify, not divide. He was, for this reason, hostile to the denominational schools of his day. He would probably have been hostile to the selective system. He would certainly have been hostile to faith schools.[20]

Green's impact came, not so much from his publications, which were prolix and diffuse; and his one substantial work of political thought, *The principles of political obligation*, was published after his death. It came from his lectures and sermons and, perhaps above all, from the force of his example. It was, at bottom, a moral inspiration. 'His existence', declared Edward Caird, 'was one of the things that gave reality to the distinction between good and evil'.[21] It is hard to imagine any Oxford tutor exerting a similar impact today. Tutors today are scholars, not preachers, and would think it illegitimate to seek to influence the ethical or political outlook of their pupils.

Green told his pupils to search for the common good. This common good was exemplified as much in civic society as in the state. Nevertheless, Green believed, like his master, Hegel, that the state could be a civilizing force; and the consensus which he legitimised and helped to create proved to be a collectivist one, although Green himself was far from collectivist in outlook. The new consensus reacted sharply against the Gladstonian ideal of limited government. By the time of Gladstone's death in 1898, Gladstonianism, the doctrine of the limited state, already appeared obsolete, and was under attack from all sides—from the Bismarckian nationalists of the Right—the National Efficiency school—and from the New Liberals of the Left. Green was a 'public moralist', defined by Collini as someone who tended to concentrate 'on failings of character as the chief source of civic as well as private woe'.[22] He was a moralist who believed strongly in the ameliorative effects of education. The teacher, in words used by Jean Floud in the 1960s, would be both a 'missionary in the slums' and a 'crusader in the suburbs'.[23] Of those celebrated in this collection, only Norwood perhaps was an obvious moralist, with his concern, typical of the public school headmasters of his era, for the building of 'character'.[24] All of the mandarins, however, shared Green's belief in the ameliorative effects of education. They were sure that more and better education would lead, not only to greater efficiency, but also to greater justice. They were all public moralists in a deeper sense than that used by Collini, in that they were sure that the expansion of education would transform the character of those who were being educated, rendering them more altruistic and public-spirited, more aware of the demands of the common good.

II

Was it, however, mere coincidence that the seven celebrated in this collection should all have been, at one time or another, Oxford dons? George and Teresa Smith suggest that, for Halsey, and presumably the others discussed in this collection, the Oxford connection was a mere coincidence. There was, they believe, nothing specifically Oxonian about Halsey's contribution, nothing that Oxford gave him that could not have been given by another university.

Oxford was, however, the centre of philosophical Idealism, and it was the vocabulary of Idealism, as mediated for English consumption by Green, which gave those celebrated here the ideology of citizenship, with its characteristic vocabulary of duty and responsibility. That was by no means accidental. The reasons for Green's influence lie deep in the history of Oxford. It is difficult to imagine that influence being as strong in any other university of the time. For:

> Oxford, as early as the thirteenth century, accepted the sovereignty of Aristotle, and the authority of antiquity; it pursued a general and encyclopaedic wisdom, and it discovered the fountain of that wisdom in the past. Cambridge was later in finding a single acknowledged master; but that master, when he came, was one of its own sons, Isaac Newton, and he was a master of deep and ascertained knowledge in the one field of natural philosophy.[25]

In the 19th century, Cambridge came to emphasise mathematics and the natural sciences, while Oxford remained loyal to theology, philosophy and the classics. Cambridge was also a pioneer in the development of the study of economics which was emancipating itself from its philosophical foundations, and had no need for philosophical underpinnings such as would be provided by Idealism. As José Harris has pointed out, 'Of the major social sciences in Britain only economics remained largely wedded to an individualist and positivistic tradition'.[26] Neo-classical economics, as adumbrated by Alfred Marshall, and solidified in the Cambridge economics tripos, created in 1903, was the only genuine social science—perhaps it still is—in the sense of being a discipline with agreed foundations and axioms, whose conclusions were entirely independent of the political stance of the person deriving them. It aspired to the condition, therefore, of mathematics and the natural sciences. Other areas of the study of society, such as sociology, remained tied to philosophy, tending to blend moral philosophy, and sometimes preaching and moralising, with social inquiry. They were to remain somewhat innocent of statistical and quantitative approaches; and, in any case, sociology, studied at the London School of Economics from 1895, the year of its foundation, did not reach Oxford until the 1960s; even then, it was studied only as an optional component of the Politics part of the PPE school, founded in 1923. 'The history of nineteenth-century Oxford', Leslie Stephen believed, 'is the history of its preachers'.[27]

It is perhaps not surprising that Oxford did not develop any equivalent to the Cambridge economics tripos. Green had aspired to produce a theology for an age of religious doubt, a theology with civic uplift. His interest in philosophy, he confessed to his friend Scott Holland, was 'wholly religious'.[28] Thus, when Oxford began to take the study of society seriously, its emphasis came to be philosophical and historical—moralistic—rather than behavioural. The belief at Oxford was that economics and the study of society should be informed by philosophy. Instead of an economics tripos, therefore, Oxford instituted PPE. The culture at Oxford was to remain philosophical and ruminative, while at Cambridge it became scientific and analytical. In Oxford, mathematics and the natural sciences were emphasised much less than philosophy and the classics. The radical Liberal politician, John Morley, was much gratified, in later life, by a conversation with a bishop 'who knows his Aristotle', adding 'I suppose Cambridge men have some other sort of intellectual link'.[29] Norwood, an archetypal Oxford man, devoted three chapters of his book, *The British tradition of education*, published in 1929, to religion, which 'lies at the base of all education', and none to science.[30] For, as Leslie Stephen, a Cambridge man had noticed, 'You cannot appeal to men's souls in the name of the differential calculus'.[31] Idealism, it has been held by one authority, 'was at least partly responsible for the powerful anti-vocational bias that characterized British educational institutions for much of the twentieth century'.[32]

It was the philosophical tradition, and a peculiarly moralistic kind of political theory, which informed Oxford's view of educational problems. That view would have been very different in a university at which the study of empirical sociology and other forms of social science had been dominant; and it was a view which was to become outdated with the rise of the social sciences and the development of a genuine professional expertise in them.

Green had been a philosopher, who aspired perhaps to be a philosopher king. Of the other six discussed in this collection, four—Sadler, Norwood, Bullock and Halsey—were involved in giving advice to government. All were meritocrats, men who had risen through ability, rather than connections or inherited wealth. But, with the exception of Green and Crosland, they rose through patronage. Sadler had worked in the university extension movement with Arthur Acland. When Acland became Vice President of the Committee of Council on Education, a forerunner of the Board of Education, he appointed Sadler Director of the Office of Special Inquiries and Reports. Fisher's name was suggested for the 1912 Commission on the Indian Public Services by the Marquess of Crewe, and he later came to the attention of Lloyd George. Norwood in turn attracted Fisher's eye as a distinguished public school headmaster, 'the most interesting Head Master I have yet met'.[33] Halsey had been a friend of Crosland, and also of Philip Williams, one of Crosland's closest friends who, like Halsey, was a Fellow of Nuffield.

Patronage, Disraeli believed, was 'the outward and visible sign of an inward and spiritual grace, and that is Power'.[34] It depended very much on the whim of ministers. There are two graphic illustrations of how the system worked, in the post-war era, under both Labour and Tory governments. There is no reason to believe that things had been different in earlier times.

Barbara Castle, Health and Social Security Secretary in the 1974–76 Wilson government, tells in her diaries of a dinner in November 1975 with her Health Minister, David Owen, her special advisers, Jack Straw and Brian Abel-Smith, and various leaders of the public service unions.

> Over drinks before the meal, I had casually raised the question of the chairmanship of the Royal Commission on the Health Service. Had they any suggestions? To my surprise, Audrey (Audrey Prime of NALGO) said enthusiastically, 'Yes, Merrison.' [Dr Alexander Merrison, Vice-Chancellor of Bristol University.] David and I were rather taken aback, but as she had served with him on the Merrison Committee [a Committee of Inquiry into the Regulation of the Medical Profession, which had reported in April 1975], she was in a better position than any of us to judge his attitudes to the NHS and the things in which we believe. She was emphatic that he was a dedicated supporter of the NHS and she was sure he would have no truck with private financing and all that nonsense.[35]

David Owen later admitted to Peter Hennessy that he had been 'party' to rigging a Royal Commission. 'I plead guilty', admitting that the Merrison Commission 'was rigged … I would claim that it was done for higher motives. But it was rigged'.[36]

The second exhibit, equally graphic if more artless, comes from the memoirs of Marmaduke Hussey, who was offered the chairmanship of the BBC in 1986.

> On the following Tuesday the telephone rang about 9.30 in the evening. 'Oh, Dukie, it's Douglas Hurd here, with a very odd question to ask you. Would you like to be Chairman of the BBC?' 'Good Lord, no!' I said. 'That's a ridiculous idea. I'm far too old and it's an appalling job anyway'.[37]

But, eventually, Hussey was persuaded to accept it.

From 1994, however, the likelihood of such telephone calls was greatly reduced following the reforms of the Committee on Standards in Public Life, chaired by Lord Nolan. For the Nolan Committee laid down rules for public appointments. In future, such appointments would have to be publicly advertised, and candidates would have to put their names forward for them. One cannot imagine the seven mandarins putting themselves forward in this way. They would, with the exception of Crosland, have regarded it as unseemly self-advertisement.

Two of the seven discussed in this collection—H. A. L. Fisher and Anthony Crosland—became politicians with executive authority, not merely advisers. Fisher, however, was a politician of a rather peculiar sort. He was catapulted, by Lloyd George, from the position of Vice-Chancellor of Sheffield University, into office as President of the Board of Education, in December 1916, when the Lloyd George coalition government was formed. A constituency, Sheffield Hallam, was found for him and he was returned unopposed. In 1918, Fisher removed himself from the popular electoral fray entirely, by becoming MP for the Combined English Universities, which he represented until leaving the Commons in 1926. Fisher, like the other outsiders brought into the Lloyd George coalition government, never possessed an independent political base of his own. His authority depended entirely upon the support of the Prime Minister. That support was given only so long as political conditions remained favourable to the expansion of education. When, with the Geddes axe of 1921, conditions turned unfavourable, Lloyd George withdrew his support for educational reform and education suffered severe expenditure cuts.

Anthony Crosland's career was more orthodox than Fisher's, since he was elected to the Commons and sat as a Labour backbencher for some years before entering government. Yet, although Crosland held a number of Cabinet posts, culminating in that of Foreign Secretary, he is likely to be remembered more by his books, and in particular by *The future of socialism*, published in 1956, long before entering government, rather than for anything which he achieved as a minister. It was in *The future of socialism*, that Crosland put forward his theory that education, rather than public ownership, was the prime means to equality. Crosland, so Halsey believed, had established education 'as a serious alternative to nationalisation in promoting a more just and efficient society'.[38] This hypothesis—that educational reform could promote 'a more just and efficient society'—came to be tested—tested to destruction one might say—when Crosland became Secretary of State for Education in 1965.

Five of the seven celebrated here—Green, Sadler, Fisher, Crosland and Halsey—were party men. Green and Sadler were strong Liberals. Fisher was a Coalition Liberal—if the Coalition Liberals can be called a party—and became sympathetic to the National Government in the 1930s. Crosland and Halsey were Labour. Yet they tended, with the exception perhaps of Halsey, to favour a broadly non-ideological approach to educational problems. All of them had what E. C. Bentley, inventor of the clerihew, called 'a cross-bench mind'. 'To put it shortly', one of Bentley's friends told another, 'You have a cross-bench mind'. 'You may put it even more shortly', the other replied, 'I have a mind'.[39] Sadler, although unwilling to assist a Conservative government, sought to establish an independent research unit in the Board of Education, which would be insulated from the short-term outlook of party politicians. He favoured a broadly non-ideological approach to educational problems, writing to Robert Morant in 1903:

> the true function of the Office of Special Inquiries and Reports is not limited to the promotion of the purely administrative purposes of the Board. ... Its most important and responsible task is to undertake the dispassionate examination of educational problems and to lay before the country an impartial and accurate survey of the facts *on both sides* of great educational questions, in order that readers may draw their own conclusions and that there may thus be formed in regard to national education that sound and enlightened public opinion, on the existence of which, far more than on Departmental control, the prospects of wise educational Development depend.[40]

Fisher, after serving Lloyd George, offered his services unsuccessfully to Bonar Law and to the Earl of Balfour, Lord President in Stanley Baldwin's 1924–9 Conservative government. Anthony Crosland felt that he had more in common with a fellow 'moderate' on the other side of the House, the Tory baronet, Sir Edward Boyle, than with the extremists in his own party.[41] Halsey has been a committed socialist all his life, and yet, significantly, his work was used by Margaret Thatcher as Secretary of State for Education, during the last phase of the period of post-war consensus, the years of the Heath government.

Norwood and Bullock, unlike the other five, did not align themselves publicly with any party, and Bullock specifically chose to sit on the cross-benches in the House of Lords. It is probable, however, that generally, Norwood voted Conservative or Liberal—he and Fisher are the only two of the seven whom one can envisage regularly voting Conservative—while Bullock generally voted Labour before 1981, but became in that year a founder-member of the SDP. As cross-bench minds, the seven were obvious fodder for Royal Commissions, government committees and working parties, bodies which proliferated in the late 19th century and for much of the 20th. 'We are born', Bagehot believed, 'with a belief in a green cloth, clean pens and twelve men with grey hair'.[42] We are, no doubt, no longer born with that belief.

What particular qualities did these mandarins have that made them so amenable to their patrons? A rather artless Cabinet memorandum of 1954 by the Postmaster General, Earl de la Warr, who was searching for an inaugural chairman and committee of the Independent Broadcasting Authority, declared that 'The Authority would have an advisory function, and the qualities required in the Chairman and members were tact and sound judgment rather than energy and administrative ability'.[43] It was the world of C. P. Snow, the world of the tap on the shoulder. The mandarins triumphantly passed the test allegedly used by Margaret Thatcher—is he one of us? They were valued by government for possessing the qualities that de la Warr needed for the IBA committee, 'tact and sound judgment'—though Sadler perhaps lacked this latter quality. But they also had drive and administrative energy as well.

The seven were not appointed as advisers for any particular expertise which they possessed. Indeed, until the latter part of the 20th century, the disciplines upon which the study of education depended, such as sociology and psychology, were in an underdeveloped state, and there were no real experts on whom governments could call. 'Political and social data were regarded as something to be acquired by common sense and practical experience; specialized social research was unnecessary.'[44] 'There is nothing of which I have so great a horror', Norwood declared, 'as the expert'.[45] What the seven mandarins had was not so much expertise as wide experience—experience primarily of the universities and of the public schools. Most of them had less experience of the maintained sector. Nevertheless, as a Permanent Secretary told Peter Hennessy in the early 1980s, '*They* [i.e. those appointed to public bodies] are the real amateur element in the system, *not* us'.[46] They were prime examples of what Jeremy Bentham called 'the lay-gent'.[47]

All seven of those celebrated believed that the state must play a greater role in education. It was, indeed, under Fisher that the state became, for the first time, the major source of funds in both primary and secondary education, and it was Fisher who established the UGC. Norwood believed that the state should establish a tripartite system of secondary education, suited to three kinds of young mind, while Crosland believed that the government should 'request' local authorities to establish a comprehensive system. It was, moreover, Crosland who gave the Comptroller and Auditor General power, for the first time, to audit the funds of universities.

The history of British educational policy in the 20th century can almost be summed up in the phrase—the expansion of the state. At the beginning of the century, the British state was, by comparison with states on the Continent, 'peculiarly reluctant to intervene in the educational market-place'. By the end of the century, however, there was 'a national system of education with a core curriculum and a uniform method of financing. … It took some time, but the state and its chosen experts had triumphed in the end'.[48] By 1987, a year before the Education Reform Act, one authority on British government believed that we had become, in Maitland's phrase, 'a "much-governed nation", with councils, boards, departments and authorities of many kinds exercising ... numerous ... and extensive ... powers ... in the name of social justice and the common good'.[49] A few years earlier, in 1980, as Geoffrey Caston points out, Alan Bullock had become so worried by the increasing role of the state and by the over-emphasis upon institutions, that he was moved to say, 'Today we are so impressed by the need for planning in education, so overawed by the bureaucratic structures we have created, that it is easy to conclude that only through these means can new initiatives take effect'.

III

Why are these seven gurus likely to be the last of their kind? Why has the era of the Oxford mandarin come to an end?

Those celebrated in this collection held a view of the role of education derived, as we have seen, less from the social sciences than from a philosophical standpoint—what one might call a world-view, a world-view whose origins lie, in large part, with Green. Or perhaps it would be more precise to say that much of the language of reform was the language of citizenship and community derived from Green. The seven, moreover, tended to believe that the academic guru had a special status in educational debate, and that he had something of importance to say about the nature of the good society.

Such a standpoint seems, from the vantage-point of the early 21st century, somewhat quaint. Admittedly, there is much talk, especially in New Labour circles, about the importance of citizenship and the teaching of civics. Yet this talk lacks the under-pinning of a world-view, the underpinning of Idealist philosophy which informed earlier discussion. Interestingly enough, Tony Blair seemed, before becoming Prime Minister, eager to find philosophical backing for his instinctive ideas about community and social responsibility. But he had to search for such backing in the work of figures such as John Macmurray and Donald Mackinnon, moralists only marginally related to philosophical discussion in the universities. No reputable philosopher in the universities would be willing to take on the mantle of Green today. The idea that philosophy should provide a world-view is now quite outdated. Since the 1930s, philosophy has become professionalised, concerning itself more closely with the analysis of language and of meaning.

Idealism has come to be tainted both in practice and in theory. During the First World War, liberals such as Hobhouse came to believe that it had provided the ideological basis for the very Prussianism which Britain was fighting against. In his preface to *The metaphysical theory of the state* (1918), a critique of the Idealist, Bosanquet's book, *The philosophical theory of the state* (1899), Hobhouse wrote 'In the bombing of London I had just witnessed the visible and tangible outcome of a false and wicked doctrine, the foundation of which lay, as I believe, in the book before me'.[50] Idealism was attacked for reifying the state and for encouraging a false sense of mysticism about it. Moreover, the notion of positive freedom came to seem something of a conjuring trick, designed to obscure the conflict between the state and the individual and to define away the difficult issue of the appropriate balance between freedom and coercion.[51] Such feelings were intensified during the inter-war years when the rise of Fascism and National Socialism served to cast further opprobrium on doctrines which seemed to exalt the state. There was, as a result, an aversion, after the Second World War, to grand theory, to ideology and to total explanations—the result, of course, of the experience of Nazism and Communism. On the Left, growing interest in Marxism in the 1930s also served to undermine Idealism. For the Marxist saw it as his task to 'unmask' doctrines of duty and citizenship as attempts to prop up a decaying capitalist society, doomed inevitably to collapse. The moralism of Green and his followers seemed of little relevance to a society riven by mass unemployment, a society in which the rhetoric of altruism served only to hide the reality of sharpening class antagonisms.

During the inter-war years, there was, in David Marquand's words, 'a sharp break in the intellectual and cultural climate. ... It was the age of the spare, the hard, the reductionist, the pared-down, the *mechanical*'.[52] The moralistic Idealism of Green was a prime victim of this intellectual and cultural change.

> The task of the intellectual and the artist was to cut through richly textured inevitably misleading surfaces in order to expose the secret realities beneath. Hegelian idealism gave way to logical positivism, and later to linguistic analysis; moral earnestness to a hard-edged, often mocking, pretended realism. The style and content of late Victorian and Edwardian public discourse came to seem vague, empty, self-deceptive and even hypocritical—ripe for unmasking and debunking. Lytton Strachey's 'eminent Victorians' were, at best, pompous deluded fools; at worst, dishonest rogues.

Strachey's portrait of Dr Arnold was devastating. What, one wonders, would he have made of Norwood?

> By the same token, the 'soft' essentially moralistic themes of pre-1914 political debate—citizenship and its obligations ... gave way to the 'hard' themes of class conflict and economic organization. ... As a result, talk of citizenship in the nineteenth-century sense of the term—citizenship as a strenuous, testing collective moral enterprise that depended on a capacity for personal growth and the exercise of self-discipline—began to seem empty, self-indulgent and, worse still, quaint and old-fashioned.[53]

Technical developments in philosophy seemed to show that the whole idea of a political or social philosophy was somehow illegitimate, something that belonged to the pulpit not the university. Logical positivism, as Marquand has noticed, is a typical intellectual product of the reductionist, pared-down ethos of the inter-war years. It purported to show that all statements which were neither empirical statements of fact nor a priori tautologies were illegitimate. After 1945, logical positivism was translated into political theory by T. D. Weldon, in his books, *The vocabulary of politics* (1953); and *States and morals* (1962).[54] Weldon shared the positivist view that the philosopher could have nothing to say about the good society, or about why one set of social arrangements should be preferred to another.

Logical positivism was succeeded by variants of linguistic philosophy, influenced by Wittgenstein, Austin and Ryle, which held that the true business of philosophy was the analysis of language, rather than the production of moral and political theories.

The philosopher came to be seen not as a preacher but as an analyst, subversive of all ideals, for none of them could be logically validated. The introduction to the first volume of an influential series of essays, *Politics, philosophy and society*, published in 1956, baldly declared that 'For the moment, anyway, political philosophy is dead'.[55] The second series, published in 1962, contained an essay by Sir Isaiah Berlin, Chichele Professor of Political Theory at Oxford, entitled 'Does Political Theory Still Exist?'[56] It would have been difficult to give a positive answer to this question until 1971, the year of the publication of John Rawls's *A theory of justice*. Yet, the rehabilitation of what might be called traditional political philosophy has not led to the rebirth of the mandarin. For although Rawls, and those who came after him, were seeking to answer traditional questions, they were doing so with the refined and pared-down tools of 20th-century analytical philosophy. They were professional philosophers, not ruminative generalists.

Of course, many of those celebrated in this collection—certainly Bullock, Crosland and Halsey—regarded themselves as empiricists, not philosophers of education. Halsey was a professional social scientist, while Crosland, in writing *The future of Socialism*, consciously thought of himself as revising classical socialism, and doing for the British Labour Party what Eduard Bernstein had sought to do for the German Social Democrats. That revision of classical socialism consisted of displacing nationalisation from its central position as one of the aims of socialism, and reformulating social democracy on an empirical, rather than a dogmatic, basis. One wonders, however, how empirical the mandarins actually were. Would any evidence from the social sciences have convinced Norwood that there were not three types of mind; would any evidence have convinced Crosland or Halsey that educational egalitarianism was harmful? They were, after all, working in the tradition of Green who, as Melvin Richter emphasises, 'although ostensibly welcoming the findings of science and history ... sought to build his new foundations for belief on ground which could not be undermined by any empirical evidence whatever'.[57] In 1879, Graham Wallas had heard Green present an argument for human immortality 'on the ground that, since we only know of the existence of our bodies from the testimony of our conscious mind, there was no reason to suppose that the dissolution of the body affected the continued existence of the mind'. Wallas asked whether the same argument applied to the conscious mind of dogs. Green replied that he was not interested in dogs.[58] Idealism was indeed a closed system of thought, and some of those influenced by Green had minds which, like his, were impervious to empirical evidence.

Governments believed that the mandarins celebrated here had the precious ability to consider educational problems dispassionately. The seven exerted much of their influence through committees of the Great and the Good. But the Great and the Good disappeared with the advent of Margaret Thatcher's government in 1979, a real watershed in British politics. Margaret Thatcher took the view that there was no position above politics. People were either for her or against her. The consensus position was not, as it seemed, a neutral position—indeed no such position existed. It was, instead, a position dedicated to the expansion of the state, dedicated in fact to the preservation of that very 'socialism' or social democracy which she sought to combat. It was for this reason that the era which began in 1979 saw the demise of the Royal Commission, that favourite playground of the Great and the Good. Since 1979, just three Royal Commissions have been established, none of them on educational matters. Royal Commissions thus became 'the most elevated and distinguished casualties of the Thatcher years'. There was no longer any need for 'cartographers of the middle way'.[59]

Moreover, modern governments operate on a much more rapid time-scale than they did in the past. They seek solutions in weeks not years; and they seek solutions to immediate practical problems, not sermons on the good society. Oxford is, no doubt, just as well placed to provide solutions as it was to offer sermons. But the universities no longer have a monopoly on policy advice, finding themselves increasingly supplanted by think-tanks, whose work is geared to providing practical solutions rapidly and without fuss. The close networks linking government with Oxford colleges, whether Balliol, All Souls or Nuffield, no longer exist, while the prestige and self-confidence of Oxford, as of other universities, has been heavily undermined. It is perhaps significant that, in his valedictory lecture, delivered in July 2005, Sir Andrew Turnbull, the retiring Cabinet Secretary and Head of the Home Civil Service, mentioned the great diversity of sources of advice available to government. 'We no longer claim a monopoly over policy advice. Indeed we welcome the fact that we are much more open to ideas from think-tanks, consultancies, governments abroad, special advisers, and frontline practitioners'. The list conspicuously excludes the universities. Perhaps it was an accidental omission.

IV

But perhaps the main reason for the decline of the Oxford mandarin lies in changing attitudes towards the state. The seven figures celebrated in this collection all saw themselves as benevolent guardians, and Green had shown that the state also could be moralised into becoming a benevolent institution. In 1934, a Manchester local government official was to claim that this had in fact now occurred. For the state, 'has evolved from being the embodiment of force and developed gradually until in modern days it emerges as guide, philosopher and friend'. It is, José Harris comments, 'hard to imagine similar sentiments being expressed at that time by his opposite numbers in much of Western Europe'.[60]

The seven mandarins believed that it was for the state to decide how the schools and the universities should be organised and financed. Norwood and Crosland disagreed about whether the tripartite system should be preserved. But they agreed that the decision was one for the public authorities to make. Both were, in their different ways, collectivists. In her memoirs, *The path to power*, Margaret Thatcher writes that in fighting for the grammar schools,

> we were defending a principle—namely that the state should select children by the simple criterion of ability and direct them to one of only two sorts of school—that is far more consistent with socialism and collectivism than with the spontaneous social order associated with liberalism and conservatism. Selection by ability is, after all, a form of manpower planning.[61]

The seven would probably have agreed with Douglas Jay's celebrated dictum in his book, *The socialist case*. 'In the case of nutrition and health, just as in the case of education, the gentleman in Whitehall really does know better what is good for people than the people know themselves'.[62] This may indeed have been true in 1947 when the second edition of *The socialist case* was published. For the Second World War seemed to have reinforced social solidarity and a sense of mutual obligation: it emphasized once again the need for the virtues of citizenship as preached by Green and the Idealists, and it gave a new impetus to the work of Edwardian social reformers such as Beveridge and Temple, reformers who were later to be sneeringly accused by Correlli Barnett of seeking to build the 'New Jerusalem' without thinking sufficiently about the industrial foundation needed to sustain it.[63] It was the sense of national solidarity which provided the essential ideological basis for the social reforms of the Attlee government, reforms which seemed to make traditional socialism, based as it was upon the nationalisation of the means of production, distribution and exchange, redundant. The Attlee government indeed gave the Idealist philosophy of fellowship and citizenship an unexpected second innings. By 1956, Anthony Crosland, in *The future of socialism*, was able to argue that capitalism had been fundamentally transformed. The mixed economy of the 1950s had become a quite different animal from capitalism as classically conceived by Karl Marx. Indeed, in Crosland's view, it should no longer be called capitalism at all. For a transformation had occurred in the ethic of managers of large private businesses such that they too were coming to act in accordance with principles of duty and citizenship. They too were in the process of becoming socially responsible citizens just as Green would have wished.

The philosophy of state action reached its apogee in the years following the Second World War when the 'post-war settlement' legitimised the role of government.[64] For governments could, so it was believed, ensure—through intelligent macro-economic policy and consultation with the forces of organised labour—ever-higher living standards as well as a steadily expanding welfare state and wider educational opportunities for all. But this required, as Green had noticed, a society in which civic cohesion and a sense of mutual obligation were strong. It also required deference to 'the gentleman in Whitehall'. For the philosophy of Idealism was, in the last resort, a patronising philosophy. It required the mandarins to do good to others, to remove 'obstacles' to their self-realisation, 'obstacles' that they might perhaps have been unaware of. 'We, as middle-class socialists', the leader of the Labour Party, Hugh Gaitskell, told his Shadow Cabinet colleague, Richard Crossman in 1959, 'have got to have a profound humility. Though it's a funny way of putting it, we've got to know that we lead them because they can't do it without us, with our abilities, and yet we must feel humble to working people'.[65]

Respect for authority and respect for the rights of others were the key components of the post-war settlement. Leaders could only lead, and gurus could only pontificate, if followers were willing to follow, and if the flock were willing to listen. 'The real slavery of today', Bernard Shaw had argued as early as 1891, 'is slavery to ideals of goodness'.[66] As memory of wartime conditions receded, people sought to emancipate themselves from that slavery.

The philosophy of Idealism was an austere philosophy, based upon what Oscar Wilde in *The soul of man under socialism* called 'the sickly cant about Duty', and 'the sordid necessity of living for others'.[67] The culture of social obligation and mutual respect came gradually to be undermined by the new forces of consumerism, home ownership, affluence, greater social mobility and individualism, and people came to believe that they knew better what was good for them than the gentleman in Whitehall, or even the gentleman in County Hall. In 1971, Tony Benn was to rail against an Austrian Social Democrat, who thought that 'socialism means everybody being allowed to have a Rolls Royce'. This, Benn believed, was 'the individual escape from class into prosperity, which is the cancer eating in the Western European Social Democratic parties; it is what Crosland believes'.[68]

It was indeed what Crosland believed. Far from railing at affluence, he had welcomed it. Indeed, in *The future of socialism*, he repudiated the Puritanism which had so long appeared to be part of the socialist ethic. 'Total abstinence and a good filing-system are not now the right sign-posts to the socialist Utopia; or at least, if they are, some of us will fall by the wayside'. Labour, Crosland believed, should welcome, rather than being suspicious of, rising living standards, a greater variety of consumer goods, social fluidity and a weakening of the restraints on sexual behaviour. In the blood of socialists, Crosland insisted, there should 'always run a trace of the anarchist and the libertarian'.[69]

The trouble was, however, that a society dominated by hedonistic individualism could hardly be expected to accept the social obligations which underpinned the postwar settlement. Crosland hoped that, with a growing public sector, everyone would become as socially responsible as the managers of the large private companies whom he so admired. The transformation of character, which Green had called for, would come about, not through the moralising and preaching of Idealist philosophy, but through changes in economic structure. Yet consumer affluence and growing social mobility were coming rapidly to dissolve traditional ties of community and society. For the ambitious, local communities were becoming places of departure, not places of permanent residence to which they would remain rooted. Self-assertion, both by individuals and by powerful groups, in particular the trade unions, was coming to replace older notions of citizenship. By the 1980s, Peter Shore could lament that

> we were engaging in what I call occupational tribal warfare, as though every separate group in the country had no feeling and no sense of being part of a community, but was simply out to get for itself what it could.[70]

Leaders continued to try to lead; but the followers would no longer follow. Politicians, whether Labour or Conservative, made desperate attempts to preserve the old order, but the forces of individualism, affluence and hedonism were too strong for them. These forces succeeded in destroying both Edward Heath's One Nation brand of Toryism and Labour's politics of social obligation. For both of these political philosophies relied on a sense of civic cohesion which was rapidly passing away.

What Crosland had not understood was that the very ethic of fellowship and social service which he extolled, depended upon personal self-restraint. By the 1970s, however, restraint was disappearing in a society in which privation and unemployment were but a distant memory. Crosland's famous book, *The future of socialism*, had 'continually invoked the old communitarian catchwords of ethical socialism—whilst at the same time deriding the old culture of Puritanism and stoicism from which such ideals had sprung'.[71] It was a contradiction that Crosland could not resolve; neither could any other socialist. It was, perhaps, a contradiction incapable of resolution.

Today, living as we do in a more fluid society, in which the great corporate blocks have broken down, we can, so we think, do without benevolent guardians. Admittedly, the Blair government still clings to the idea of a national strategy in education. But national strategies have been the main ideological victims of the post-war era. 'The state', it has been said 'has been a widely acknowledged *disappointment* in our time. For it has succeeded in satisfying neither those who had hoped for very much from its expanded provision—the radical proponents of social justice—nor those who had banked on relatively little from its increased interference—the conservative apologists for social peace. We might almost call this a consensus. But if so, it is a consensus of disillusion, not of expectation'.[72] Thus, while in the 1890s, a Liberal Chancellor of the Exchequer, Sir William Harcourt, was able to declare 'We are all socialists now', meaning that we were all in favour of state action, the decline of Labour, the party of the Left, the party which believed in state action, could be reversed only after its leaders, in the 1990s, had reassured the electorate that we are none of us socialists now.

For much of the period in which those celebrated in this collection worked, public intellectuals concerned themselves with the failings of markets, and tended to the belief that government activity could remedy those failings. Today, by contrast, there is greater awareness of the failings of the state. Indeed, the most remarkable feature of the past 25 years has been the revival of the philosophy of market liberalism, a philosophy of which all seven of those celebrated here were suspicious. Analysis of the public services is now dominated by public choice theory which assumes that politicians and bureaucrats are as much motivated by self-interest as private entrepreneurs and providers. In consequence, the claims of the market are now held to trump the claims of the public domain, the domain of citizenship and duty.[73] Those who use public services are no longer seen as citizens. They have become instead consumers or clients. 'The public realm has ceased to be a realm of debate, of reflection, or of persuasion. It became a special kind of market place'.[74] In that market place, there seems no room for the mandarin. Amidst the ruins of the collapse of the post-war settlement, the Oxford mandarin has become just one, although of course by no means the most important, of the casualties.

Acknowledgements

I am grateful for many helpful comments on an earlier draft by Harry Judge and Fergus Millar. But they are not responsible for my arguments or my conclusions.

Notes

1. Cited in Alon Kadish, *Oxford economists in the late 19th Century*, Clarendon Press, 1982, p. 25.
2. Cited in Melvin Richter, *The politics of conscience: T. H. Green and his age*, Weidenfeld and Nicolson, 1964, p. 30.
3. Beatrice Webb, *My Apprenticeship* (1926), Cambridge University Press, 1979, p. 143.
4. W. H. Greeenleaf, *The British political tradition*: Volume 3: *A much governed nation*, Part. 1, Methuen, 1987, p. 37.
5. John MacCunn, *Six radical thinkers*, Edward Arnold, 1910, p. 220.
6. T. H. Green, *Prolegomena to Ethics*, Clarendon Press, 1883, para. 270.
7. Ian Bradley, *The call to seriousness: the evangelical impact on the Victorians*, Jonathan Cape, 1976.
8. Richter, *The politics of conscience*, p. 13.
9. R. G. Collingwood, *An autobiography*, Oxford University Press, 1939, p. 17.
10. See, for example, Michael Freeden, *The New Liberalism: an ideology of social reform*, Clarendon Press, 1978.
11. J. A. Spender and Cyril Asquith, *Life of Herbert Henry Asquith, Lord Oxford and Asquith*, Hutchinson, 1932, vol. 1, 36.
12. A. H. Birch, *Representative and responsible government: an essay on the British Constitution*, George Allen and Unwin, p. 101.
13. J. H. Higginson (Ed.), *Selections from Michael Sadler: studies in world citizenship*, Dejall and Meyorre, Liverpool, 1979, p. 203.
14. Bernard Allen, *Sir Robert Morant: a great public servant*, Macmillan, 1934, pp. 22, 26–27, 32–33, 44.
15. Norman Dennis and A. H. Halsey (Eds), *English ethical socialist theories: more to R. H. Tawney*, Clarendon Press, 1989, p. 159.
16. A. H. Halsey, *No discouragement: an autobiography*, Macmillan, 1996, p. 76.
17. Matt Carter, *T. H. Green and the development of ethical socialism*, Imprint Academic, Exeter, 2003, p. 1. Green himself was, however, far from being a socialist or even a collectivist, in the modern sense of the word.
18. Richter, *The politics of conscience*, p. 351.
19. T. H. Green, *The work to be done by the new Oxford High School*, 1881, Slater and Rose, Oxford.
20. On the problems created by faith schools in the modern world, see Harry Judge, *Faith-based schools and the state*, Symposium Books, Wallingford, 2001.
21. Richter, *The politics of conscience*, p. 346.
22. Stefan Collini, *Public moralists: political thought and intellectual life in Britain 1850–1893*, Clarendon Press, 1991, p. 2.
23. Jean Floud, 'The teacher in the affluent society', *British Journal of Sociology*, 1962, p. 305.
24. Chapter 3 of Collini, *Public moralists*, 'The idea of character: private habits and public virtues' offers a fascinating discussion of this topic.
25. Richter, *The politics of conscience*, p. 56.
26. José Harris, 'Political thought and the state', in: S. J. D. Green and R. C. Whiting (Eds), *The boundaries of the state in modern Britain*, Cambridge University Press, 1996, p. 19.
27. Noel Annan, *Leslie Stephen: the Godless Victorian*, Weidenfeld and Nicolson, 1984, p. 185.
28. Andrew Vincent, 'T. H. Green and the religion of citizenship' in: Vincent (Ed.), *The philosophy of T. H. Green*, Gower, 1986, p. 48.
29. P. F. Clarke, *Liberals and Social Democrats*, Cambridge University Press, 1978, p. 11.
30. Cyril Norwood, *The British tradition of education*, John Murray, 1929, p. 51.
31. Cited in Sandra M. Den Otter, *British idealism and social explanation: a study in late Victorian thought*, Clarendon Press, 1996, p. 42.
32. José Harris, 'Political thought and the welfare state 1880–1940: an intellectual framework for British social policy', *Past and Present*, 1992, p. 138. It is, however, only fair to point out that Sadler was a fervent champion of technical education.

160   *The University and Public Education*

33. PRO EP 12/246, cited in the entry on Norwood in the *Oxford Dictionary of National Biography*.
34. Robert Blake, *Disraeli*, Eyre and Spottiswoode, 1966, p. 388.
35. Barbara Castle, *The Castle diaries 1974–76*, Weidenfeld and Nicolson, 1980, Entry for 6 November, 1975, p. 541. NALGO was the union of local government officers.
36. David Owen made this confession in a Radio 3 broadcast on 4 February 1985, printed in Peter Hennessy, *The great and the good: an inquiry into the British establishment*, Policy Studies Institute, 1986, p. 15.
37. Marmaduke Hussey, *Change governs all*, Macmillan, 2001, p. 193.
38. Cited in Maurice Kogan, *Edward Boyle and Anthony Crosland: the politics of education*, Penguin, 1971, p. 19.
39. E. C. Bentley, *Those days*, Constable, 1940, p. 198.
40. Sadler M. S., Bodleian Library, Eng. Misc. C 552, fols, 57–8, 3 April 1903, cited in the *Oxford Dictionary of National Biography* entry on Sadler.
41. See Kogan, *Edward Boyle and Anthony Crosland: the politics of education*, Penguin, 1971.
42. Cited in Anthony Sampson, *The anatomy of Britain*, Hodder and Stoughton, 1962, p. 247.
43. Cited in Peter Hennessy, *The great and the good: an inquiry into the British establishment*, Policy Studies Institute 1986, p. 16.
44. Richter, *The politics of conscience*, p. 353.
45. Cited in Christopher Tyerman, *A history of Harrow School, 1324–1991*, Oxford University Press, 2000, p. 506.
46. Peter Hennessy, *The great and the good*, p. 16.
47. Jeremy Bentham, 'On the art of packing juries' in: *The works of Jeremy Bentham* (Ed.) John Bowring, William Tait and Co, 1843, vol. V, p. 159.
48. Adrian Wooldridge, 'The English state and educational theory', in: Green and Whiting (Eds), *The boundaries of the state in modern Britain*, pp. 231, 257.
49. Cited in W. H. Greenleaf, *A much governed nation*, Part 1, Methuen 1987, p. 1. Greenleaf's volumes provide a highly detailed if idiosyncratic account of the growth in the role of the state, together with its ideological underpinnings, written from an Oakeshottian perspective.
50. L. T. Hobhouse, *The metaphysical theory of the state*, Allen and Unwin, 1918, p. 6.
51. For a powerful statement of this view, see Sir Isaiah Berlin's inaugural lecture in 1958 as Chichele Professor of Political Theory at Oxford, *Two concepts of liberty*, reprinted, inter alia, in Berlin, *Liberty*, Oxford University Press, 2002.
52. Marquand, *Decline of the public*, p. 69. The Cambridge historian, Peter Clarke, was to draw a similar distinction between 'moral' and 'mechanical' reformers in his *Liberals and Social Democrats*. Those celebrated in this symposium were all 'moral' reformers.
53. Marquand, *Decline of the public*, p. 70.
54. T. D. Weldon, *The vocabulary of politics*, Penguin, 1953; *States and morals*, John Murray, 1962.
55. Peter Laslett, *Philosophy, politics and society*, 1st series, Blackwell, 1956, p. vii.
56. Peter Laslett and W. G. Runciman, *Philosophy, politics and society*, 2nd series, Blackwell, 1962.
57. Richter, *The politics of conscience*, p. 55.
58. Clarke, *Liberals and Social Democrats*, p. 14.
59. *The Listener*, 7 February 1985, cited by Peter Hennessy in *The great and the good*, p. 1 and p. 49.
60. José Harris, 'Political thought and the welfare state 1880–1940: an intellectual framework for British social policy', *Past and Present*, 1992, p. 139.
61. Margaret Thatcher, *The path to power*, HarperCollins, 1995, p. 174.
62. Douglas Jay, *The socialist case*, 2nd edn, Faber and Faber, 1947, p. 258.
63. See Correlli Barnett, *The audit of war*, Macmillan 1986.
64. See, inter alia, Paul Addison, *The road to 1945*, and Keith Middlemas, *Politics in industrial society: the experience of the British system since 1911*, André Deutsch, 1979.
65. Janet Morgan (Ed.), *The backbench diaries of Richard Crossman*, Hamish Hamilton and Jonathan Cape, 1981, pp. 769–770.
66. George Bernard Shaw, *The quintessence of Ibsenism* (1891), Constable, 1913, p. 181.

67. Oscar Wilde, *The soul of man under socialism* (1891) in Richard Ellmann (Ed.), *The artist as critic: critical writings of Oscar Wilde*, Allen, 1970, p. 255.
68. Tony Benn, *Office without power: diaries 1968–72*, Hutchinson, 1988, p. 356.
69. C. A. R. Crosland, *The future of socialism*, Cape, 1956, pp. 524, 522.
70. Cited in D. J. Taylor, *After the War: the novel and English society since 1945*, Chatto and Windus, 1993, p. 197.
71. José Harris, 'Political thought and the state', in: Green and Whiting, *The boundaries of the state*, p. 27fn.
72. S. J. D. Green and R. C. Whiting, 'Conclusion: on the past development and future prospects of the state in modern Britain' in: Green and Whiting (Eds) *The boundaries of the state in modern Britain*, p. 379. Emphasis in original. The essays in this book provide a profound analysis of the ebb and flow of the power of the state in the 20th century.
73. This theme forms the central motif of David Marquand's lament in his book, *Decline of the public*, Polity, 2004.
74. Marquand, *Decline of the public*, p. 72.

Notes on contributor

Vernon Bogdanor is Professor of Government at Oxford University. His books include *The monarchy and the constitution* (1995) and *Devolution in the United Kingdom* (1999). He edited, for the centenary of the British Academy, *The British Constitution in the 20th century* (2003) and he is also editor of *Joined-up government* (2005). He is at present preparing a book on the British Constitution to be published by Allen Lane/Penguin.

Index

academic drift 75
Access and achievement in urban areas (Ofsted, 1993) 114, 118
action-research programmes 112, 113
adult education 47
Anglicanism 29
Annan, N.G. 139
Anti-Waste Campaign 12
Arnold, Dr T. 55, 60-1
Arnold, M. 55
art education 47
Asquith, H.H. 146-7
Australian universities 76
authority 158

Balliol College (Oxford) 19, 138
Banbury, Sir F. 7
Barnett House (Oxford) 103
Baur, F.C. 23
Beerbohm, M. 126
Bentley, E.C. 152
Berlin, Sir I. 156
Berrill, K. 95
binary system: of higher education 75, 76
biography: significance to issues in the wider world 53-4
Blair, T. 70, 154
Board of Education 9-10, 51, 62
Board of Education report (1943) *see* Norwood Report
Board schools 29, 30
Bradford Grammar School 86
Briggs, A 37
Bristol Grammar School 53
Britain's economic problem (Crosland, 1953) 71

The British tradition of education (Norwood, 1929) 150
Britton, J. 89, 90
Bruce, W.N. 4
Bryce Commission (1895) 9
Bryce, J. 3, 57
Building Jerusalem: A Portrait of My Father (Bullock, 2000) 85
Bullock, A.: achievements 90-1, 97-8; biography 85-7; and the Bullock Committee 89-91; character 84-5, 87, 93-4; fundraising 92; on history 91; in the House of Lords 91-2, 152; on the humanities 95, 96-7; politics 88; relationship with Oxford 85, 86, 87, 92-5, 101; and the Schools Council 88-9; on small schools 92; view of science 92, 93, 95; working methods 89-90
The Bullock Committee (1972-75) 89-91
Bullock, F. 86
Bullock plus one conference 90
Bullock Report (DES, 1975) 86, 89-91
Burnham committees 11
Butler, R.A. 62

Caird, E. 24, 148
Cambridge University 131-2, 138, 149
Campaign for Education (1963) 87
campus planning 131-2
Cannadine, D. 68
capitalism 158
Castle, B. 150-1
Cecil, Lord H. 62
Central Advisory Councils (CACs) 77
centrality: of academia 134-6

164 Index

Centre of Educational Research and Innovation (CERI) 108
Chambers, E.K. 4
character: and the common good 148; and the concept of the gentleman 133; national 41-2; role of Oxford in forming 130, 141; shaping 25, 56
Chester, N. 42
Children and their Primary Schools (Plowden, 1967) 77, 111-12
Christed life 24
Christian socialism 139
Christianity 22-3, 24, 145-6
Circular 10/65 73, 109
citizenship: and the Continuation School 6; Green's beliefs in 20, 145, 146, 147, 148; modern view of 155, 159; and World War II 158, *see also* common good
civil service 110, 133, 146
Clarendon report (1864) 55
Clarke, F. 53
class divisions: in education 6, 7, 55, 56-8, 62-3; and equal opportunities 71, 117; and higher education 87; and mass unemployment 155; Norwood's view 135; and social reform 104-5
classical socialism 156
classics 9, 14, 129
Cockerill, G. F. 68-9
collectivism 157
Colleges of Advanced Technology 75-6
collegiate system 130-1, 137, 141
Collingwood, R.G. 20, 146
Committee of Council on Education 41
Committee on Standards in Public Life 151
Committee of Vice-Chancellors and Principals (CVCP) 9
common good: in a changing world 146-7; and character formation 148; and creating a common culture 148; definition 23, 24; in education 24, 28, 31, 148; and freedom 26-8; and property rights 27; and the role of the law 26; and social justice 25; and the state 30; view of competition 24-5, *see also* citizenship
communism 155
Community Development Programme (CDP) 114
comparative studies: and education in Germany 40-1, 45; and funding 42; guiding principles 41-2; origins 39, 40; significance 43, 47
competition 24-5
comprehensive schools: the case for 72; importance to equality 70; introduction strategy 73-4; lack of planning 110; problems in funding 80; role of research 109-10
compulsory education 28, 29, 30, 31
The Conservative enemy (Crosland, 1962) 68, 72
consumerism 159, 160
Continuation Schools: demise 12; in Germany 45; purposes 6, 7, 8, 14; and religious instruction 7-8
Corbett, A. 73
counselling 141
Cowper-Temple clause 29
Crosland, A.: on capitalism 158; character 73, 75, 76, 78, 79, 81; and classical socialism 156; comparison to Blair 70; on consumerism 159; on education 68, 71-3, 74, 152, 153; family background 78, 79; key beliefs 69-71, 79, 152; legacy 73, 79-81; limitations of beliefs 159-60; as Minister of Education 73-7; as politician 67, 151-2; relationship with Oxford 68, 79-81; view of polytechnics 74; view of the state 157; written work 68
Crosland, C.A.R. *see* Crosland, A.
Crosland Circular (Ministry of Education, 1965) 73, 109
Crosland, S. 68, 69, 73, 76, 79

culture: mandarin 145, 153, 154, 156-7, 158, 160
Curriculum and Examinations in Secondary Schools (Board of Education, 1943) 52, 53

David Copperfield (Dickens) 56
de la Warr, Earl 62, 153
debating 133
Denmark 109
Department of Educational Studies (Oxford) 93-4
Department of Social and Administrative Studies (Oxford) 103
Dickens, C. 56
Disraeli, B. 150
dons 149
dual system: of higher education 75, 76
duty *see* common good

economic development 107-8
economics 149
Education 78
Education: a framework for expansion (White Paper, 1972) 111, 113
Education Act (Fisher, 1918) 6, 8, 14, 45
Education Act (Forster, 1870) 29
education cuts 12, 14
Education Priority Areas (EPAs): Halsey's contribution 115; in other countries 114; overview 111, 112; significance of research 113, 119; and social experimentation 113; theory of poverty 77
Education Reform Council (1916) 5
educational expenditure 73
Educational priority (Halsey, 1972) 106
educational reforms: and economic constraints 12, 14; of Lloyd George 3, 4-5, 6; and the OECD 107-8; and public/private life 54; religious issues 5; role of Oxford *iii*, 106-7; in universities 10

Educative State (*Erziehungsstaat*) 146-7
élitism 75, 132-3, 133, 138
endowed schools 55
English tradition 58, 59, 60-1, 62
The English tradition of education (Norwood) 53, 60
environment 131-2, 141
equal opportunities 108, 151
equality: and citizenship 32; of competition 71; and economic growth 69; in education 72; and excellence 95; and positive discrimination 94; in provision of university places 31, 117; in public appointments 151; of resources 95
Erziehungsstaat (Educative State) 147-8
ethical socialism 160
Eton School 55
eurhythmics 47
evangelicalism 140
examinations 9, 14, 47, 88
experimental social administration 103-4, 114

fascism 155
fees 8, 72
Fisher, H.A.L.: achievements in education 14, 45, 153; biography 1-3, 13; choice as Minister of Education 3-4; curriculum committees 8-9; effect of education cuts 12; on importance of the classics 9; and intellectual aristocracy 139; introduction of national examination system 9, 14; introduction of the PhD 10; legacy 10, 14; as Member of Parliament 6-8, 12-13, 151; on Michael Sadler 44; movement away from education 11-12; and patronage 150; political beliefs 151, 152; reforms 4-5, 6, 8-11; relationship with the churches 7-8; relationship with Oxford 1, 2, 13; on T.H. Green 2; on value of juvenile/part-time education 7

Fisher's Act (Fisher, 1918) 6, 8, 14, 45
Fleming Report (Fleming, 1944) 72, 77
foreign educational practice *see* comparative studies
Forster Act (Forster, 1870) 29
free places 8
funding: and comparative studies 42; in education 12, 14, 153; for universities 91-2
The future of socialism (Crosland, 1956) 68, 69, 71, 152, 158, 159, 160

Gaitskell, H. 158
Gathorne-Hardy, J. 58
gender issues ii-iii, 2, 11, 38
Germany: in comparative studies 40-1; educational standards post World War I 5; use of continuation schools 45
Gosden, P. 44
government *see* state
graduate studies 10
grammar schools: Crosland's view 73-4; and the end of selection 73; and inequality 71; in the late 19th century 55, 56-7; and sixth form colleges 74; Thatcher on 157
grants 5, 9, 10
the Greats 129, 130
Green, T.H.: and citizenship 23, 26-8, 145-6; and educational provision at Oxford 30-1; educational views 22, 28-32; ethic of public commitment 138; on Hegel 23; legacy 147, 148; metaphysical theory 21-2; on morality 23; philosophy 21, 147, 150; political beliefs 152; and possible/ideal self 24, 26, 27; reasons for his appeal 145-6; and religion 22-3, 24; Sadler's view of 147; scope of influence 19, 20-1, 146, *see also* common good
Grigg, J. 87

Haldane, R.B. 4, 147

Halsey, A.H. 75, 77, 79; biography 104-6; on Crosland 75, 77, 79; on Green 147; on his educational research 110, 111; influences 139; as lecturer 105-6; and networking 105, 111-12; and the OECD 107-9; and patronage 150; pioneering techniques 103-4; political beliefs 152; role of Oxford 106, 112-13, 116-17, 138; significance 103, 117-19; as a socialist 156; working style 103, 105, 113, 136-7
Harris, J. 149
Harrow School 53, 54, 55, 58-61
hedonism 159
Hegelianism 23
high culture 140
higher education 74, 75, 76, *see also* individual universities
Hilton Young report (Board of Education, 1920) 8
Himmelfarb, G. 20
History of Europe (Fisher, 1935) 13
Hobhouse, L.T. 154
Hughes, T. 56
Human Science 117
humanism 96, 98
humanistic education 147
Humanities 96-7
Humanities Curriculum Project 97
humanity 23, 25

ideal self 24, 26, 27
Idealism 21, 149, 150, 154, 156, 159
Ilbert, L. 2
independent schools *see* public schools
individualism 159
inequality 6, 7, 31, 71, 112, *see also* class divisions
intellectual aristocracy 139

Jay, D. 158
Jones, Sir H. 4
Jones, T. 4, 14, 44

Jowett, B. 138
Judge, H. 90

Kaplan, M. 91
Kay-Shuttlework, J. 54
Kazamias, A.M. 40
Kekewich, Sir G. 43
King's College (Cambridge) 138, 141
Kogan, M. 78, 79, 87

Labour government 70, 154, *see also* state
ladder of learning 28, 30
A language for life see Bullock Report
law 26
Leeds University 44, 46
lifelong learning 47
linguistic philosophy 155-6
literacy 5
Lloyd George, D. 3, 11, 12-13, 151
local education authorities 6-7
logical positivism 155
London School of Economics and Political Science 136, 149
Loss and Gain (Newman, 1848) 126

Mackail, J.W. 4
Maitland, Z. 2
Manchester University 43
mandarin culture: importance post World War II 158; individual qualities 153; Oxford's role in promoting 145; reasons for demise 154, 157, 160; and the role of the state 156-7
Manpower Social Affairs and Education Directorate (OECD) 108
market liberalism 160
Marland, M. 90
Marlborough College 53
Marquand, D. 155
meritocracy 94-5, 125-8, 150
Mills, C. Wright 53-4
Minovi, R. 90
modern political history 129

moral education 47
moral equality 27-8
moral ideals 25, 27
morality 23, 29, 148, 155
Morant, R. 40-1
multiversity 137
Murray, G. 3, 7-8

NACTST *see* National Advisory Council on the Training and Supply of Teachers
National Advisory Council on the Training and Supply of Teachers (NACTST) 87-8
national examination systems *see* examinations
National Foundation for Educational Research 89
National Socialism 155
National Union of Teachers (NUT) 74
Nazism 155
negative freedom 26-7, 28, 147
Neighbourhood Renewal Unit 118
New College (Oxford) 13
Newcastle Commission (1861) 41, 55
Newman, J.H. 126
No discouragement (Halsey, 1996) 147
Nolan Committee 151
Norwood Report (1943) 52, 53
Norwood, S. 56-7
Norwood, Sir C.: biography 51, 52-3, 54, 56-8; character 52, 54, 58-9; as Head of Harrow 54, 58-61; legacy 62-3; overview of achievements 52, 153; and patronage 150; public perception of 61; relationship with Oxford 52; on religion 150; review of secondary schools 61-2; view of the state 157
Nuffield College (Oxford) 102-3
NUT *see* National Union of Teachers

Ockwell, A. 38

OECD *see* Organisation for Economic Co-operation and Development
Office of Special Inquiries and Reports 40, 41, 42
On the grading of secondary schools (Green, 1879) 30
One Nation 159
Organisation for Economic Co-operation and Development (OECD) 107-8, 109, 112
Oriel College (Oxford) 138
Oxford Access Scheme 141
Oxford Extension Movement 38-9
Oxford Magazine (May, 1883) 145
Oxford Preschool Research Group (OPRG) 115-16
Oxford Review of Education 93-4
Oxford University: admissions 94, 140; and centrality 134-6, 149, 150; in comparison with other universities 127, 149; creation of loyalties 130, 135; and economics 149; ethic of public service 79-81, 125; importance of the setting 131-2, 141; influence of philosophy 149-50; legacy 128; as a living entity 126; as a locus for educational reform 106-7, 116; and meritocracy 94-5, 125-8; outside influences 138-41; and parliamentary intervention 127-8; as a place for poor students 30-1, 141; reasons for appeal 125-8; role of history 141, 149; and self-confidence 132-3; significance of membership 30, 126-7; student support mechanisms 141; use of collegiate system 130-1, 137, 141; use of size 136-8, *see also specific colleges*

Packwood, T. 87
parental involvement 112, 118-19
part-time schooling *see* Continuation Schools
The Path to Power (Thatcher, 1995) 157
patronage 150-1

Pattison, M. 41
philosophy 20-2, 149, 154, 155-6
place: importance of 131-2, 141
Plant, R. 148
Playfair, G. 58-9
Plowden Report (Plowden, 1967) 77, 111-12
policy-related research 106
political philosophy 156
political theory 155
The politics of conscience: T.H.Green and his age (Richter, 1964) 146
Pollins, H. 38
polytechnics 74, 75, 76
pool of ability 108, 110
Pope, C.G. 59
positive discrimination 97, 118
positive freedom 27, 147, 154
possible self 24, 26, 27
postgraduate studies 10, 137
poverty 77, 108, *see also* class divisions; equality
The principles of political obligation (Green, 1884) 26
Prolegomena to ethics (Green, 1883) 24
property rights 27
public appointments: and equal opportunities 151
public examinations 9, 14, 47, 88
The public school phenomenon, 1597-1977 (Gathorne-Hardy, 1977) 58
public schools: and equal opportunities 72; and privilege 73; and social prestige 55; and state control 62, 76-7
Public Schools Commission (1965) 72, 76-7
public service: and consumerism 160; influence of T.H. Green 19, 20-1; and philosophy 22; and religion 140; role of Oxford 125

qualifications 110

reading standards *see* Bullock Report

Redcliffe-Maud, J. 35, 36, 37, 46
reforms *see* educational reforms
religion: and the common good 30; and culture 140; in education 7-8, 29; and educational reforms 5, 6, 14, 29, 30; Green's view 22-3; and idealist philosophy 21; and morality 29; relevance to choice of Oxford 139, 140
revisionism 67, 69
Richter, M. 146, 156
Rosen, H. 89, 90
Rothenstein, W. 2
Royal Commissions 157
Rugby School 55, 56

Sadler, M.: at Leeds University 44; at Manchester University 43; character 35-6, 42-3, 44; and comparative studies 40, 41-2, 47; decision making 36; as Director of the Office of Special Inquiries and Reports 40, 41, 42, 43; on German Continuation Schools 45, 47; on H.A.L. Fisher 44-5; on higher education for women 38; interest in art 46; as lecturer 39; on national character 41-2; and patronage 150; political beliefs 152; relationship with Oxford 35-6, 37, 46-7; on secondary education 39, 43-4, 47; significance 40, 43, 47-8; on T.H. Green 147; as undergraduate 37-8
Sadler Report (Sadler, 1919) 46
St Anne's College (Oxford) 31
St Catherine's (Oxford) 86, 87, 92-3
St Catherine's Society (Oxford) 31, 93
St John's (Oxford) 51-2
salaries 10-11, 12, 14
Scholares non Ascripti 31
scholarships 9, 14
school leaving ages 72
Schools Council for Curriculum and Examinations 88-9
science 45, 92, 93, 95

Scottish universities 133
Secondary Modern Schools 71
Secondary Schools Examination Council 9, 53
sectarianism *see* religion
Selby-Bigge, Sir L.A. 4, 40
selection *see* comprehensive schools; grammar schools
self-confidence 132-3, 134-6
selfhood *see* ideal self; possible self
Selleck, R. 54
setting 131-2, 141
Settlement Movement 20
Sheffield University 2-3
Shils, E. 134
Shore, P. 159
sixth form colleges 74
Soares, J: A. 93, 94
social democracy 68, 156
Social democracy in Europe (Crosland, 1975) 68
Social Exclusion Unit 118
social experimentation 113
social reform 106, 115
social research 106-7, 112, 113
Social Science Research Council (SSRC) 111
social services 117
social work 116
The sociological imagination (Mills, 1959) 53-4
sociology 106, 110, 112, 117
Spender, S. 35
Spens, Sir W. 61-2
spirituality 22
state: and the common good 28, 30; control over public schools 62, 76-7; importance post World War II 158; importance of role in education 153; influence on moral character 26, 28; new ways of problem solving 157; role in promoting mandarins 156; role in supporting universities 9
State Scholarships 9, 14

States and morals (Weldon, 1962) 155
Stenhouse, L. 97
Stephen, L. 149, 150
superannuation schemes 11, 12
systemic research 40

Taunton report (1869) 55
Tawney, R.H. 7, 147
Taylor, A.J.P. 7
teacher salaries 10-11, 12, 14
teacher training: Bullock's view 87-8; crisis 11; improving provision for 11; lengthening 72; school-based 93
technical education 74
technological universities 75-6
Thatcher, M. 156, 157
theory of poverty 77
think-tanks 157
Tom Brown's schooldays (Hughes) 56
Toynbee, A. 22
tradition 53, 56, 59-60, 62, 63
Turnbull, Sir A. 157
Tyerman, C. 59

ultra-meritocracy 97
unemployment 155
unitary system: of higher education 75, 76
United Kingdom (UK) 75
United States of America (USA) 108, 134

University of Calcutta 46
University College (Oxford) 46
University Extension Movement 38-9
University Grants Committee 9, 95
University of Oxford Convocation 39
university support centres 141
Urban Programme 113
USA *see* United States of America

The vocabulary of politics (Weldon, 1953) 155
vocational education 74
voluntary schools 29

Walcott, F.G. 56
Wallas, G. 156
Weaver, T. 75
Webb, B. 146
Weldon, T.D. 155
welfare state 158
Wilson, J.D. 4, 6
women educational reformers 54
women's causes *see* gender issues
Woodward, Sir L. 36
Woolf, V. 2, 14
World War I (1914-18) 5

Young, M. 111

Zones d'Education Prioritaire (ZEP) 114
Zuleika Dobson (Beerbohm) 126

For Product Safety Concerns and Information please contact our EU
representative GPSR@taylorandfrancis.com
Taylor & Francis Verlag GmbH, Kaufingerstraße 24, 80331 München, Germany

www.ingramcontent.com/pod-product-compliance
Lightning Source LLC
Chambersburg PA
CBHW060513300426
44112CB00017B/2650